Mind the Children

Mind the Children

How to Think About the Youth Mental Health Collapse

Naomi Schaefer Riley
and Sally Satel

AEI PRESS

Publisher for the American Enterprise Institute
WASHINGTON, DC

Library of Congress Cataloging-in-Publication Data

Names: Riley, Naomi Schaefer editor | Satel, Sally L. editor
Title: Mind the children : how to think about the youth mental health collapse / [edited by] Naomi Schaefer Riley and Sally Satel.
Description: Washington, DC : AEI Press, publisher for the American Enterprise Institute, [2025] | Includes bibliographical references and index. | Summary: "Mind the Children: How to Think About the Youth Mental Health Collapse edited by Naomi Schaefer Riley and Sally Satel is a collection of writings from medical professionals, researchers, and journalists delving into different aspects of the youth mental health crisis. Adults' plan to make children's lives easier may actually be setting them more adrift, and to reverse the trend, we must examine the root causes. Across 11 chapters, experts explore various aspects of the crisis—including social media and screen time, the decline in institutions such as marriage and religion, and changes in attitudes around children's independence—and what parents, teachers, and policymakers can do to help"—Provided by publisher.
Identifiers: LCCN 2024061428 (print) | LCCN 2024061429 (ebook) | ISBN 9780844750781 hardback | ISBN 9780844750798 paperback | ISBN 9780844750804 ebook
Subjects: LCSH: Adolescent psychology—United States | Teenagers—Mental health—United States | Teenagers—United States—Social conditions | Parent and teenager—United States
Classification: LCC BF724 .M55 2025 (print) | LCC BF724 (ebook) | DDC 155.5—dc23/eng/20250314
LC record available at https://lccn.loc.gov/2024061428
LC ebook record available at https://lccn.loc.gov/2024061429

© 2025 by the American Enterprise Institute for Public Policy Research. All rights reserved. No part of this publication may be used or reproduced in any manner whatsoever without permission in writing from the American Enterprise Institute except in the case of brief quotations embodied in news articles, critical articles, or reviews. The views expressed in the publications of the American Enterprise Institute are those of the authors and do not necessarily reflect the views of the staff, advisory panels, officers, or trustees of AEI.

Publisher for the American Enterprise Institute
for Public Policy Research
1789 Massachusetts Avenue, NW
Washington, DC 20036
www.aei.org
Printed in the United States of America

Contents

1. What's the Matter with Kids? 1
   Naomi Schaefer Riley and Sally Satel

2. Kids, the World Is Not Bad and Broken 9
   Robert Pondiscio

3. The Tyranny of Happiness and Its Consequences 23
   Lawrence H. Diller

4. Coming of Age in a Postmarital Culture 39
   Kay Hymowitz

5. Who Does Hyperbolic News Hurt the Most? 51
   Zach Goldberg

6. America's Social Experiment with Gender 77
   Leor Sapir

7. Cannabis, Psychosis, and the Teen Brain 99
   Ken C. Winters and Holly B. Waldron

8. Help Kids Resist the Lure of Screens 115
   Paul E. Weigle

9. The Benefits of Religious Optimism 131
   Michelle Shain

10. Let Kids Do More on Their Own 147
    Camilo Ortiz and Lenore Skenazy

11. Fixing the Mental Health Provider Shortage 161
    Alice Lloyd Rahn

12. Our Generational Challenge: A Gen Z Perspective 177
    Kate Farmer

13. Conclusion 187
    Sally Satel and Naomi Schaefer Riley

About the Authors 191

Index 195

1

What's the Matter with Kids?

NAOMI SCHAEFER RILEY AND SALLY SATEL

In a post on X in September 2023, education expert Doug Lemov described visiting his daughter's school after cell phone use was restricted. For anyone who has been following the debate about kids and screen time, the results were not surprising. "So many students sitting in groups in the cafeteria, laughing & talking . . . chatting in the hallways . . . it's a different place," wrote Lemov. He also asked a teacher about the biggest change in the school. The response? "Kids are in class so much more! They used to 'go to the bathroom' all the time, but now it's clear they were just using their phones."[1]

The story illustrates not only how much phones have affected kids' lives but also how easy it is for adults to overlook some of the most significant ways we have made kids' lives harder by trying to make them easier. The contributors to *Mind the Children* find that American children and teens may be suffering from *aegrescit medendo*, a medical condition in which the cure is worse than the disease.

We have made them miserable by trying to make them happier. Giving children the internet at their fingertips and the ability to remain in constant communication with their friends and parents once seemed like a way to give them a leg up. But now, widespread smartphone use is almost universally acknowledged to have been detrimental to some students' intellectual, social, and emotional development.

It's hard to learn in school if you're spending a significant amount of time in the bathroom. It's easy to get frustrated with your classes if you don't understand what's going on. It's hard to remember there's a world outside social media if you never get to spend a few hours without access to the internet. And it's hard to gain any kind of independence if you are never more than a text message away from your mother.

Stories about the growing mental health crisis among young people are ubiquitous. According to the *New York Times*,

> in 2019, 13 percent of adolescents reported having a major depressive episode, a 60 percent increase from 2007. Emergency room visits by children and adolescents in that period also rose sharply for anxiety, mood disorders and self-harm. And for people ages 10 to 24, suicide rates, stable from 2000 to 2007, leaped nearly 60 percent by 2018.[2]

There is now general agreement that things got worse during the pandemic. The US surgeon general recently issued a report on young people's "devastating" mental health challenges.[3] School closures and other lockdown measures led to high levels of isolation among young people. Physical and emotional abuse of children by their caregivers seemed to rise as well. As rates of substance abuse—and overdose deaths—increased among adults, thousands of children lost one or both parents. Finding therapists and counselors proved all but impossible for many families during this time. The effects of all this could be seen in our medical facilities: Emergency room visits for suicide attempts rose 51 percent for adolescent girls and 4 percent for adolescent boys between early 2019 and early 2021.[4]

The problem is broad, and its causes are varied. Different segments of the population have been affected differently. There is no single answer to the question of how we got here or what we can do to help our children get back on track. But *Mind the Children* examines all the major causes the media has covered and a number of others that have been overlooked. The book also offers several potential solutions—for families, mental health practitioners, and policymakers.

While screen time is a significant factor in the decline in teen mental health, there are other (often related) contributors worth examining. The easiest place to start is parenting. How can we understand the prevailing style of modern parenting? Mostly, it involves giving kids few boundaries and a lot of choices. In an effort to make our kids happier, we are providing them with all the comforts of the modern world and offering them few rules to navigate its abundance. This situation has wreaked havoc for many adults, who often become paralyzed by the freedom they are offered. It's no wonder this is having deleterious effects on children.

Moreover, children's feelings have simply become more important to parents and caregivers over the past 40 or so years. Children are encouraged to identify and talk about those feelings, and adults are encouraged to pay close attention. This has led, as one of our contributors puts it, to the "tyranny of happiness." Adults have become uncomfortable with children feeling even temporarily distressed, especially if their distress results from reasonable limits their parents or teachers placed on them.

What we do to prevent or relieve a child's distress is important in his or her development. Sometimes the distress is simply a symptom of boredom. This is both a cause and effect of the overuse of screen time. If children never have to entertain themselves, they will never find ways of entertaining themselves. The screen—whether it's a video game or social media—will also fill the void.

On the one hand, interactions through video games or online communication can help connect a child who is isolated from his or her peers. Not only does screen time achieve the benefit of entertaining kids; it is also good for creating healthy bonds with other children. But depending on the interaction, it can also lead to conflict or distress, from which teens might retreat—thus further isolating them. Kids glued to a device seemingly don't need to develop the skills required for face-to-face communication. In reality, they miss out on the emotional benefits that come with that kind of contact. And no one needs to be reminded anymore about the detriments of social media.

The freedom to define oneself also seems like it would be a great boon to young people—but sometimes that freedom can go too far. When young people are liberated from the structures adults place on them, they can be who they want to be and form attachments with other young people of the same or a different sex. They can even redefine their gender. Adults are finally allowing young people to be true to themselves. But the relentless focus on discovering one's identity comes from parents and teachers, not to mention political activists.

But it turns out there are real consequences to offering children all the choices in the world, problems that result from asking preschoolers to construct their identity from scratch, telling them that even the most basic facts they think they know about themselves are up for debate. Where is a child to begin if not by knowing whether they are a boy or a girl?

The breakdown of American families has been calling children's identity into question for decades. What does it mean for a child not to know who their father is? In a country where 40 percent of births are out of wedlock, this kind of real identity crisis is widespread.[5] The point is not simply that children from broken homes are more likely to experience mental health crises. Rather, as one of our contributors explains in Chapter 4:

> If kids are depressed and anxious, it is in part because older generations have shredded the most legible scripts for becoming an adult—namely, those of marriage and parenthood. Fickle as they may be, marriage and parenthood offer people guidance on how to form the stable, intimate connections that are so essential to human flourishing.

There are other scripts, too, that children have lost (or been denied access to), such as those offered by religion. While adults may have thought skipping religious services or Sunday school would be liberating for children, it turns out that the messages about life's meaning and purpose and the rituals and sense of community that come with religious ties provide young people with a much-needed anchor in the modern world. The association between religious belonging and youth mental health was brought home by the pandemic. While lockdown policies isolated many young people, others held fast to their communities—sometimes even in violation of those policies—and wound up faring much better.[6]

In the absence of institutions like family and faith, our country has turned to schools as the bulwark against the youth mental health crisis. We have tasked the nation's teachers with engaging in social and emotional learning, among other pedagogical tools. Though often lacking the time and training to be therapists for the young people in their classes, teachers are trying to help students cope with the problems they are experiencing at home and their feelings about the wider world. But there is little evidence that their efforts are effective. Many students see school as a way to escape problems they experience at home. Meanwhile, these students have been falling behind academically since the pandemic and need more, not less, instruction in core subjects like reading and math.[7] And so their frustration grows.

Parents are also pressing schools to do more to accommodate not only their children's learning disabilities but also ADHD, anxiety, discipline problems, and dysphoria. While teen drug use is down from a decade earlier, those who use high-potency cannabis over many months or years significantly elevate their risk of chronic psychosis. Distinguishing between necessary accommodations and those aimed at protecting youth from experiencing any distress is often lost in these negotiations. These accommodation efforts also take time away from schools' academic mission.

And when it comes time to finding actual psychologists and psychiatrists to help children who truly need mental health care, the situation is bleak. The shortage of these providers is affecting families at both ends of the economic spectrum, but it is particularly hard for families that cannot pay out of pocket for mental health care. The pipeline of trainees going into this work is not robust, and the clinicians who are highly competent and in demand quickly determine they will be better off not taking insurance and certainly not taking Medicaid.

The messages kids are getting at school about the world may also be contributing to their mental health deficits. A popular YouTube video about climate change shown to elementary schoolchildren predicts that the world as we know it could end by 2030.[8] While purveyors of these messages believe they will spur children to action, the truth is that many of these ideas simply lead to children feeling helpless and in despair.

The political messages young people are getting from the wider world—more from the left than the right—also seem to encourage passivity, a sense that there is nothing they can do to solve their own problems. Conversations about systemic racism and sexism and ideas about how trauma is simply passed down biologically from one generation to the next can leave young people (and older people too) feeling as though we are all just doomed. Not only does this mean people are less likely to improve their communities, but it also contributes to deteriorating mental health.

Mental health professionals generally agree that for young people (or anyone) to feel positive about themselves, they need to have some sense of autonomy and independence, a feeling that they know and can accomplish things. "Helicopter parenting," which has become the de facto method of parenting for upper- and middle-class families, has considerably hindered children's ability to do anything on their own. Yet children who can walk to school by themselves, make themselves breakfast, or put up a lemonade stand by themselves feel better about themselves. They also have the confidence to take on bigger responsibilities as they get older.

Understanding the causes of the current mental health crisis can guide us in devising solutions. Encouraging kids to perform more tasks on their own may actually reverse some of the sense of helplessness they are feeling. There are other "therapies" that don't require professionals. Short-term interventions like exposure therapy and cognitive behavioral therapy could help children combat some of their anxiety and depression—and they may not require a new infusion of professionals into the workforce.

The scope of the youth mental health crisis is broad, and we can blame no single cause for the deficits that millions of children seem to be facing. But *Mind the Children* offers a variety of answers from medical professionals, researchers, and journalists who have explored one aspect in particular depth. We hope this volume will provide a comprehensive picture of these factors and the relationship among them.

It is hard to find a parent in America today who does not want their child to be happy. But we find ourselves moving further and further away from that end. Maybe we are working toward the wrong goal. Instead, we must help our children find purpose and meaning in life and equip them to be independent even if it means allowing them to take risks and make mistakes, form significant bonds with other people even if those bonds sometimes lead to sadness, and live in their community even if that means sacrificing individual freedom. Adults' plans to help children achieve short-term happiness—through more freedom, fewer attachments, loosened rules, and fewer moments of boredom and discomfort—have led them adrift. This book will explore how we got here and how we can get back.

Notes

1. Doug Lemov (@Doug_Lemov), "Visiting my daughter's high school today. They've recently restricted cellphone. So many students siting in groups in the cafeteria, laughing & talking," X, September 28, 2023, 12:44 p.m., https://x.com/Doug_Lemov/status/1707436196983353373; and Doug Lemov (@Doug_Lemov), "Answer: 'Kids are in class so much more! They used to 'go to the bathroom' all the time but now it's clear they were just using their phones," X, September 28, 2023, 12:46 p.m., https://x.com/Doug_Lemov/status/1707436589016572285.

2. Matt Richtel, "'It's Life or Death': The Mental Health Crisis Among U.S. Teens," *New York Times*, April 23, 2022, https://www.nytimes.com/2022/04/23/health/mental-health-crisis-teens.html.

3. Vivek H. Murthy, *Protecting Youth Mental Health: The U.S. Surgeon General's Advisory*, US Office of the Surgeon General, 2021, 3, https://www.hhs.gov/sites/default/files/surgeon-general-youth-mental-health-advisory.pdf.

4. Ellen Yard et al., "Emergency Department Visits for Suspected Suicide Attempts Among Persons Aged 12–25 Years Before and During the COVID-19 Pandemic—United States, January 2019–May 2021," Centers for Disease Control and Prevention, June 18, 2021, https://www.cdc.gov/mmwr/volumes/70/wr/mm7024e1.htm.

5. Elizabeth Wildsmith, Jennifer Manlove, and Elizabeth Cook, "Dramatic Increase in the Proportion of Births Outside of Marriage in the United States from 1990 to 2016," Child Trends, August 8, 2018, https://www.childtrends.org/publications/dramatic-increase-in-percentage-of-births-outside-marriage-among-whites-hispanics-and-women-with-higher-education-levels.

6. See, for example, Janhavi Ajit Vaingankar et al., "Religious Affiliation in Relation to Positive Mental Health and Mental Disorders in Multi-Ethnic Asian Population," *International Journal of Environmental Research and Public Health* 18, no. 7 (April 2021): 1–16, https://www.mdpi.com/1660-4601/18/7/3368; W. Justin Dyer, Ali Crandall, and Carl L. Hanson, "COVID-19 Stress, Religious Affiliation, and Mental Health Outcomes Among Adolescents," *Journal of Adolescent Health* 72, no. 6 (June 2023): 892–98, https://www.jahonline.org/article/S1054-139X(23)00017-4/fulltext; and Sriya Iyer, Shaun Larcom, and Po-Wen She, "Do Religious People Cope Better in a Crisis? Evidence from the UK Pandemic Lockdowns" (working paper, University of Cambridge, Faculty of Economics, Cambridge, UK, January 30, 2024), https://www.econ.cam.ac.uk/research-files/repec/cam/pdf/cwpe2403.pdf.

7. Nation's Report Card, "Scores Decline Again for 13-Year-Old Students in Reading and Mathematics," accessed May 24, 2024, https://www.nationsreportcard.gov/highlights/ltt/2023.

8. Robert at Children's Climate Championship, "A Message to COP28 Delegates from the World's Kids," YouTube, December 10, 2023, https://www.youtube.com/watch?v=7Ka9SHOQXvc.

2

Kids, the World Is Not Bad and Broken

ROBERT PONDISCIO

Adults charged with caring for children want them to be clear-eyed about the world, both its wonders and its dangers. But if they interrogate their instincts, many—perhaps even most—adults at least tacitly believe it is in children's best interests for them to be on their guard as they move through the world. This seems like common sense: A naive, credulous, or overly trusting child is more likely to be taken advantage of or even stumble into danger.

What if this common impulse is wrong?

If it could be demonstrated that viewing the world as dangerous and the people in it as untrustworthy damages mental health and well-being, would that change how adults encourage children to see things? Would teachers' approach to curricula, the books they assign, and the historical narratives students discuss in class change if it could be demonstrated that cultivating a more positive view of the world and humanity correlates with better mental health?

As teachers—and often parents—we pride ourselves on being "real" and "authentic" with kids. We think we are motivating and "empowering" them to tackle real-world problems or inspiring them to be "change agents" as adults by presenting a clear-eyed view of the problems that beset modern life, including poverty, racism, "threats to democracy," and climate change. Educators treat this as a mark of our seriousness and sophistication.

But that well-intended impulse may have exactly the *opposite* effect on students' lifelong mental health, well-being, and life satisfaction. An emerging and intriguing body of research, almost entirely foreign to K–12 educators, strongly suggests that adults do children no good by encouraging them to view the world as bad and broken. On the contrary, this research suggests, adults' common impulses have been misleading them all along.

Primal World Beliefs

About a decade ago, a team of researchers led by University of Pennsylvania psychologist Jeremy Clifton began identifying, collecting, and categorizing common beliefs about the world. Clifton and his colleagues culled descriptions from hundreds of religious texts, philosophical treatises, political speeches, novels, and films. They electronically scanned a database of more than 2.2 billion tweets, searching for those that started with the phrase "The world is . . ." Their inventory grew to more than 1,700 unique claims about the nature of human existence.[1]

Clifton and his colleagues called these fundamental assumptions "primal world beliefs." Known also as "primal beliefs" or simply "primals," these beliefs subconsciously shape people's perceptions, thoughts, emotions, and behaviors. A closer look at primals research offers a key to understanding how a seemingly healthy distrust of the world and humanity might paradoxically fail to make children safer or happier.

The researchers categorized their "Primals Inventory" into three clusters that represented humanity's most basic beliefs about the world's general character, dubbing them the "Big Three" sets of primal beliefs.[2] People tend to believe the world is (1) safe or dangerous, (2) enticing or dull, and (3) alive or mechanistic.[3]

When walking alone at night in an unfamiliar neighborhood, for example, someone with a primal belief that the world is dangerous is more likely to feel anxious and vigilant, constantly looking around and feeling threatened. A person with a primal belief in a safe world might feel more at ease, trusting that they are unlikely to encounter any harm during their walk.

Presented with the prospect of a party with lively music and conversation, a person with a primal belief that the world is enticing will feel excited and eager to attend. Conversely, someone with a primal belief in a dull world might find the prospect uninteresting and prefer to stay home with a book.

Looking at a beautiful sunset, a person with a primal belief in an alive world might perceive the sunset as living and vibrant, feel a deep connection with nature, or have a sense of awe, wonder, or even the divine. Their companion, whose primal beliefs tilt toward a mechanistic world, might appreciate the same sight from a scientific or aesthetic perspective without attributing any consciousness, meaning, or purpose to the natural phenomenon.

Clifton observed that, like personality traits, primals are relatively stable over time. They're not easily visible; you can't detect someone's primals on sight. More pertinently, you can't reliably infer them, even if you know about a person's life history and experiences. One might assume that a person whose life has been beset by challenges—growing up in poverty, for example, or suffering trauma—is more likely to adopt negative primals than is someone whose life has been comparatively friction-free. Clifton noted that expectation: "Many researchers intuit that the rich will see the world as a *Good* place and privileged racial majorities will see the world as more *Just* and *Abundant* than minorities."[4]

But perhaps surprisingly, Clifton's research on primal world beliefs suggests perceptions of the world are actually the product of beliefs about the world, not the other way around. In other words, people generally don't adopt primal beliefs based on their life experiences. Rather, people's primal beliefs influence how they explain the world to themselves—and this seems to profoundly affect their general well-being. As Clifton and coauthor Peter Meindl wrote in a *Journal of Positive Psychology* article, "Regardless of occupation, more negative primals were almost never associated with better [life] outcomes. Instead, they predicted less success, less job and life satisfaction, worse health, dramatically less flourishing, more negative emotion, more depression, and increased suicide attempts."[5]

This is a potentially crucial insight for teachers and parents. First, the emerging body of research on primal world beliefs appears to fly in the face of much contemporary pedagogical thought and practice in K–12 education, including many ideas undergirding curriculum development, social and emotional learning (SEL), and "trauma-informed pedagogy." Moreover, many parents believe that raising their children with a pessimistic world outlook will prepare them for life's harsh realities and thus help them develop resilience. But Clifton and Meindl found that this common approach is linked to adverse effects in children, including increased anxiety, cynicism, and a limited sense of possibility.

People who hold sunnier primals—viewing the world as generally safe and intriguing—seem more likely to flourish. "Safe world belief was strongly correlated with increased life satisfaction . . . including among jobs where the ability to spot threats are useful, such as law enforcement," Clifton and Meindl found. "The seemingly widespread meta-belief that associates negative primals with positive outcomes is unsupported."[6] Clifton put things even more bluntly in a 2022 interview with *Education Week*, in which he offered the following advice: "*Don't* assume teaching young people that the world is bad will help them. *Do* know that how you see the world matters."[7]

In recent decades, however, teachers and parents seem to have drifted toward presenting to children a darker view of the world. In their 2021 paper, Clifton and Meindl reported that 53 percent of parents "preferred dangerous world beliefs for their children" and "expressed the belief that their children would most benefit by being taught to see the world as dangerous, declining, competitive, fragile, unjust, barren, not funny, and full of physical threats."[8] No similar data exist on teachers, but many features of contemporary education at least tacitly impart to children a view of the world as bad and broken. Much of today's pedagogical thought, practice, and training instructs teachers that many or even most children have suffered adverse life events that are tantamount to trauma.[9]

Where is this turn toward a darker outlook on the world presented to children? Perhaps the most vivid illustration is found in the evolution of young adult (YA) literature.

The Dark Turn in YA Literature

Over the past several decades, the books most assigned to and read by young people have shifted from the uplifting tales and didactic stories of a century ago—which were marked by clear distinctions between good and evil—toward darker themes of pathology and even depravity.

Beginning in the mid-19th century and for decades afterward, the McGuffey reader was the most common textbook in America's public schools. "What is most impressive in the McGuffey Readers is the morality," historian Henry Steele Commager observed. "There is rarely a page but addresses itself to some moral problem, points some moral lesson." He continued, "Industry, sobriety, thrift, propriety, modesty, punctuality, conformity—these were the essential virtues, and those who practiced them were sure of success."[10]

The YA literature genre that emerged in the 1960s and 1970s, by contrast, began to embrace stories with greater realism. This period emphasized "relatable" characters facing many of the same challenges and struggles as the reader, with authors exploring themes related to family dynamics and personal growth. Books like *The Outsiders* by S. E. Hinton (1967) portrayed the struggles of teenagers from different social classes. *Go Ask Alice* by Beatrice Sparks was a publishing sensation in 1971 for its frank description (for its time) of teenage drug addiction. Though their tone was still generally optimistic, these books certainly showed a trend toward tackling more mature subjects. In that regard, they heralded much grittier YA fare in the years to come.

By the late 1990s and early 2000s, YA literature took a much darker turn. Popular novels challenged traditional social norms and gave young readers a chance to explore their own questions about growing up and navigating life's complexities, ostensibly to provide them with a more authentic portrayal of the challenges they might face. Bestselling coming-of-age stories included *The Perks of Being a Wallflower* by Stephen Chbosky—a story about a young boy navigating adolescence that discussed sexuality, drug use, rape, and mental health—and *Thirteen Reasons Why* by Jay Asher, which explored sexual assault, bullying, and depression in light of a high school freshman girl's suicide.

More recently, *The Hate U Give* by Angie Thomas (2017) focused on questions of race, identity, and social justice through the experience of a young black girl who becomes an activist after witnessing her friend's fatal shooting by a police officer. These are but a few prominent examples of YA literature, which began to lean heavily into darker themes.

Perhaps the starkest example of YA literature's dark turn is the popular 2008 novel *The Hunger Games* by Suzanne Collins. The first in a trilogy of dystopian novels, the book tells the story of a group of teenagers who are forced to compete in nationally televised fights to the death in a decadent successor nation to the United States. As of 2024, over 100 million copies of *The Hunger Games* have been sold.

The Hunger Games series spawned one of the most successful movie franchises in Hollywood history, grossing $3 billion worldwide. While dystopian tales have always appealed to younger readers, previous generations would have been appalled that mainstream culture would one day see child slaughter, even in fiction, as a form of entertainment. Yet many contemporary readers find the stylized brutality of *The Hunger Games* less discomfiting than even more gritty and "authentic" novels that dwell on depression, self-harm, abuse, and addiction, nearly to the point of fetishizing them.

The educational establishment has largely embraced YA literature's dark turn. Mainstream education organizations have broadly supported assigning "realistic" YA books in school, arguing they engage students and promote discussions about important topics. The National Council of Teachers of English (NCTE), for example, promotes students' right to access a wide range of literature, including books with mature themes. The NCTE provides recommendations for YA books that can be included in classrooms to "promote open inquiry, critical thinking, diversity in thought and expression, and respect for others."[11] These lists often feature books that tackle themes such as racial and gender identity, sexual abuse, and suicide.

Note that this catastrophizing of contemporary life is not limited to YA fiction. Civic education, a founding purpose of American public education, has in recent years evolved into "action civics," in which students are expected to identify and develop solutions to real-world problems. Peter Wood of the National Association of Scholars criticizes this form of civic education for replacing instruction in how the government works in favor of "Neo-Marxist 'social justice' propaganda, vocational training for left-wing activism, and Alinsky-style community organizing techniques adapted for use in the classroom."[12] Fundamentally, the problem—as I noted in a March 2022 essay published in *Commentary*—is that this approach risks pathologizing childhood, signaling to kids that American life is bad and broken and citizenship is merely an effort to address our myriad ills.[13]

These trends in educational thought and practice may have accelerated in recent years, but the phenomenon is not new. When the American Educational Research Association issued its comprehensive review of teacher education in 2005, it reported,

> Over the last decade or so, conceptualizing teaching and teacher education in terms of social justice has been the central animating idea for educational scholars and practitioners ... who connect their work to larger critical movements.... Advocates of a

social justice agenda want teachers to be professional educators as well as activists committed to diminishing the inequities of American society.[14]

This almost axiomatically requires problematizing the world to children. Exemplifying this tendency are recent fights over critical race theory in K-12 education—which proponents argue helps students understand how racism has shaped American society and critics hold merely encourages a view of the world as divided into oppressors and oppressed.[15]

Author and journalism professor Steve Salerno noted,

> It is difficult to understand why educators would so determinedly insist on immersing students in an unsavory worldview, portraying life in terms of its anomalies and unorthodoxies, as if there's something wrong with you if there's nothing wrong with you.[16]

He expressed concern that adolescents might be inclined to "seek membership" in groups that get all the attention. "Are high rates of depression and suicide an organic outgrowth of life's legitimate trials—or are they a crisis manufactured, at least in part, by painting life as so much more trying than it is?"[17]

People like Salerno are onto something. Especially over the past decade or so, ideas previously considered to be in the domain of psychology have begun creeping into the classroom, further embedding young minds with the thought that the world is bad and broken.

The Rise of Therapeutic Education

In their 2018 book *The Coddling of the American Mind: How Good Intentions and Bad Ideas Are Setting Up a Generation for Failure*, social psychologist Jonathan Haidt and First Amendment lawyer and advocate Greg Lukianoff explored the rising trend of emotional fragility and intolerance among young Americans. They delved into "safetyism," an overemphasis on protecting individuals from discomfort and opposing viewpoints.

Haidt and Lukianoff posited that nurturing children in an environment that overly prioritizes emotional safety establishes a cycle in which they become increasingly delicate and less resilient. This leads adults to think children need heightened protection, which only exacerbates kids' fragility and diminished resilience. While the authors do not discuss primal world beliefs (their book predates Clifton's first published papers), their argument is a book-length anticipatory critique of what we might call *institutional* negative primals: beliefs that the world is filled with unsafe ideas from which students need protection.[18]

Lukianoff and Haidt delved into the evolving interpretation of the term "trauma," which the *Diagnostic and Statistical Manual of Mental Disorders* (DSM) once used to refer exclusively to physical damage such as a traumatic brain injury. But in its 1980 revision, the DSM recognized for the first time post-traumatic stress disorder as a mental disorder—the first use of the term "trauma" to describe a nonphysical injury. "By the early 2000s, however, the concept of 'trauma' within parts of the therapeutic community had crept down so far that it included anything 'experienced by an individual as physically and emotionally harmful,'" the authors observed, "'with lasting adverse effects on the individual's functioning and mental, physical, social, emotional, or spiritual well-being.' The *subjective experience* of 'harm' became definitional in assessing trauma."[19]

This echoes a similar trend that has emerged largely unchallenged in K–12 education—namely, trauma-informed pedagogical practices aiming to establish safe spaces and nurturing settings for students. The US Department of Health and Human Services frequently cites statistics suggesting that over two-thirds of US students confront at least one traumatic event before their 16th birthday.[20] Alarming figures like these and a nascent body of literature on the consequences of "toxic stress" for learning have sparked an upsurge of interest in trauma-informed practices. Exemplifying this phenomenon is the rise of therapeutic education, which has swiftly integrated psychological concepts with classroom methodologies under the banner of SEL. A recent survey of teachers in 11 states found virtually unanimous agreement that "training in trauma-informed classroom practices is something all teachers need."[21]

The roots of K–12 education's interest in trauma-informed practices can be traced to a 1998 joint study by Kaiser Permanente and the Centers for Disease Control and Prevention. This research scrutinized trauma's long-term health repercussions for over 17,000 patients, identifying links between "adverse childhood experiences" (ACEs)—such as abuse, neglect, and household dysfunction—and a broad spectrum of mental and physical health issues.[22] Outcomes like criminality, incarceration, homelessness, and premature mortality were all correlated with early-life adversity. Adults encountering four or more ACEs were markedly prone to depression and suicide attempts. Consistent with the expanded definition of "trauma" that Haidt and Lukianoff detailed, numerous hardships experienced during childhood—including exposure to substance abuse, domestic violence, or parental divorce—contributed to an individual's ACE score.

But some of the same researchers who published the original 1998 study, the source of so much of education's focus on trauma-informed practices, recently raised questions about its applications and interpretations. In the *American Journal of Preventive Medicine*, these scientists cautioned:

> Unlike recognized public health screening measures, such as blood pressure or lipid levels that use measurement reference standards and cut points or thresholds for clinical decision making, the ACE score is not a standardized measure of childhood exposure to the biology of stress.[23]

They pronounced themselves "concerned that ACE scores are being misappropriated as a screening or diagnostic tool to infer individual client risk."[24] Though the paper was not aimed at educators, its pointed critique of ACE screening seems particularly relevant to classroom practice.

The obvious danger is that teachers may simplistically interpret or overestimate the effects of trauma, with serious consequences for student achievement in the form of lowered standards and diminished expectations. Teachers' attitudes and beliefs might also rub off on students. According to Clifton, the processes by which people develop their primals are unclear and subject to further study, but it is reasonable to infer that parents and other influential adults play a significant role.

Similarly, overexposure to unsettling news and events—school shootings, political instability, and the threat of climate change, for example—

may contribute to a sense of trauma. And it is not uncommon for teachers to project onto students their own anxieties. In the days following Donald Trump's 2016 election, for example, the nation's largest teachers union published advice for its members on discussing the election with students on the assumption, as one teacher said, that "the election results will have a traumatic experience on our students."[25]

Incorporating Primal World Beliefs in K–12 Education

None of this chapter's discussion should be mistaken as minimizing concerns about students' mental health. Nor should it be construed as arguing that concerns for their well-being are misguided—particularly as evidence continues to accumulate about learning loss, behavioral challenges, and high rates of absenteeism in the aftermath of COVID-driven school closures and disruptions to children's lives and routines. The *Washington Post* reported that more than 75 percent of schools surveyed in spring 2022 said teachers and staff had voiced concerns about student depression, anxiety, and trauma.[26] A survey that the Centers for Disease Control and Prevention conducted from January to June 2021 revealed that 37 percent of students at public and private high schools said "their mental health was not good most or all of the time during the pandemic," a figure that included roughly half of girls and about a quarter of boys.[27]

As the contours of students' mental health struggles have continued to emerge post-COVID, so too have calls for schools to prioritize SEL. Proponents uphold it as a necessary and unobjectionable method to build students' emotional self-regulation, making it not just positive but potentially lifesaving given rising teen suicide rates. But critics have charged that SEL is a Trojan horse that inserts ideological indoctrination, critical race theory, or gender ideology into classrooms.[28]

The larger concern, however, may be the assumptions undergirding SEL's increasing dominance in classroom culture and practice. Bluntly, the question is whether, by inflating unfortunate but common events to the magnitude of trauma, SEL advocates are in danger of pathologizing childhood.

SEL has drifted ever closer to becoming the central purpose of schooling, without a full and appropriate discussion of its priorities, role, and methods. As I argued in an October 2021 American Enterprise Institute report, the unexamined rise of "therapeutic education" risks making teaching akin to therapy, social work, or even clerical ministry while failing to sufficiently consider the downsides of doing such sensitive work haphazardly.[29] SEL has been promoted as intertwined with, even *inseparable* from, schools' academic mission.

But SEL further enshrines an assumption that children are not resilient but fragile, traumatized by life events that, while upsetting, may neither meet the standard for trauma nor counterbalance the ameliorating effects of close family ties or other stabilizing influences in a child's life. It is reasonable to wonder whether this further signals to impressionable children that the world is filled with dangers. In sum, education at large seems poised to adopt an institutional primal world belief that the world is dangerous, requiring constant vigilance and putting students in need of continual reassurance.

Consider the potential effect of teaching children that the world is bad and exposing them to credible and influential adults who hold or promote a dark view of the world and humanity. This practice is born of the common but demonstrably mistaken notion that teaching kids to view the world as bad and broken is in their best interest, and educators regard it as a mark of intellectual seriousness, sophistication, and authenticity. The effects could be particularly harmful if this is a dominant theme of kids' K–12 experience.

By contrast, awareness of primal world beliefs and their influence offers teachers and parents a promising alternative to today's pessimistic educational paradigms. While research on primal world beliefs is in its infancy—the first paper published on the topic didn't appear until 2019—the lack of attention to primals in K–12 education is surprising, given their numerous applications. "If you see the world as an enticing place, you are probably a more curious person than someone who sees the world as dull," Clifton noted.[30] Teachers turn cartwheels, sometimes literally, trying to engage students and spark their curiosity.

"We found very little evidence, very few places, where seeing the world as a bad place was tied to good things," Clifton concluded in one discussion about primal world beliefs. Healthy and successful people tend not to be "people who see the world as a dangerous place. They're people who see it as safe."[31]

Parents have a role too. "Almost every day that my daughter was in high school, she was taught about the dangerous world—about bad people, dangerous forces in nature, and a bleak future for our country," wrote columnist and academic Arthur C. Brooks. "She told us about the doom and gloom each evening at dinner, and my wife and I could see her growing pessimism." In response, Brooks counsels parents to avoid cultivating "fear primals" and instead teach kids "love primals." "People are made for love," he writes, "and we can find something lovable in just about everyone we meet."[32]

Research on how primal world beliefs affect mental health and well-being is in its infancy, but for now, Clifton counsels those who care about children not to assume teaching them that the world is bad is helpful. "Personally, I plan to teach my daughter specific bad things to watch out for but, on balance, the world is good," Clifton says. "There's beauty everywhere—we have only to open our eyes to see it."[33]

Notes

1. J. D. W. Clifton et al., Primals Inventory, American Psychological Association, 2019, https://psycnet.apa.org/doiLanding?doi=10.1037%2Ft79109-000.

2. Jeremy D. W. Clifton and Eric S. Kim, "Health in a Crummy World: Implications of Primal World Beliefs for Health Psychology," *Medical Hypotheses* 135 (February 2020), https://myprimals.com/wp-content/uploads/2020/01/healthyinacrummyworld.pdf.

3. Jer Clifton, "What Are Your 3 Deepest Beliefs About the World?," *Psychology Today*, March 28, 2022, https://www.psychologytoday.com/us/blog/primal-world-beliefs-unpacked/202203/what-are-your-3-deepest-beliefs-about-the-world.

4. Jeremy D. W. Clifton, "Testing If Primal World Beliefs Reflect Experiences—or at Least Some Experiences Identified *ad hoc*," *Frontiers in Psychology* 11, no. 1145 (June 23, 2020), https://www.frontiersin.org/journals/psychology/articles/10.3389/fpsyg.2020.01145/full.

5. Jeremy D. W. Clifton and Peter Meindl, "Parents Think—Incorrectly—That Teaching Their Children That the World Is a Bad Place Is Likely Best for Them," *Journal of Positive Psychology* 17, no. 2 (2022): 182–97, https://ppc.sas.upenn.edu/sites/default/files/parentsprimalbeliefs.pdf.

6. Clifton and Meindl, "Parents Think—Incorrectly—That Teaching Their Children That the World Is a Bad Place Is Likely Best for Them."

7. Jer Clifton, "Don't Try to Toughen Students Up, Research Says," *Education Week*, April 27, 2022, https://www.edweek.org/leadership/opinion-dont-try-to-toughen-students-up-research-says/2022/04.

8. Clifton and Meindl, "Parents Think—Incorrectly—That Teaching Their Children That the World Is a Bad Place Is Likely Best for Them."

9. Robert Pondiscio, "The Unbearable Bleakness of American Schooling," *Commentary*, March 2022, https://www.commentary.org/articles/robert-pondiscio/american-schooling-bleak-broken.

10. Henry Steele Commager, foreword to *McGuffey's Sixth Eclectic Reader* (Toronto, ON: New American Library of Canada Limited, 1962), viii, x.

11. National Council of Teachers of English, "NCTE Intellectual Freedom Center," https://ncte.org/resources/ncte-intellectual-freedom-center.

12. Peter Wood, "Why We Need a Civics Alliance," National Association of Scholars, March 22, 2021, https://www.nas.org/blogs/article/nas-announces-the-civics-alliance.

13. Pondiscio, "The Unbearable Bleakness of American Schooling."

14. Marilyn Cochran-Smith and Kenneth M. Zeichner, eds., *Studying Teacher Education: The Report of the AERA Panel on Research and Teacher Education* (New York: Routledge, 2005), https://psycnet.apa.org/record/2005-07530-000.

15. Cochran-Smith and Zeichner, eds., *Studying Teacher Education*.

16. Steve Salerno, "The Unbearable Darkness of Young Adult Literature," *Wall Street Journal*, August 28, 2018, https://www.wsj.com/articles/the-unbearable-darkness-of-young-adult-literature-1535495594.

17. Salerno, "The Unbearable Darkness of Young Adult Literature."

18. Greg Lukianoff and Jonathan Haidt, *The Coddling of the American Mind: How Good Intentions and Bad Ideas Are Setting Up a Generation for Failure* (New York: Penguin Random House, 2018).

19. Lukianoff and Haidt, *The Coddling of the American Mind*, 26 (cleaned up).

20. US Department of Health and Human Services, Substance Abuse and Mental Health Services Administration, "Understanding Child Trauma," June 6, 2024, https://www.samhsa.gov/child-trauma/understanding-child-trauma.

21. Melissa Ezarik, "Survey: Teachers Need Training in Trauma," *District Administration*, May 8, 2020, https://districtadministration.com/survey-teachers-need-training-in-trauma.

22. Vincent J. Felitti et al., "Relationship of Childhood Abuse and Household Dysfunction to Many of the Leading Causes of Death in Adults," *American Journal of Preventive Medicine* 14, no. 4 (May 1998): 245–58, https://www.ajpmonline.org/article/S0749-3797(98)00017-8/fulltext.

23. Robert F. Anda, Laura E. Porter, and David W. Brown, "Inside the Adverse Childhood Experience Score: Strengths, Limitations, and Misapplications," *American Journal of Preventive Medicine* 59, no. 2 (August 2020): 293, https://www.ajpmonline.org/article/S0749-3797(20)30058-1/fulltext.

24. Anda, Porter, and Brown, "Inside the Adverse Childhood Experience Score," 293.

25. Cindy Long, "'I'm Going to Reassure Them That They Are Safe': Talking to Students After the Election," *NEA Today*, November 9, 2016, https://www.nea.org/nea-today/all-news-articles/im-going-reassure-them-they-are-safe-talking-students-after-election.

26. Donna St. George and Valerie Strauss, "The Crisis of Student Mental Health Is Much Vaster Than We Realize," *Washington Post*, December 5, 2022, https://www.washingtonpost.com/education/2022/12/05/crisis-student-mental-health-is-much-vaster-than-we-realize.

27. Katherine Schaeffer, "In CDC Survey, 37% of U.S. High School Students Report Regular Mental Health Struggles During COVID-19 Pandemic," Pew Research Center, April 25, 2022, https://www.pewresearch.org/short-reads/2022/04/25/in-cdc-survey-37-of-u-s-high-school-students-report-regular-mental-health-struggles-during-covid-19.

28. Protect Our Kids Now, "Social Emotional Learning: A Critical Race Theory Trojan Horse," February 2023, https://protectourkidsnow.org/social-emotional-learning-a-critical-race-theory-trojan-horse.

29. Robert Pondiscio, "The Unexamined Rise of Therapeutic Education: How Social-Emotional Learning Extends K–12 Education's Reach into Students' Lives and Expands Teachers' Roles," American Enterprise Institute, October 13, 2021, https://www.aei.org/research-products/report/the-unexamined-rise-of-therapeutic-education-how-social-emotional-learning-extends-k-12-educations-reach-into-students-lives-and-expands-teachers-roles.

30. Shanker Vedantam and Jer Clifton, "How Your Beliefs Shape Reality," Hidden Brain Media, https://hiddenbrain.org/podcast/how-your-beliefs-shape-reality.

31. Vedantam and Clifton, "How Your Beliefs Shape Reality."

32. Arthur C. Brooks, "Don't Teach Your Kids to Fear the World," *The Atlantic*, September 1, 2022, https://www.theatlantic.com/family/archive/2022/09/the-best-way-to-teach-kids-about-danger/671310.

33. Clifton, "Don't Try to Toughen Students Up, Research Says."

3

The Tyranny of Happiness and Its Consequences

LAWRENCE H. DILLER

Aristotle remarked in his *Rhetoric* that young people "are high-minded, for they have not yet been humbled by life nor have they experienced the force of necessity.... They think they know everything, and confidently affirm it."[1] The Greek philosopher captured a perennial sense of worry that older generations show toward the youth, one that certainly hasn't gone away. But as a behavioral-developmental pediatrician with training in family therapy, I think it's safe to say that despite adults' persistent worries, kids these days *are* facing something new and worse.

In my over 40 years of private practice—seeing more than 5,000 children and their families from across the income spectrum and of varying demographic backgrounds—I've noticed troubling trends that mirror those of the wider population of young people. Rates of anxiety and depression have markedly increased for all teens. This increase has especially affected girls, who now outnumber boys in terms of anxiety and depression by a two-to-one ratio.[2] The percentage of youths receiving mental health services has spiked for both sexes and all races. Seventeen percent of teens and 15 percent of college-age young adults have engaged in some form of self-injury at least once.[3] A report by the Centers for Disease Control and Prevention in 2021 found that nearly 60 percent of female students experienced "persistent feelings of sadness or hopelessness" in the past year, while almost 25 percent "made a suicide plan." Completed suicide rates increased by 29 percent between 2012 and 2022, becoming the third leading cause of death for teens age 15 to 19.[4]

Though these trends seem to have started with the rise of social media and accelerated during the COVID-19 pandemic, youth mental health had been shaped before by two broad influences, one economic and the other psychological. To be clear, the greatest factors contributing to children's poor mental health are living in poverty and experiencing violence and their parents' substance abuse. But the biggest changes in children's mental health in the past 40 years have occurred among the middle class. The economic trend is perhaps more straightforward: Income disparities between low- and high-income Americans have risen since the 1980s, and people's happiness has become more closely tied to their economic status in recent decades.[5] Unhappy parents living amid these trends may find it more difficult to be consistent with their affection and discipline toward their children, contributing to more emotional and behavioral problems among kids.

The psychological trend is less noticed but arguably just as relevant, if not more. In a nutshell: Over the past 50 years, children's feelings about themselves, especially negative feelings like sadness and low self-esteem, have become far more important to their parents and teachers. This trend has concurrently shrunk the window of normalcy in describing differences in children (there are more children with psychiatric diagnoses), limited ways to teach children how to cope (especially regarding discipline), and greatly increased the roles of professionals (psychiatrists, psychologists, and special education teachers) whom parents have entrusted to address their worries about their children's feelings. To understand how it began, let's examine how parents, teachers, and medical professionals have overemphasized preserving positive feelings—or what I've come to think of as the "tyranny of happiness."

The Tyranny of Happiness

In his 2003 book *Therapy Culture: Cultivating Vulnerability in an Uncertain Age*, the British sociologist Frank Furedi notes a variety of economic and social factors starting at the end of the 19th century that led to kids' feelings becoming more central. Furedi posits that improvements in economic standing led initially to the wealthy spending more time and money with professionals seeking mental health relief. He suggests that a trend toward managing individual needs rather than those of the community (especially organized religion) also contributed to the growing importance of feelings for everyone, adults and children alike. The cultural importance of feelings strongly established itself by the mid-1960s in the United States.[6]

In the years since Furedi's book was published, the tyranny of happiness has only become more dominant, reaching young people of all ages. It also affects parents and other caregivers (e.g., teachers and preschool providers) who are uncomfortable with children feeling even temporarily distressed, especially if their distress results from reasonable limits being placed on them. Many upscale preschools, for example, have gone so far as to eschew the use of time-outs (now euphemistically called "break time") when dealing with an unhappy or out-of-control child.[7] Some consider this approach to be abusive or worry it might lead to permanent negative memories (a *forme fruste*, or clinical harbinger, of post-traumatic stress disorder). Similarly, teachers and principals I interact with in my practice have told me that at many schools, teachers routinely ask their entire class to leave the room rather than sending out the offending child. Many school districts now forbid a teacher or principal from escorting a kindergartner or first grader out the classroom, likely for fear of legal repercussions. Only staff, likely connected to special education services and specially trained in escort or restraint, are allowed to touch the child.

Unfortunately, these well-meaning, labor-intensive alternatives—as well as others, such as talking things through, offering choices, or having a separate teacher assigned to help the child navigate his or her feelings— have never been proven to be effective in children from middle- or upper-class families. Efforts to avoid conflict and negative feelings may also unintentionally make a situation worse. The use of sedating psychiatric drugs in one inpatient unit increased significantly when the staff was instructed to abandon time-outs and attempt more cognitive behavioral approaches.[8] Removing the entire class is likewise far more damaging to disruptive kids' self-image than being escorted to the principal's office. Their behavior has a visible impact on many more people. When the entire class departs, disruptive children feel worse about themselves than they would have if they had just been removed. For many persistent and intense children (especially boys), these alternative and seemingly positive approaches simply don't work.

The mindset that stems from the tyranny of happiness follows kids as they grow older. Avoiding unhappiness at all costs has led to a generation of children unprepared to face social (and educational) rigors, especially during puberty and adolescence.[9] Learning to accept and cope with stress at an early age prepares children for a time when caregivers are much less able to affect and rearrange the child's environment. This is particularly true for tweens facing the social cauldron of middle school and high school students beginning to face the choices of adulthood.

Teens have become more uneasy with emotional and physical intimacy—with profound and measurable implications. Reports of first sexual intercourse and physical intimacy appear later and later in the teenage years.[10] Young teens are also avoiding sexuality in another way: In vast numbers, they are refusing the traditional gender binary. Though an exploration of the transgender phenomenon is beyond the scope of this chapter, it's striking how many preteens and teens who have completed or partially completed transitioning have avoided close emotional and physical relationships, saying that they are just not interested in or ready for that kind of experience.[11]

The tyranny of happiness influences all aspects of child-rearing and teaching. Parents and teachers are under extraordinary pressure to "get it right" with their children. The fear of failing them drives parents first to their pediatrician and then to therapists and specialists like me in search of solutions to their kids' problems. Psychiatric diagnoses offer an attractive shortcut but unfortunately few answers. As a result, children are getting diagnosed with externalizing and anxious disorders earlier and in greater numbers than ever.

For example, diagnoses like attention deficit hyperactivity disorder (ADHD) and autism spectrum disorder (ASD) have exploded over the past three decades.[12] Moreover, higher medication rates have followed the higher rates of diagnoses. I estimate that approximately one-third of my referrals go about their lives comfortably *without* psychiatric medication. And yet, most American child psychiatrists employ only medications in their practices.[13]

Medication can work in the short term, but so can nondrug interventions. Medications prioritize efficiency and cost, but nondrug interventions prioritize engagement with the child, family, and school. I've never been against children's use of medications, but I am against medication as the first and only intervention for children's problems. This overall reliance on medication has not resulted in any obvious improvements on the epidemiological scale. Nevertheless, medical practitioners and insurance companies are exacerbating the tendency to diagnose young people with various disorders.

Expansive and Expensive Diagnoses

No biological test (blood, brain scan, etc.) or psychometric assessment can reliably diagnose psychiatric conditions in children or adults. Instead, a diagnosis is based on criteria spelled out by "expert" opinion in the *Diagnostic and Statistical Manual of Mental Disorders* (DSM), now in its fifth edition.

But broadened diagnostic criteria for ADHD and ASD in the DSM now capture many more children than in the past. Moreover, numerous new diagnoses—such as sensory processing disorder, pathological demand avoidance, avoidant/restrictive food intake disorder, and sluggish cognitive tempo—will likely be recognized in future DSMs because research and insurance dollars follow their inclusion. And when parents searching for answers find these disorders promoted online, they come to expect professionals to diagnose them.

As a result of its broader definition and the increased expectation of receiving one, a psychiatric diagnosis has come to imply that children's mental health challenges are inherent, biological, or genetic. Rather than thinking a young patient *won't* do something (be it homework, chores, or orders), a diagnosis justifies the view that he or she simply *can't*. Under this mindset, holding him or her accountable would be the same as punishing a child with a congenitally short leg for not running as fast as other kids. In fact, most treatment guidelines for the above conditions call for accommodations for the child's problem (e.g., more time for tests, more choice, and more one-on-one sessions with teachers) to avoid conflict.

With the ever-growing number of potential diagnoses and diagnosed children, the window of normalcy for children has narrowed. Unsurprisingly, that has led to more diagnoses. Nearly 20 years ago, I explored this phenomenon in my book *The Last Normal Child: Essays on the Intersection of Kids, Culture, and Psychiatric Drugs*. At that time, I was treating a 12-year-old boy who had been doing poorly in school. His motivation was inconsistent.

But he was feeling bad about his performance. I didn't think that this boy had ADHD, but I knew that by using the criteria to diagnose ADHD, I could rationalize giving him medication that would likely improve his performance and have him feel better about himself. It was a pivotal case for me in that I began giving medication to children I didn't feel were seriously impaired by their mental conditions but whose situations would be improved by medication. I mused that if I could justify calling this boy's problems "ADHD" and treating him with medication—meaning he was abnormal—there might come a time when there were no more "normal" children.[14] Since then, the trend of giving medication to children like this boy has become only more pronounced.

If a diagnosis is supposed to explain what's affecting a child, delineate the natural course of a disease, and determine specific treatment, child psychiatric diagnoses generally fail on all three counts. Except for a small minority of children, individual diagnoses today rarely offer a good description of the cause, the likely course of the problem, or specific treatments.

This doesn't mean the psychological problems children and teens face have no basis in biology. Indeed, biology probably plays the largest role in behavior. But it is not the *only* factor in problem creation. By contrast, consider the *won't* versus *can't* example from above. In my practice, I prefer to treat children's problems with a position that acknowledges aspects of both *can't* and *won't*: "It's *harder* for them to do it, but under the right conditions they can." This approach allows for accommodation *and* accountability, with rewards and consequences as reinforcers. Punishment is the third rail in child psychology, but entirely avoiding it eliminates a potent motivator. No child should experience repetitive ineffective punishments. Yet if a sanction's short-term consequences improve behavior or performance, it should be part of the armamentarium for parents and teachers.

Child psychiatry, however, has been passive about its interventions—except the vastly increased use of psychiatric drugs. A child psychiatrist can double his or her hourly earnings by seeing four 15-minute "med-check" visits, rather than one 50-minute consultation with a child or his family.[15] Insurance companies reimburse at rates that reinforce this practice (though most child psychiatrists are so busy they no longer participate with insurance companies).

Another failure of the child mental health industry has been that it remains oriented toward the individual, evaluating and treating only children and teens. Parents, if involved, are seen only intermittently, and they are regularly kept out of the treatment for "confidentiality" concerns. Psychoanalytic theory has been abandoned by most of psychiatry, yet it remains a potent theoretical framework in play therapy for younger children. While cognitive behavioral therapies are currently popular, virtually all treatments that have included parents have been shown to be more effective than treating the child alone.[16]

More and more effort, money, and time are spent on a diagnosis. The "psychoeducational" evaluations of the 1970s to the 2000s have morphed into the current "neuropsychiatric" evaluation. The former involved some two to three hours of testing. Reports ran to about 12–15 pages, including a modest number of treatment recommendations, at a cost in today's dollars of around $2,000 to $2,500. Neuropsychiatric evaluations today, by contrast, are much more involved. Many parents have told me that waiting lists run up to six months for an exam that can include five or six hours of evaluation and cost between $5,000 and $6,000. Generated reports run over 50 pages, with over 40 recommendations.[17] It is rare to find a neuropsychiatric report on a child that doesn't include a diagnosis of ADHD and a recommendation to further investigate the use of medication.

Lost Opportunities and Confusion at Schools

The increased demand for extensive neuropsychological testing has had school psychologists trying to catch up to their private counterparts. School psychologists, already overburdened with extraordinary caseloads, spend an overwhelming amount of time testing, writing reports, and attending Individualized Educational Program (IEP) assessment meetings with school personnel and parents. Any counseling is deferred to less-trained school counselors.

The IEP meeting has also grown in scope, time, and inefficiency. I've attended at least 200 IEP meetings over the years. The school staff is always pleased and surprised to see a medical professional, even if—as has been the case for me lately—only virtually. But these meetings have deteriorated over the years. They are meant to communicate to the parents the school's sense of their child's strengths and weaknesses; to determine what, if any, interventions the child qualifies for; and to establish what services the school can provide. Picture a parent—usually the mother—surrounded by four or five experts, each of whom reports the results of their testing. Any patient can usually remember two or at most three things a doctor shares in delivering a diagnosis. In these meetings, the school staff inundates parents with test scores and opinions presented in a quasi-legal atmosphere. Meetings that were once 30–45 minutes long now routinely run for 90 minutes. What is a parent, school, or child supposed to do with all this information?

This isn't meant as a criticism of public schools, which have borne the brunt of the decline of children's mental health. Under the Individuals with Disabilities Education Act (IDEA), not only do learning problems fall under the educational responsibility of the school district, but so do mental health concerns. But over the years, federal and state budgets have funded, at most, only 50 percent of special education costs.[18] Individual districts are left to make up the difference: They must balance the rights and needs of special education students with those of the other children in the regular classroom.

We are thus diagnosing more students—some unnecessarily—but also failing to fully fund the diagnoses and support we are prescribing. This underfunding of special education puts pressure on school districts to limit services that cost money. Special education student services cost the school district three times as much as services for children in the general education classroom.[19] The classic snake-eats-its-tail paradox follows. As more funds are directed to special education, student-to-teacher ratios rise in the general classroom. As there are more students for the individual teacher in the general classroom, more children with borderline coping skills deteriorate and become eligible for special education services. And on it goes.

The greatest special education drain on school budgets is the district's responsibility to pay for a private educational placement when there isn't a satisfactory environment in the public setting. A small industry has developed consisting of specialty lawyers hired by wealthier families to sue the school district to pay for private day school and residential therapeutic boarding schools. In some cases, these schools can cost between $60,000 and $80,000 a year.[20] Based on previous court decisions, school districts have decided not to fight most suits and settle, generally paying for a portion of the costs involved in private placement. Insurance companies and the family pick up the balance. One wealthy school district in my area has reserved two beds always available at a long-term residential therapeutic school because it is cheaper than fighting lawsuits and settling on an alternative private setting.

One can question the school's overall mandate to take on this much responsibility for children's mental health. In an ideal world, the school's access to the family through the child is an opportunity to potentially intervene early with family dysfunction that contributes in part to the child's school problems. But in most school districts, counselors may contact parents only with the child's permission (over age 12), except in life-threatening situations.[21] Meeting the child alone is better than nothing—but sometimes not much better than nothing and therefore a relative waste of school resources and money.

Identifying mental health problems like depression and anxiety through school-based general screenings has been controversial and is often resisted by the community.[22] Ideally, earlier recognition might result in earlier intervention. But concerns arise about stigmatization and treatment, given that counseling is often unavailable in many communities. In consequence, earlier diagnoses result in only an earlier administration of psychiatric medications. Whether drugs alone are better than no treatment at all is a reasonable question. However, drugs are not a morally equivalent substitute for treatments that engage the child and family.

The Recent Past and the Path Forward

It's important to note that not all the trends I've observed over the past 40 years have worsened children's mental health and treatment. Fathers, for example, are more involved in treatment. All but maybe 20 fathers of my patients out of some 5,000 elected to be involved in their children's treatment, especially if I called them directly and requested their participation. The "sense" that fathers are important for the evaluation and treatment of children's mental health has become much more accepted and routine.

Two drugs have made a significant difference in children's mental health. Concerta (methylphenidate), a long-acting stimulant used to treat ADHD since 2000, eliminated the lines forming at lunchtime for students' second dose of Ritalin, the previous variety of methylphenidates that was much shorter acting. A child or teen can take Concerta at 8:00 a.m., and the effects will last until 6:00 p.m. Eliminating the need for a second and third dosage significantly improved compliance and reduced the stigma students who needed to take the drug felt. Now there are over a dozen long-acting stimulant preparations for ADHD. But Concerta was the first.

Additionally, Prozac (fluoxetine), the first selective serotonin reuptake inhibitor (SSRI), was introduced in 1987 as an antidepressant and has proved to be reasonably effective in treating depression, anxiety, and a slew of similar psychiatric conditions. Similar to Concerta, there are now a half dozen SSRI medications. They are more effective with adults than children. They are also infinitely safer than their predecessors. A chief method of suicide in America was once overdosing on antidepressant medication.[23] Prozac, by contrast, does not pose that risk.

Moreover, applied behavioral analysis (ABA) has provided an effective way to treat autism. In the 1970s and '80s, an autism diagnosis was one of the worst pieces of news doctors could deliver to parents. It was believed to be neurologically based and incurable. But reports from the University of California, Los Angeles, in the late 1980s showed a return to normal functioning for most of the autism-diagnosed preschoolers exposed to 40 hours a week of ABA.[24] Subsequent studies showed much more modest success ranges, but the overall effect was consistent: A group of children appeared "normal" at age 5 if they maintained two to three years of treatment.[25]

Nevertheless, the tyranny of happiness and the related expansion of treatment with, at best, mixed results continue. Finding solutions to the multiple trends contributing to the crisis in children's mental health and treatment is a humbling exercise. Though some of the macro trends are unlikely to change soon, parents, teachers, mental health professionals, insurance companies, and policymakers can make adjustments to ameliorate the most harmful consequences for children. The following seem to me like a promising way to start.

Everyone. We must stop worrying so much about our children's feelings. The "tyranny of happiness" creates enormous pressures on children, parents, and teachers. In his recent book *The Anxious Generation: How the Great Rewiring of Childhood Is Causing an Epidemic of Mental Illness*, the social psychologist Jonathan Haidt asks parents specifically to resist "safetyism" by allowing their children more freedom to explore their environments without adult supervision. He acknowledges that the process intentionally exposes them to more risks of physical and emotional injury but importantly allows them more opportunities to develop self-awareness and self-protective skills.[26]

Parents. Parents should talk less and take action sooner when setting limits with their children. This approach to parenting is encapsulated in the parenting manual *1-2-3 Magic*. Too many children, especially boys, struggle with the current cognitive behavioral approaches to setting limits. In *Magic*, the ritual of counting improves parents' effectiveness in discipline by their talking less, giving fewer chances, and taking an immediate action (reward or consequence). Alternative guides do not have the evidence to support their use. *Magic* does.[27]

Parents should require that children and teens turn in all their screens by 9:00 or 10:00 p.m. School administrators should set limits to cell phone access at school.

Schools. Policymakers need to ease the burden on public schools to provide an optimal education for all students. Requiring school districts to pay for private schools or residential therapeutic placements must be more restricted. Legislation or court rulings must limit the extent of IDEA.

The IEP meeting needs serious reform to move from its current quasi-legal process to one that effectively communicates the child's strengths and weaknesses to parents and leaves time for a discussion of reasonable and achievable accommodations and interventions. Small-group instruction for children in elementary school and a study hall period for middle and high school students are the most effective ways to help disabled children learn successfully at school.

School psychologists and counselors should be encouraged to include parents in treating children at school.

Medical Practitioners. The five-hour, 50-page neuropsychological evaluation is a relative waste of public and private resources. Professional educational and mental health organizations (e.g., the American Academy of Child and Adolescent Psychiatry, American Academy of Pediatrics, and National Association of School Psychologists) should speak out against these excesses. Insurance companies often refuse to pay, and parents are left spending their own dollars.

Dispense with the requirement of a psychiatric diagnosis for insurance companies to pay for eight to 10 outpatient visits. Employment assistance programs do not require a psychiatric diagnosis. Families seeking assistance for their children's problems should be enough. However, any treatment beyond 10 sessions should require a review or second opinion from a noninvolved mental health expert.

Insurance Companies. Insurance companies should reevaluate their support of individual therapy for children given its poor track record compared with family- and parent-involved treatments. Payment for ongoing play therapy often delays implementation of more effective interventions. Exceptions should be made for major child trauma, suspected abuse, and high-conflict divorce.

Insurance companies must end differential (i.e., higher pay) for psychiatrists when they prescribe medication versus when they offer cognitive or psychotherapeutic interventions. The higher pay is a financial incentive that further prioritizes medication as a first-line intervention for children's emotional and behavioral problems.

Conclusion

I've been extraordinarily fortunate to be able to pursue a professional career that has allowed me to serve so many families. I have been able to do what I thought made the most sense and worked best, medically and ethically, in my practice, despite the many cultural, political, and economic challenges. I hope the next generation of mental health experts and policy-makers will try, as I have, to find workable, multidisciplinary approaches to address what has become an increasingly concerning emotional landscape for children and teens.

Notes

1. Aristotle, *Rhetoric*, trans. J. H. Freese (London: William Heineman, 1926), 249–51, http://www.perseus.tufts.edu/hopper/text?doc=Perseus%3Atext%3A1999.01.0060%3Abekker+page%3D1389a.

2. Centers for Disease Control and Prevention, National Center for HIV, Viral Hepatitis, STD, and Tuberculosis Prevention, *Youth Risk Behavior Survey: Data Summary & Trends Report: 2011–2021*, 2023, 60, https://www.cdc.gov/healthyyouth/data/yrbs/pdf/YRBS_Data-Summary-Trends_Report2023_508.pdf.

3. Qingqing Xiao et al., "Global Prevalence and Characteristics of Non-Suicidal Self-Injury Between 2010 and 2021 Among a Non-Clinical Sample of Adolescents: A Meta-Analysis," *Frontiers in Psychiatry* 13, no. 912441 (August 10, 2022): 1–16, https://www.frontiersin.org/journals/psychiatry/articles/10.3389/fpsyt.2022.912441/full.

4. Centers for Disease Control and Prevention, National Center for HIV, Viral Hepatitis, STD, and Tuberculosis Prevention, *Youth Risk Behavior Survey*, 2.

5. Jean M. Twenge, *Generations: The Real Differences Between Gen Z, Millennials, Gen X, Boomers, and Silents—and What They Mean for America's Future* (New York: Atria Books, 2023).

6. Frank Furedi, *Therapy Culture: Cultivating Vulnerability in an Uncertain Age* (London: Routledge, 2004).

7. Katherine Martinelli, "Are Time Outs Harmful to Children?," Child Mind Institute, October 30, 2023, https://childmind.org/article/are-time-outs-harmful-kids.

8. Gabrielle A. Carlson et al., "Behavior Modification Is Associated with Reduced Psychotropic Medication Use in Children with Aggression in Inpatient Treatment: A Retrospective Cohort Study," *Journal of the American Academy of Child and Adolescent Psychiatry* 59, no. 5 (May 2020): 632–41, https://www.jaacap.org/article/S0890-8567(19)31435-2/abstract.

9. Jonathan Haidt, *The Anxious Generation: How the Great Rewiring of Childhood Is Causing an Epidemic of Mental Illness* (New York: Penguin Press, 2024).

10. Mike Stobbe, "Pandemic Sent High School Sex to New Low, Survey Finds," Associated Press, April 27, 2023, https://apnews.com/article/teen-sex-survey-high-school-3d45d0441f531d1da9f5b44373becee4.

11. Robin Respaut and Chad Terhune, "Putting Numbers on the Rise in Children Seeking Gender Care," Reuters, October 6, 2022, https://www.reuters.com/investigates/special-report/usa-transyouth-data.

12. Melissa L. Danielson et al., "ADHD Prevalence Among US Children and Adolescents in 2022: Diagnosis, Severity, Co-Occurring Disorders, and Treatment," *Journal of Clinical Child & Adolescent Psychology* 53, no. 3 (2024): 343–60, https://www.tandfonline.com/doi/full/10.1080/15374416.2024.2335625; and Ginny Russell et al., "Time Trends in Autism Diagnosis over 20 Years: A UK Population-Based Cohort Study," *Journal of Child Psychology and Psychiatry* 63, no. 6 (June 2022): 674–82, https://acamh.onlinelibrary.wiley.com/doi/10.1111/jcpp.13505.

13. Dorothy E. Stubbe and W. John Thomas, "A Survey of Early-Career Child and Adolescent Psychiatrists: Professional Activities and Perceptions," *Journal of the American Academy of Child and Adolescent Psychiatry* 41, no. 2 (February 2002): 123–30, https://www.jaacap.org/article/S0890-8567(09)60654-7/abstract.

14. Lawrence H. Diller, *The Last Normal Child: Essays on the Intersection of Kids, Culture, and Psychiatric Drugs* (Westport, CT: Praeger, 2006).

15. From one insurance company, I am paid $150 for a 15-minute med-check visit, of which I can do potentially four in an hour. I am paid $337 if I spend 45–50 minutes in a psychotherapy session in which I am also prescribing a medication.

16. Stephen Pilling et al., "Recognition, Intervention, and Management of Antisocial Behaviour and Conduct Disorders in Children and Young People: Summary of NICE-SCIE Guidance," *BMJ* 346, no. 7902 (April 6, 2013): 33–35, https://www.bmj.com/content/346/bmj.f1298.

17. Recent patient's father, phone call with the author, August 2024.

18. US Department of Education, Institute of Education Sciences, National Center for Education Statistics, "Public School Revenue Sources," May 2024, https://nces.ed.gov/programs/coe/indicator/cma/public-school-revenue.

19. Louis Freedberg, "California Spending over $13 Billion Annually on Special Education," EdSource, November 8, 2019, https://edsource.org/2019/california-spending-over-13-billion-annually-on-special-education/619542.

20. For example, the average cost of attending a private residential school in California is $73,155. Boarding School Review, "Best California Boarding Schools (2024–25)," accessed September 27, 2024, https://www.boardingschoolreview.com/california.

21. Carolyn Stone, "Confidentiality, Privileged Communication and Your Legal Muscle," ASCASchoolCounselor, March 1, 2012, https://www.schoolcounselor.org/Magazines/March-April-2012/Confidentiality,-Privileged-Communication-and-Your.

22. University of California, Los Angeles, Center for Mental Health in Schools, *Screening Mental Health Problems in Schools*, January 2007, https://smhp.psych.ucla.edu/pdfdocs/policyissues/mhscreeningissues.pdf.

23. Shitij Kapur, Tammy Mieczkowski, and J. John Mann, "Antidepressant Medications and the Relative Risk of Suicide Attempt and Suicide," *Journal of the American Medical Association* 268, no. 24 (December 23, 1992): 3441–45, https://jamanetwork.com/journals/jama/article-abstract/402188.

24. O. Ivar Lovaas, "Behavioral Treatment and Normal Educational and Intellectual Functioning in Young Autistic Children," *Journal of Consulting and Clinical Psychology* 55, no. 1 (February 1987): 3–9, https://psycnet.apa.org/doiLanding?doi=10.1037%2F0022-006X.55.1.3.

25. Kristen R. Choi et al., "Patient Outcomes After Applied Behavior Analysis for Autism Spectrum Disorder," *Journal of Developmental and Behavioral Pediatrics* 43, no. 1 (January 2022): 9–16, https://journals.lww.com/jrnldbp/abstract/2022/01000/patient_outcomes_after_applied_behavior_analysis.2.aspx.

26. Haidt, *The Anxious Generation*.

27. Seven peer-reviewed articles supporting the effectiveness of 1-2-3 *Magic*'s approach are available at California Evidence-Based Clearinghouse for Child Welfare, "1-2-3 Magic: Effective Discipline for Children 2–12," March 2023, www.cebc4cw.org/program/1-2-3-magic-effective-discipline-for-children-2-12.

4

Coming of Age in a Postmarital Culture

KAY HYMOWITZ

Of the many possible causes proposed to explain the sadness of today's adolescents, one in particular seems to dominate: the omnipresence of cell phones and social media. The timing makes a lot of sense. Adolescent mood disorders, depression, and even suicide became more common starting around 2012, only a few years after the widespread adoption of smartphones. Since 2014, the proportion of teens who say they use the internet "almost constantly" has doubled.[1]

This technological theory, however, raises further questions. If cell phones and social media are so noxious, why did American kids become enthralled by them so easily? Would a resilient, optimistic, energetic population of teens have succumbed in such a dramatic fashion to the bullying of digital gossip and the outlandish trend chasing of Instagram and TikTok? As the writer Isaac Wilks has astutely observed, "None of the analysts have sufficiently explained *why* and *how* American young people were primed for such a swift emotional implosion when life was digitized."[2]

One potential answer has lurked silently in the background of discussions about the mental health problems facing 21st-century adolescents: the fraying of the family.

America's family troubles didn't start in the 2010s, of course. The institution of marriage was first shaken in the late 1960s and early 1970s. Researchers have been studying the impact of its decline on children ever since, finding correlations between family breakdown and a host of childhood problems.[3] One of them—especially relevant to the current debates about technology and mental health—is that kids growing up in what used to be called "broken homes" are at greater risk of depression, especially during adolescence.[4]

But the problem is even more fundamental. Fifty years of family upheaval has eroded the traditional way young people thought about their futures and in so doing changed the emotional ecosystem of adolescence. If kids are depressed and anxious, it is in part because older generations have shredded the most legible scripts for becoming an adult—namely, those of marriage and parenthood. Fickle as they may be, marriage and parenthood offer people guidance on how to form the stable, intimate connections that are so essential to human flourishing.

The decline of marriage and parenthood affects kids from all family backgrounds. Whether they are children of parents who had a screaming divorce or an amicable one, children who grew up with a single mother and didn't know their fathers, or those lucky ones who grew up with some postmodern version of *The Adventures of Ozzie and Harriet*, all suffer from a lack of legible scripts to walk them through to adulthood. Like a digital pied piper, social media arrived at the perfect cultural moment to seduce a population of young people bereft of cultural guidance.

The Adolescent Script

"What do you want to be when you grow up?"

Most American kids start hearing this question in the nursery school dress-up corner. At that early age, the answer may be something like an astronaut, a police officer, or (as my youngest responded when she was 3 years old) "a singer, because all you have to do is sing." Amusing as these responses may be, the question itself is revealing. It communicates two expectations about growing up in fluid, postindustrial homes: Adults expect children to choose and plan their future, and the consequential question facing children revolves around the kind of work they will do.

The career question becomes even more central for teens, affecting their education and their sense of themselves as future adults. It's a subject of discussion with counselors and teachers. It may guide them and their parents in choosing schools to attend and classes to take. The career question might determine what after-school and summer programs they sign up for. It will certainly be the subject of college essays and interview questions for those who apply.

Important as it is, however, the career question is a narrow one, limited to a person's vocation. It doesn't address their more personal aspirations.

It doesn't, in other words, question whether young people aspire to get married and have kids themselves.

Until the recent past, silence on the question of conjugal identities was understandable. Getting married and having children was just what nearly everyone did. Kids grew up seeing parents, grandparents, aunts, uncles, and neighbors living with their wives or husbands. Those households generally had either children in the house or grown children nearby. In 1965, three-fourths of all households consisted of married couples. Bachelors and divorcées existed, of course, but children encountered them only rarely. So few children lived with a single parent that they were barely a blip on statistical charts.[5]

Educators reinforced this presupposed social order. To prepare for their future lives as wives and mothers, girls took "home ec" to learn how to cook and plan thrifty, healthy meals for their families. Boys, meanwhile, took "shop" to learn skills they might use in their work or around the house where they raised their families. Absurd as it sounds in an age of Tinder hookups, some girls had "hope chests" in which they collected clothing and household items they planned to use in married life.

Without question, freedom from strict social rules about sex and marriage has benefited untold numbers, especially sexual minorities. That said, the lack of guiding scripts about marriage and parenthood has left kids today disoriented amid a wave of social change. Their current unhappiness tells us something about the pitfalls of growing up in a postmarital society. To understand why this is true, it's helpful to take a brief detour into the anthropological record of adolescence.

Marriage, Parenthood, and Human Anthropology

Throughout human history, the young were all but universally expected to eventually begin a new family, meaning they would marry and have children. Every culture has passed down established life scripts—a series of stages for young people to traverse to become adult men and women—to guide the next generation in this process. Yes, these scripts varied from culture to culture and era to era. In some cultures, marriage was monogamous; more often it was polygamous. Usually the bride moved in with her husband's family, but in some cases couples lived in separate nuclear households. Although for us modern skeptics the nuclear family is a social construct, an artifice of time and place to be debated and transformed, for most humans, the family forms before them seemed just as natural as the local flora and fauna.

To Westerners who take the modern welfare state for granted, it may not be obvious why marriage and the family have been a cultural universal.[6] The answer is that together they mitigated numerous problems underlying human biology and psychology.

Marriage helped support the human propensity toward pair bonding and the urge to procreate. It reduced sexual competition. It contained the sexual energies of the young, "of fertile daughters and lusty sons," as Alice Schlegel, perhaps the leading anthropologist of adolescence, and Herbert Barry put it.[7] It tied men to their children, thereby improving the young's chances of survival (and, for that matter, the group's).

Historically, weddings weren't seen as a celebration of an individual couple's happiness but rather as the moment when young men and women stepped into their crucial role of forming the next generation of families. Whatever their specific rules and with only extremely rare exceptions, families (i.e., married couples with children) have been fundamental to sustaining complex social groups—whether clans, towns, countries, or religions.[8]

Saying that marriage and parenthood were cultural universals for adults doesn't mean that every individual married and had children. Even in pre-industrial cultures, where single adults could not survive on their own, there were alternatives—including for sexual minorities.[9] But much like marriage, these alternatives were tightly scripted, with a shared understanding of the role these singles would play within the social order.

This family- and clan-centered past amounts to far more than an anthropological curiosity; it helps clarify the strange predicament facing today's adolescents. Adolescence, the period between puberty and social and economic maturity, has always been what the writer Martin Gurri calls a "liminal" space.[10] It's the greenroom where the young loiter before stepping onto the public stage of full, generally married, adulthood—where the young reach sexual maturity, court, and pair off. Even if no one put it precisely this way in freer, modern cultures, one of the main functions of adolescence was to equip young people to find a suitable and hopefully lifelong companion.

But today, teens are being asked to make up their own scripts about marriage and family, whole cloth. Their pessimism about both prospects suggests it's a monumentally difficult task.

As Marriage Declined, Gen Z Took Note

Given America's disappointing record in both marriage and childbearing, Generation Z has good reason to be wary. Marriage rates have declined by 60 percent since their grandparents were coming of age.[11] Forty percent of married couples break up.[12] The percentage of women who never marry is 29 percent, close to a historical high.[13] Forty percent of Gen Z kids were born to unmarried mothers. True, many of those infants will live with both parents, but the odds are those dads will move out by the time their child is in third grade. In the United States, unmarried cohabitation tends to be a fragile, short-term arrangement.

Adding to cynicism about family life is the simple fact that, like most un-partnered humans, single parents are probably looking for intimate companionship regardless of earlier romantic disappointments. Some of those companions will become trusted and beloved stepparents for children in the house. However, many will be only one in a series of itinerant roommates.[14] As the psychologist Rob Henderson writes in his recent memoir, "I lived in so many homes and saw so many breakups growing up and the lesson this imparted was that all relationships are fleeting, and everyone is replaceable."[15]

If Gen Zers have grown up to be skeptical about marriage, they won't get much of a counterargument from their parents. In a Pew survey released in 2023, parents were asked what they viewed as the most important priority for their children.[16] Understandably, there was almost universal agreement—among 88 percent of respondents, specifically—that financial independence is extremely or very important. More surprising, even delusional to those of us who are grandparents, were the measly 22 percent who put much stock in their children eventually marrying and having children at all.

Other studies reveal a similarly odd apathy among American parents toward their own descendants. The instability of cohabitation when compared to marriage is as strong a finding as any in family research.[17] Still, one Gallup poll shows Americans were 16 percentage points more likely to approve of out-of-wedlock birth in 2015 than in 2000.[18] Moreover, 40 percent of American adults are indifferent to whether couples with children should marry.[19]

Pop culture reflects this increasing apathy toward marriage. Take two of the most popular, marriage-centered TV shows of the past quarter century: *The Bachelor* and its spin-off, *The Bachelorette*. Even our marriage-averse culture has managed to stomach 28 and 20 consecutive seasons, respectively, of both shows. There are still *Bachelor* and *Bachelorette* fangirls—the show's viewership overwhelmingly skews female—who covet a diamond ring. But ratings for these reality shows have plummeted since the early aughts, when the franchise was must-see TV. Viewership for *The Bachelor* peaked at nearly 26 million viewers in 2002; by 2023, it had dropped below three million viewers.[20]

There have always been singles, of course. But in recent years, marriage has been increasingly viewed as a threat to autonomy and self-development. In a 2023 "Singles in America" survey organized by the Harris Poll, a market research firm, participants were asked why they prefer to remain single. Eighty-four percent of singles answered that they preferred remaining unmarried because they could "move anywhere without considering a partner," "focus more on [their] personal growth," and have the "freedom to do whatever [they] want without justification, discussion, or compromise."[21]

From Child-Free to Childish

Given the dramatic drop in stable families and worsening attitudes toward the prospects of marriage, it's not surprising that our culture in general—and Gen Z in particular—has also eschewed another previously assumed script: parenthood.

A helpless infant limits an individualist's independence and self-exploration, two essential values of our postmarital culture. Millennials are on track to be the most childless generation in American history, with some demographers projecting that 25 percent of that cohort will not have kids.[22] But Gen Z will probably outdo them. Forty-four percent of childless individuals between the ages of 18 and 49 say they are unlikely to ever want children.[23]

This reluctance to become parents is sometimes cast as a matter of social and global justice. After all, each baby born represents another two dirty carbon footprints defiling an already polluted planet. But while the 20-something anti-natalist social justice warrior may be the subject of quotable trend pieces, she is not typical of childless Zoomers and millennials. Only 5 percent of those who don't plan to have children cite global climate worries. The majority (56 percent) of childless adults younger than 50 say, simply, that they "just don't want to have kids."[24]

Nowhere is this apathy about children more on display than in the online spaces teens today frequent. The subreddit "r/Childfree" boasts 1.5 million members. Child-free TikTok has over 242 million views. Instagram is also a carnival of child-free accounts. One popular TikToker hosts a #freebirthcontrol series reminding followers of all the reasons having kids is ruinous: sagging breasts, varicose veins, cluttered homes, and interrupted sleep and meals.[25] Some of the reasons her followers offer for their natal preferences don't inspire much hope about the depth or farsightedness of the next generation: "I like to walk around the house naked," "I love spicy food," "my partner and I are both gamers," and "the cables all over the living room would be dangerous for a young child."[26]

The superficiality of explanations like these suggests that Gen Z has become not only more child averse than previous generations but also more childish. As the psychologist Jean Twenge observed, "18-year-olds now act more like 15-year-olds used to, and 15-year-olds more like 13-year-olds. Childhood now stretches well into high school."[27]

Only about half of Gen Z men have any interest in dating, and Gen Z women are even more indifferent to the idea.[28] Furthermore, the sexes have grown strangely indifferent to sex itself. Even as the media continued to be hypersexualized in the early 21st century—*50 Shades of Grey*, *Euphoria*, and the normalization of sex work—teens just started saying no. The percentage of high school juniors who have ever had sexual intercourse declined from 62 percent in 1991 to 42 percent today. This "sex recession," as described by the writer Kate Julian, has experts at a loss, but it is entirely in keeping with the other ways young people are shying away from adulthood and mature relationships.[29]

Mistrust of intimacy and dating go a long way toward explaining "the sex recession" among young people. Why date if you don't think anything meaningful can come of it, especially if you are surrounded by so much mistrust of the opposite sex? One popular meme highlights the sort of "red flags" that might signal "toxic power dynamics in relationships." Another, under the rubric "beige flags," is closer to mean-girl bitchiness.[30] TikTok posts catalog men's quirky, awkward, or gross habits that turn women off. These "icks" might include videos of a guy falling off his bike, not wiping food from his face, or standing with his feet pointed outward.[31]

And of those teens who do date, many end up in relationships that aren't conducive to marriage or parenthood. Often, they end up in mere "situationships." As the term suggests, situationships are impromptu, temporary, and directionless, somewhere between casual dating and "friends with benefits." The Tinder report *Future of Dating 2023*, written by "arguably one of the world's most famous and respected matchmakers," finds close to 80 percent of those age 18–25 say their own self-care is their most important consideration when dating, and 79 percent want their prospective partners to make their own well-being a priority too.[32]

Situationships seem like the perfect invention for a generation preferring self-care over genuine attachment. That it gets the seal of approval from an expert matchmaker speaks volumes about culture's suspicion of any attachment that calls for compromise. To the zealous individualist, compromise suggests self-abnegation. Romance and love are just not part of the picture.

Freedom Without Scripts

It's an article of American faith that people have the right to live their lives the way they want. That's why people have always clamored to come to the US, why many today brave the Darién Gap, coyotes, and treacherous rivers to get through the southern border. For most people living in America, the freedom to craft their own life is the whole point.

Arguably, young people today have been born in an America at the pinnacle of its promise of freedom. Outside of making enough money to feed and shelter themselves—and even that they might be able to finesse with a little help from their friends, family, and the government—there is far less pressure to conform to social expectations. People can marry, or not. They can have children, or not. They can raise a child alone. They can raise a child with a partner but leave when love grows cold or when they simply get restless. They can have children with different partners, and no one will say a thing against it (at least not out loud). They can bed down in a "polycule" of straight and gay men and women. They're so free they can even change their sex or pronounce themselves free of any gender.

At its best, this extraordinary freedom means "you get to curate your own life," as Bella DePaulo, psychologist and author of *Single at Heart: The Power, Freedom, and Heart-Filling Joy of Single Life*, puts it in her celebration of unmarried life.[33] But it's one thing to be an adult who, having grown up in a specific culture, tries to "curate" her own life; it's another to be a child without enough experience of life's inevitable constraints to evaluate the scripts, institutions, and norms she's supposed to curate.

In their current unhappiness, the young are signaling that unguided freedom has been a recipe for disenchantment and loneliness for them. Humans can't create themselves de novo. They understand the world and their own identity through the language and concepts their culture provides them. Children's brains, larger than those of any other species, have evolved to latch on to local cultural norms, just as they have evolved to learn the language they hear spoken around them.

Growing up in a culture that has lost faith in its most fundamental, normative institutions—marriage and the family—and a culture increasingly untethered from the social forms of the human past, adolescents don't "find their authentic self." They fill themselves up with fragments of "wisdom" they pick up on the internet. Their mental health diagnoses, their perpetual adolescence, and their disembodied social connections may give temporary relief to their emptiness and confusion, but they do little to guide them toward a fulfilling social embeddedness.

"Good ideology, wrong species," the biologist E. O. Wilson once remarked about Communism.[34] The same goes for adolescence without a script.

Notes

1. Jonathan Haidt, Zach Rausch, and Jean Twenge, *Adolescent Mood Disorders Since 2010: A Collaborative Review*, New York University, https://docs.google.com/document/d/1diMvsMeRphUH7E6D1d_J7R6WbDdgnzFHDHPx9HXzR50/edit?pli=1; and Emily A. Vogels, Risa Gelles-Watnick, and Navid Massarat, "Teens, Social Media and Technology 2022," Pew Research Center, August 10, 2022, https://www.pewresearch.org/internet/2022/08/10/teens-social-media-and-technology-2022.

2. Isaac Wilks, "The Zoomer Question," *American Affairs* 7, no. 2 (Summer 2023): 192–208, https://americanaffairsjournal.org/2023/05/the-zoomer-question.

3. Melissa S. Kearney, *The Two-Parent Privilege: How Americans Stopped Getting Married and Started Falling Behind* (Chicago: University of Chicago Press, 2023).

4. Issar Daryanai et al., "Single Mother Parenting and Adolescent Psychopathology," *Journal of Abnormal Child Psychology* 44 (October 2016): 1411–23, https://link.springer.com/article/10.1007/s10802-016-0128-x.

5. US Department of Education, Institute of Education Sciences, National Center for Education Statistics, "Indicator 11. Children of Single Parents," 1996, https://nces.ed.gov/pubs98/yi/y9611a.asp; and US Department of Education, Institute of Education Sciences, National Center for Education Statistics, "Indicator 11. Family Formation," 1996, https://nces.ed.gov/pubs98/yi/y9611c.asp.

6. Donald E. Brown, "Human Universals, Human Nature & Human Culture," *Daedalus* 133, no. 4 (Fall 2004): 47–58, https://www.jstor.org/stable/20027944.

7. Alice Schlegel and Herbert Barry III, *Adolescence: An Anthropological Inquiry* (New York: Free Press, 1991), 18.

8. Cai Hua, *A Society Without Fathers or Husbands: The Na of China*, trans. Asti Hustvedt (New York: Zone Books, 2001).

9. Some cultures, for example, had accepted scripts for homosexual men. The Hijras of India, who dressed and behaved like women, had a spiritual function in their tribe. In Polynesia, effeminate boys called *fa'afafine* were raised as girls, and they were expected to perform female roles like helping mothers and grandmothers cook and tend children. There were admittedly fewer roles for unmarried women. Before the 17th century in Europe, apart from the nuns "married" to the Catholic Church, the unmarried female was simply "a girl," not an adult. By the 17th century, when the age of marriage began to rise in Northern Europe, the percentage of single women, especially poorer women in towns and cities, rose. However, outside of service, there were almost no ways for women to earn a living. For all too many unattached women, the only path to survival was witchcraft or sex work. Vaibhav Saria, *Hijras, Lovers, Brothers: Surviving Sex and Poverty in Rural India* (New York: Fordham University Press, 2021); Patrick Abboud, "Fa'afafine: The Boys Raised to Be Girls," SBSNews, July 16, 2013, https://www.sbs.com.au/news/article/faafafine-the-boys-raised-to-be-girls/5tmlnxjaj; and Judith M. Bennett and Amy M. Froide, eds., *Singlewomen in the European Past, 1250–1800* (Philadelphia, PA: University of Pennsylvania Press, 1998).

10. Martin Gurri, "The Psychopathology of Digital Life," *Discourse*, May 24, 2023, https://www.discoursemagazine.com/p/the-psychopathology-of-digital-life.

11. Julissa Cruz, "Marriage: More Than a Century of Change," National Center for Family & Marriage Research, 2013, https://www.bgsu.edu/content/dam/BGSU/college-of-arts-and-sciences/NCFMR/documents/FP/FP-13-13.pdf.

12. Jaden Loo, "Divorce Rate in the U.S.: Geographic Variation, 2022," National Center for Family & Marriage Research, 2023, www.bgsu.edu/ncfmr/resources/data/family-profiles/loo-divorce-rate-US-geographic-variation-2022-fp-23-24.html.

13. Cruz, "Marriage."

14. Pew Research Center, "A Portrait of Stepfamilies," January 13, 2011, https://www.pewresearch.org/social-trends/2011/01/13/a-portrait-of-stepfamilies.

15. Rob Henderson, "Life Is Characterized by a Fair Bit of Suffering. What Will Sustain You?," Rob Henderson's Newsletter, March 17, 2023, https://www.robkhenderson.com/p/life-is-characterized-by-a-fair-bit.

16. Pew Research Center, "Parenting in America Today," January 24, 2023, https://www.pewresearch.org/social-trends/2023/01/24/parenting-in-america-today.

17. Richard V. Reeves, "Parenting, Cam Newton, and Marriage vs. Cohabitation," *Wall Street Journal*, January 12, 2016, https://www.wsj.com/articles/BL-WB-60258.

18. Frank Newport, "Americans Continue to Shift Left on Key Moral Issues," Gallup, May 26, 2015, https://news.gallup.com/poll/183413/americans-continue-shift-left-key-moral-issues.aspx.

19. Jeffrey M. Jones, "Is Marriage Becoming Irrelevant?," Gallup, December 28, 2020, https://news.gallup.com/poll/316223/fewer-say-important-parents-married.aspx.

20. Jamie Burton, "'The Bachelor' Franchise's Painful Decline," *Newsweek*, July 4, 2024, https://www.newsweek.com/bachelor-bachelorette-franchise-painful-decline-1809593.

21. Harris Poll Thought Leadership Practice, "Singles in America Survey," January 2023, https://theharrispoll.com/wp-content/uploads/2023/01/Singles-in-America-Survey-January-2023-.pdf.

22. Lyman Stone, "1 in 4: Projecting Childlessness Among Today's Young Women," Institute for Family Studies, December 7, 2022, https://ifstudies.org/blog/1-in-4-projecting-childlessness-among-todays-young-women.

23. Anna Brown, "Growing Share of Childless Adults in U.S. Don't Expect to Ever Have Children," Pew Research Center, November 19, 2021, https://www.pewresearch.org/short-reads/2021/11/19/growing-share-of-childless-adults-in-u-s-dont-expect-to-ever-have-children.

24. Brown, "Growing Share of Childless Adults in U.S. Don't Expect to Ever Have Children."

25. Zoomie (@zoomie), TikTok video, January 21, 2022, https://www.tiktok.com/@zoomie/video/7055800214040579374.

26. Zoomie (@zoomie), "'Uncommon' Reasons Not to Have Kids," TikTok video, May 31, 2023, https://www.tiktok.com/@zoomie/video/7239509429509492014.

27. Jean M. Twenge, "Have Smartphones Destroyed a Generation?," *The Atlantic*, September 2017, https://www.theatlantic.com/magazine/archive/2017/09/has-the-smartphone-destroyed-a-generation/534198.

28. Daniel A. Cox, "From Swiping to Sexting: The Enduring Gender Divide in American Dating and Relationships," AEI Survey Center on American Life, February 9, 2023,

https://www.americansurveycenter.org/research/from-swiping-to-sexting-the-enduring-gender-divide-in-american-dating-and-relationships.

29. Kate Julian, "Why Are Young People Having So Little Sex?," *The Atlantic*, December 2018, https://www.theatlantic.com/magazine/archive/2018/12/the-sex-recession/573949.

30. Eddieman143, "What Are Some Red Flags in a Relationship That Most People Don't Realize Is a Red Flag?," Reddit, 2022, https://www.reddit.com/r/AskReddit/comments/rt057n/what_are_some_red_flags_in_a_relationship_that; and Style Girlfriend, "How Not to Raise 'Beige Flags' in Dating," February 20, 2024, https://stylegirlfriend.com/beige-flags-dating-tiktok-trend.

31. Syd Robinson, "25 'Icks' About Men That No One Talks About but Are Very, Very, Unsettlingly Real," BuzzFeed, February 18, 2024, https://www.buzzfeed.com/sydrobinson1/icks-about-men-tiktok.

32. Tinder, "Welcome to a Renaissance in Dating, Driven by Authenticity," press release, May 22, 2023, https://www.tinderpressroom.com/2023-05-22-welcome-to-a-renaissance-in-dating,-driven-by-authenticity.

33. Daniel de Visé, "A Record Share of Americans Is Living Alone," *The Hill*, July 10, 2023, https://thehill.com/policy/healthcare/4085828-a-record-share-of-americans-are-living-alone.

34. Josh Getlin, "Natural Wonder: At Heart, Edward Wilson's an Ant Man. But It's His Theories on Human Behavior That Stir Up Trouble," *Los Angeles Times*, October 21, 1994, https://www.latimes.com/archives/la-xpm-1994-10-21-ls-53158-story.html.

5

Who Does Hyperbolic News Hurt the Most?

ZACH GOLDBERG

There's no consensus on why teen mental health in the US has worsened in recent years, but any viable explanation must account for two important factors. First, it must explain the timing of increases in negative mental health outcomes (i.e., why present trends started in the past decade and not earlier). Second, it must account for why such increases were larger among some groups and smaller among others.

Given those criteria, the most persuasive theory centers on the meteoric rise of social media and smartphones. Between 2006 and 2011, the share of Americans age 12-17 who reported using social media at least several times a day grew by 20 percentage points (from 11 percent to 31 percent), compared with just 10 points (6 percent to 16 percent) among those age 22 or older. The share of US high schoolers who reported spending three or more hours of recreational screen time (e.g., using social media, watching videos, and playing video games) jumped significantly between 2009 and 2013—from 25 percent to 41 percent. As of 2021, this figure stood at 73 percent, though revisions to this question's response options that year complicate comparisons with earlier years.[1]

There's good evidence that the rise in smartphone and social media use both precedes and coincides with an uptick in negative mental health outcomes among teens and young adults.[2] At the same time, worsening mental health has not affected all groups equally. Young women, for example, have been more affected than men. Similarly, political liberals have been more affected than conservatives.

Why has this new technology affected some groups more than others?

Over the past several years, social media has amplified exposure to distressing news and information, the sort that highlights human suffering and politically divisive rhetoric. Content that evokes moral outrage tends to be shared more frequently and gets more views on social media.[3] For some young minds online, this content has minimal impact. For others, however, the high frequency of hyperbolic news could be exacerbating certain predispositions that contribute to poorer mental health.

The psychological harms of social media vary from person to person. That said, the increased frequency of hyperbolized news today only makes matters worse for many young people. To understand why, consider the relationship between mental health and certain personality traits.

Personality Traits and Mental Health

Several personality traits influence how much and how often an individual engages with social media and its psychological effects. Let's focus on five of the most important ones, also known as the Big Five personality traits.

- **Neuroticism.** Characterized by heightened emotional sensitivity, individuals with high levels of neuroticism often experience intense feelings of anxiety, sadness, and anger in response to even minor stressors.[4] Furthermore, neuroticism shapes coping strategies and problem-solving behaviors—often not in a good way, as evident in behaviors like social media procrastination and excessive rumination.[5] This can make meeting long-term goals harder and amplify self-dissatisfaction. Indeed, research indicates that those with higher levels of neuroticism are at greater risk of depression,[6] generalized anxiety,[7] and eating disorders.[8]

- **Justice Sensitivity.** Justice sensitivity is a nuanced trait marked by hypervigilance and acute negative emotional reactions to perceived injustices, whether suffered by the individual ("victim sensitivity") or others ("observer sensitivity"). Those with high justice sensitivity have a lower threshold for injustice, leading them to recall more (in)justice-related stimuli and interpret ambiguous situations negatively.[9] They are prone to ruminate over perceived injustices, experiencing and expressing more potent negative emotions in response to them.[10] Although these tendencies can inspire prosocial action, they can also carry mental health risks, as regular vigilance for and negative emotional reactivity to exploitation and victimization may exact a psychological toll, including through depression, eating disorders, and intentional self-harm.[11]

- **Agreeableness.** Agreeableness prompts individuals to deeply resonate with the emotions and suffering of others, whether they are close associates or strangers.[12] While agreeableness could foster prosocial behaviors and attitudes,[13] when empathic concern exceeds certain bounds or is poorly regulated, it can exact a psychological toll. Individuals with heightened empathic abilities may experience intense interpersonal guilt, often fixating on their perceived shortcomings in relieving others' pain or their direct or indirect contribution to it.[14] Additionally, the vulnerability to emotional contagion—the unconscious mirroring of others' distress—among these individuals can escalate to emotional overload and significant personal distress if not properly managed.[15]

- **Openness and Intellect.** Also known as "openness to experience," the openness and intellect trait reflects a tendency to seek novel stimuli. It encompasses two overlapping but distinct aspects: intellect, characterized by a keen interest in and engagement with abstract information, and openness, which signifies a strong receptiveness to sensory experiences. Though the trait contributes to various positive life outcomes, some of its facets may act as a double-edged sword.[16] Specifically, it is marked by heightened sensitivity to sensory stimuli,[17] which amplifies both positive and negative emotions.[18] Thus, in environments like social media, where negative stimuli often predominate, the psychological well-being of individuals with higher aesthetic and emotional openness may be more volatile and prone to deteriorating.

- **Conscientiousness.** On the flip side of neuroticism is the broader personality trait of conscientiousness. Marked by a propensity for organization, diligence, and goal-driven behavior, conscientiousness *can* serve as a buffer against mental health problems. Individuals high in this trait often trust their ability to navigate challenges more.[19] This self-efficacy can protect against mental health issues that crop up when facing adversity.[20] Conscientious individuals exhibit stronger tendencies toward impulse control and delayed gratification, which helps them focus and block out distractions (e.g., social media notifications).[21] They also demonstrate more effective emotional regulation, allowing them to recover more easily from negative emotions.[22]

While the Big Five traits may independently influence mental well-being, a growing body of research indicates that these effects may also be interdependent, with their strength varying according to a person's scores on other personality dimensions.[23] For example, the adverse impact of neuroticism on depression tends to be significantly more pronounced in individuals with low conscientiousness.[24] More recently, evidence for a "worst two out of three" principle has emerged: Individuals exhibiting high-risk levels in any two traits and a low-risk level in a third display an internalizing symptom severity similar to those with high-risk levels across *all* three traits. In particular, the protective effects of higher extraversion on depression are largely neutralized in individuals who also score high in neuroticism and low in conscientiousness.

These findings suggest that the cumulative effect of personality profiles within groups—such as between sexes or political orientations—could be a key factor in understanding their relative risks and experiences of mental health issues.

In addition to their general relationship with mental health, many of the Big Five personality traits show distinct associations with online habits. For instance, traits like openness, neuroticism, and extraversion are all significantly positively correlated with frequency of social media use.[25] Individuals scoring higher in openness tend to look for novel information, including intellectually stimulating and emotionally engaging content. This leads to greater information-seeking behaviors on social media,[26] more consumption of digital news,[27] and more time spent searching for information in general.[28] Conversely, extroverted individuals often use social media for entertainment and to further social goals like connecting with others and boosting their social status.[29] This is reflected in their social media usage patterns, which are marked by larger online (and offline) social networks[30] and a higher frequency of updating profile statuses[31] and posting and commenting on messages and pictures.[32]

For those scoring high in neuroticism, frequent social media use is more attributable to escapism, anxiety, insecurities about real-life social interactions, and weaker impulse control. Research suggests that neurotic individuals turn to social media at least partly to distract themselves from or cope with offline pressures and responsibilities.[33] The relative anonymity of online platforms may also provide them with a more comfortable environment for self-expression and interaction, which can be stressful in person. Combined with poor impulse control, these factors can intensify the urge for virtual escapism, which perhaps explains why neuroticism consistently emerges as the strongest personality predictor of social media and smartphone addiction.[34]

Implications for the Relationship Between Social Media and Mental Health

What do these personality traits have to do with mental health and the prevalence of hyperbolic news online? In essence, excessive social media use may amplify exposure to negative and catastrophizing news and information. This can be particularly triggering for individuals higher in neuroticism, the compassion-related facets of agreeableness, and emotional openness.

Data from the Pew Research Center's American Trends Panel, plotted in Figure 1, reveal that the frequency of observing social media content that elicits negative or internalizing (e.g., feeling depressed or lonely) versus positive (e.g., feeling inspired, connected, or amused) emotions varies as a function of panelists' scores on the Big Five personality domains.[35] For instance, higher levels of neuroticism, openness, and agreeableness all predict a higher reported frequency—and higher levels of conscientiousness a lower reported frequency—of encountering social media content that elicits negative or internalizing emotions. Again, these traits are closely linked with justice sensitivity, which predisposes individuals to be perceptually vigilant toward perceived injustices and inequalities and to react to them with stronger negative emotion.[36]

Figure 1. Effects of the Big Five Personality Domains on the Frequency of Encountering Emotional Social Media Content

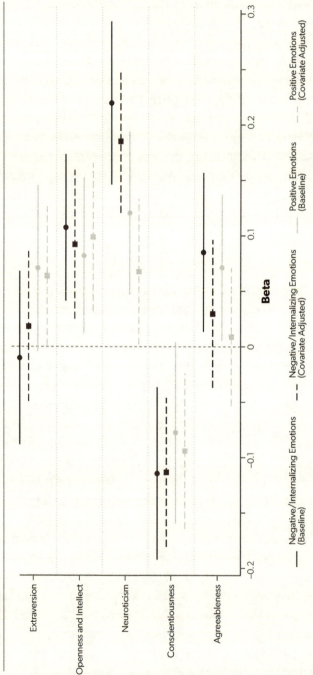

Note: The analysis includes data from 2,030 participants. Markers show expected changes in negative or positive emotions when a personality score increases by one standard deviation. Error bars represent the uncertainty of these estimates. If a marker crosses the vertical dashed line, the effect is not statistically significant. Dashed error bars indicate estimates adjusted for factors such as age, gender, income, and education. Personality traits were measured in 2014, and emotional responses to social media were assessed in 2018.
Source: Pew Research Center, American Trends Panel, Waves 3 and 35.

Figure 2. The Effects of Encountering Emotional Social Media Content (Circa 2018) on Subsequent Internalizing Symptoms

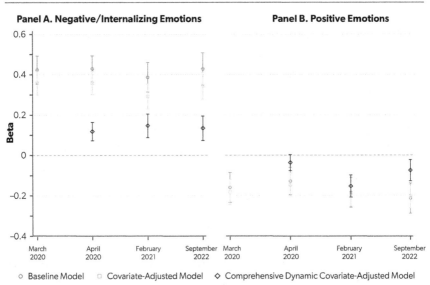

Note: This figure illustrates how negative and positive emotions triggered by social media content in 2018 predict internalizing symptoms (such as anxiety and depression) from 2020 to 2022 among 2,030 participants. In Panel A, circle markers represent the effect of negative emotions (feeling depressed or lonely) on internalizing symptoms, while in Panel B, circle markers show the effect of positive emotions (feeling inspired, amused, or connected). Square markers indicate estimates adjusted for demographic and socioeconomic factors, including age, gender, income, and education. Diamond markers further adjust for previous internalizing symptoms, providing a comprehensive analysis of these relationships. Error bars depict 95 percent confidence intervals, and any marker that touches the dashed line signifies that the effect is not statistically significant. Emotions were measured in 2018 using four-point scales, and internalizing symptoms were tracked across four points from 2020 to 2022.
Source: Pew Research Center, American Trends Panel, Waves 35, 64, 66, 83, and 114.

Because social media content is frequently about injustice, engaging with that content habitually could, over time, lead to psychological strain among justice-sensitive individuals. Consistent with this, Figure 2 shows that the frequency of exposure to content that triggers negative or positive emotions doesn't merely reflect momentary feelings. Rather, frequent exposure predicts longer-term mental health outcomes.

Specifically, the higher the average frequency at which panelists reported (circa 2018) encountering social media content that made them feel "depressed" and "lonely," the more frequently they reported experiencing internalizing symptoms at each of the four points from 2020 to 2022.[37] This relationship persisted and remained significant not only when accounting for differences in background factors like age, income, and education but also when considering the panelists' earlier levels of mental health.[38]

There are at least several plausible, nonexclusive interpretations for these patterns. One interpretation is *selective exposure*: Individuals high in neuroticism and low in conscientiousness—or those with greater internalizing symptoms—may actively seek out or pay more attention to distressing social media content.[39] This pattern of doomscrolling (i.e., the habitual excessive consumption of negative news on social media) has been linked with poorer mental health, higher levels of neuroticism, and lower levels of conscientiousness.[40]

Alternatively, or in addition to influencing exposure levels and exposure recall, mental health conditions and associated personality dimensions may shape an individual's *emotional responsiveness*. For instance, a news item that might evoke a mild emotional response, if any, from someone who is more conscientious and less neurotic could provoke a stronger reaction among their more neurotic and less conscientious counterparts.

Crucially, selective exposure and emotional responsiveness may also be influenced by moral-ideological orientations, which are in turn linked to the personality traits mentioned earlier. For example, justice sensitivity, certain aspects of neuroticism like withdrawal, the openness aspect of openness and intellect, and the compassion facet of agreeableness are all positively related—and conscientiousness is negatively related—to egalitarian and anti-hierarchy ideological orientations.[41] Ideological egalitarians tend to be more sensitive to social inequality and more likely to attribute poverty and group disparities to systemic forces like discrimination.[42] As a result, they are more prone to attend to and be emotionally affected by portrayals of inequality on social media, which may amplify distress and feelings of helplessness, ultimately undermining mental health.

Personality Traits, Gender, and Ideology

With the role of personality traits and social media exposure more clearly laid out, we can now have a better sense of the relatively poorer mental health outcomes of girls and liberals in the digital age.

In a 2018 study, psychologists Petri Kajonius and John Johnson analyzed one of the largest US personality datasets. They found that women tend to score significantly higher than men on personality traits positively associated with internalizing disorders, including neuroticism, the aesthetic and emotional facets of openness, and the compassion facet of agreeableness.[43] Another study made a similar finding in 2021 regarding political orientation, showing that liberals scored higher on these traits and lower on conscientiousness than conservatives.[44] And yet another study demonstrates that these differences extend to justice sensitivity, with women and liberals of both sexes scoring significantly higher than men and conservatives on all dimensions (i.e., observer, beneficiary, perpetrator, and victim sensitivity) of the construct.[45] These are just some examples. As a whole, the existing data strongly suggest that girls and liberals tend to score significantly higher than boys and conservatives on personality traits associated with mental health challenges and excessive social media use.

Recall that previous research has linked higher neuroticism and lower conscientiousness to excessive internet and social media use and higher openness and intellect to more frequent internet and social media use and digital news consumption. Sex and ideological differences in these personality traits—particularly neuroticism and conscientiousness—may thus explain why girls and liberals of both sexes use social media more frequently and exhibit greater digital connectivity in general than their male and conservative counterparts.

For instance, data from the Monitoring the Future survey indicate that 57 percent of 12th-grade girls reported using social media three hours or more during a typical day between 2018 and 2022, compared with 36 percent of their male peers. The pattern held for liberal girls compared with liberal boys (59 percent to 35 percent) and for conservative girls and conservative boys (47 percent to 31 percent).[46] Data pooled from three 2023 Kaiser Family Foundation surveys show even starker disparities in internet use for young adults age 18–29, with 79 percent and 76 percent of liberal girls and boys, respectively, indicating they are online "almost constantly," compared with 59 percent and 47 percent of conservative boys and girls, respectively.[47]

Naturally, those who spend more time on social media and the internet in general will have more opportunities to be psychologically affected by digital content and less time to engage in offline activities beneficial to mental well-being. Differences in time spent online and on social media could thus contribute to the relatively greater deterioration of girls' and liberals' mental health.

Yet sex and ideological differences in emotional responses to social media content and interactions and in attention to certain kinds of content may be equally, if not more, relevant to understanding the current mental health divide. For instance, due to higher levels of neuroticism, emotional and aesthetic openness, empathic concern, and justice sensitivity, we might expect girls and liberals to be more emotionally affected by negative or depressing (and positive) social media content. Moreover, girls and liberals may be more likely to seek out or interact with such content.

This could explain why, as shown in Figure 3, females and liberals report encountering social media content that triggers feelings of depression and loneliness at significantly higher frequencies than males and conservatives do. Crucially, these differences narrow substantially when controlling for neuroticism, agreeableness, conscientiousness, and openness.

If girls and liberals are more likely to have stronger emotional reactions to negative social media content, it follows that on average frequent social media use will be relatively more psychologically consequential for them than for boys and conservatives. Unfortunately, the existing publicly available data do not permit an adequate or complete test of this hypothesis. They do, however, provide some general support for it.

While restricted to sex differences and encompassing overall screen time rather than exclusive social media use, the data plotted in Figure 4 show that the relationship between daily screen time and negative mental health outcomes has generally become stronger over time for high school girls compared with boys. This is especially true for the

Figure 3. Sex and Ideological Differences in Encountering Social Media Content That Triggers Negative or Internalizing Emotions

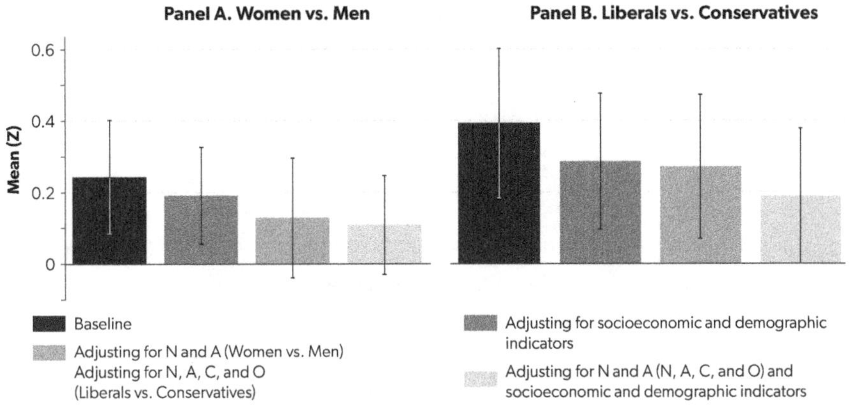

Panel A. Women vs. Men

Panel B. Liberals vs. Conservatives

- Baseline
- Adjusting for N and A (Women vs. Men) Adjusting for N, A, C, and O (Liberals vs. Conservatives)
- Adjusting for socioeconomic and demographic indicators
- Adjusting for N and A (N, A, C, and O) and socioeconomic and demographic indicators

Note: This figure compares the frequency with which women versus men (Panel A) and liberals versus conservatives (Panel B) encounter social media content that triggers negative emotions, such as depression and loneliness. The bars represent standardized differences between these groups. Socioeconomic and demographic factors include age, race, income, education, marital status, and region. The third bar shows estimates further adjusted for personality traits—specifically neuroticism and agreeableness for sex differences and neuroticism, agreeableness, openness, and conscientiousness for ideological differences. The data are weighted and corrected for attrition.
Source: Pew Research Center, American Trends Panel, Waves 35, 64, 66, 83, and 114.

relationship between screen time and reporting a major depressive episode (i.e., feeling sad or hopeless almost every day for two weeks or more). The relationship was near zero in 2003 and has been increasing ever since, particularly from 2011 onward, coinciding with the rise of smartphones and social media. In contrast, the effect for boys has seen minimal change overall.

A similar hypothesis can be tested for political leanings using the 2018 AARP Brain Health and Mental Well-Being Survey. Figure 5 illustrates the average score differences on a seven-item anxiety index and a 20-item depression index between self-identified liberals and conservatives. These individuals reported using social media for more than two hours at a time at least several times a week (36 percent of the sample), compared with those who rarely do (46 percent of the sample). Among liberals, those who

Figure 4. The Relationships Between Daily Screen Time and Negative Mental Health Outcomes Among High School Students, by Sex

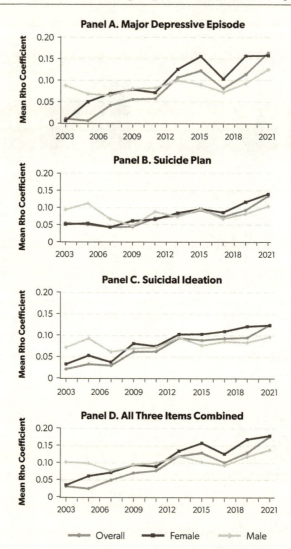

Note: The lines represent average Spearman rank correlation coefficients between hours spent on digital activities—such as gaming, watching videos, texting, and using social media—and mental health indicators, including major depressive episodes, suicidal ideation, and suicide plans. Data are weighted and corrected for attrition. Additionally, a summary measure of suicidal behaviors is presented in Panel D.
Source: Centers for Disease Control and Prevention, "Youth Risk Behavior Surveillance System (YRBSS)," https://www.cdc.gov/yrbs/index.html.

Figure 5. The Effects of Frequent Social Media Use on Internalizing Symptoms, by Ideology

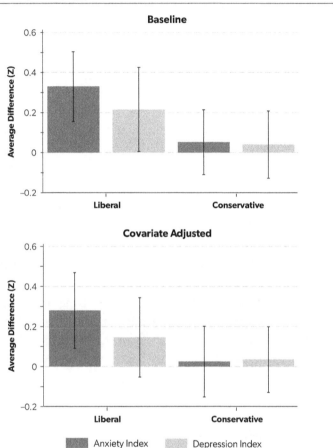

Note: This figure displays the average differences in standardized anxiety (darker gray bars) and depression (lighter gray bars) scores between liberal and conservative respondents who engage in social media or internet use for more than two hours at a time at least several times a week, compared with those who do so less frequently. The bars represent these differences, with bars in the bottom panel indicating estimates adjusted for demographic and socioeconomic factors such as age, sex, race, education, and income. The analysis includes data from approximately 2,100 participants and ensures consistent sample sizes by excluding respondents with missing data on any covariates. The findings suggest that frequent social media use is associated with higher anxiety and depression scores among liberals, while such differences are negligible among conservatives.

Source: Laura Mehegan and Chuck Rainville, *2018 AARP Brain Health and Mental Well-Being Survey*, October 10, 2018, https://www.aarp.org/pri/topics/health/conditions-treatment/brain-health-mental-well-being.

use social media more frequently showed a greater proclivity for depression than did those who reported never using social media for more than two hours at a time over the past year. In contrast, these differences among conservatives were negligible.

The Mental Health Cost of the News Becoming More Woke

The preceding findings indicate that girls and liberals likely have different social media experiences—gravitating toward different apps, interacting with different kinds of content, and having differing emotional responses to even the same content—than their male and conservative counterparts do. However, the kinds of social media experiences people have, and particularly the content they encounter, are at least partially influenced by the broader media and political context.

This is important as, since around 2011, media attention to societal issues like racism, inequality, discrimination, and sexism has surged to unprecedented levels.[48] Concurrently, the underlying sentiment in headlines has become decidedly more negative and pessimistic.[49] Of course, some of this is attributable to the rise of Donald Trump and his presidency, which served to intensify these trends and, consequently, the alarm many liberals felt.

Given the increasing interplay between social media and mainstream news media, these trends are naturally also apparent in—and, at least in some instances, likely influenced by—social media discourse. For instance, data from StoryWrangler, a web-based tool that tracks the use and salience of different terms in discourse on X (previously Twitter), show that few posts featured social justice–related terms like "racism," "sexism," "oppression," and "injustice" until roughly 2014–15, when the use of these terms surged. And while their frequency of use has either leveled off or declined since 2020, they generally remain well above the rates of the pre–"Great Awokening" era—a period preceding the mass liberalization of racial attitudes, particularly among Democrats and liberals, following the rise of Black Lives Matter in 2014.

As the tenor and content of media coverage have become more negative and alarmist, so too have perceptions of sociopolitical issues among

Figure 6. Trends in Sociopolitical Awareness Among 12th Graders, by Ideology and Sex (1976–2022)

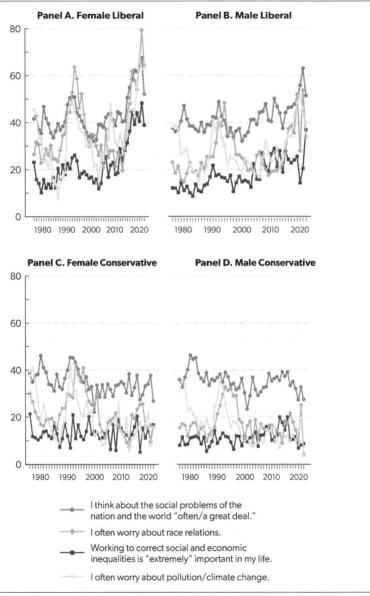

Note: Data are weighted.
Source: National Addiction & HIV Data Archive Program, "Monitoring the Future (MTF) Public-Use Cross-Sectional Datasets," https://www.icpsr.umich.edu/web/NAHDAP/series/35/studies.

liberal girls and boys. As shown in Figure 6, young liberals—and liberal girls especially—have become much more socially and politically conscious over the past 10 years.[50] For instance, the share of liberals who say they frequently think about the "social problems of the nation and the world" has reached record highs, as has the share saying that working to "correct social and economic inequalities" is "extremely" important for them. Concerns about race relations and the environment have also surged among liberals while changing remarkably little among conservatives of both sexes.

Despite the significant educational and socioeconomic advancements women have achieved since the 1950s, Figure 7 shows that liberals now perceive greater discrimination against women in various contexts (including in accessing higher education) than ever recorded. Concurrently, the share of female liberals who think their sex will prevent them from obtaining their desired careers "somewhat" or "a lot" shot up by more than 30 points between 2012 (36 percent) and 2019 (67 percent). In contrast, perceptions of discrimination against women are lower among conservatives of both sexes today than they were in the late 1970s, if they've changed at all.

At the very least, such perceptions of discrimination are unlikely to enhance—and could very well worsen—psychological well-being. Indeed, perceiving discrimination and unfairness, whether directed at oneself or one's social group, has been associated with lower self-esteem and elevated anxiety and depressive symptoms.[51] By promoting alarmist portrayals of social issues that increase feelings of despair and undermine perceptions of personal agency—namely, the belief that life chances are dictated by external oppressive forces—the surge in news and social media content on racial and gender inequality could have worsened mental health outcomes for young Americans, especially liberal females.

To the extent that media-driven increases in "woke" (i.e., bias-centered) narratives of inequality have contributed to liberal-conservative differences in mental health, such differences should shrink considerably when woke beliefs are held constant. Supporting this hypothesis, Figure 8 uses data from the 2022 Cooperative Election Study to show that a four-item index of "racial wokeness" alone accounts for more than half the conservative-liberal difference in self-rated mental health. For perspective, religiosity alone accounts for just under a third of this gap, while controlling for self-rated physical health, sexual orientation, and all other

Figure 7. Perceptions of Discrimination Against Women Among 12th Graders, by Sex and Ideology (1976–2022)

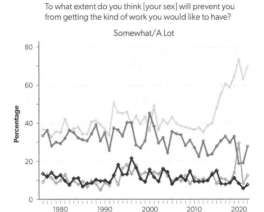

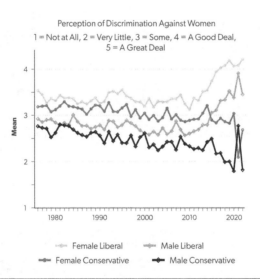

— Female Liberal   — Male Liberal
— Female Conservative   — Male Conservative

Note: In Panel A, the lines represent the percentage of respondents who believe that their gender will somewhat or greatly hinder them from achieving their desired careers, compared with those who do not perceive such barriers. Panel B illustrates the average level of perceived discrimination against women across various contexts, including leadership roles, political office, education, and equal pay. These perceptions are measured using a standardized seven-item index, in which higher scores indicate greater perceived discrimination. The data are weighted to ensure representativeness.
Source: National Addiction & HIV Data Archive Program, "Monitoring the Future (MTF) Public-Use Cross-Sectional Datasets," https://www.icpsr.umich.edu/web/NAHDAP/series/35/studies.

Figure 8. Ideological Differences in Self-Rated Mental Health

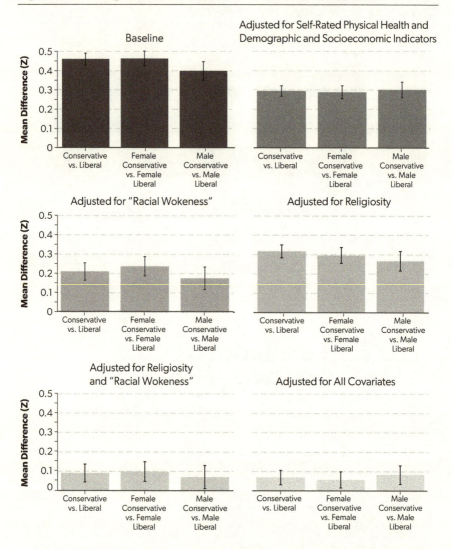

Note: The analysis accounts for various demographic and socioeconomic factors, including age, sex, race, education, income, religiosity, and self-rated physical health. Key variables examined are a four-item racial wokeness index and measures of religiosity. The data are weighted to ensure representativeness.

Source: Brian Schaffner, Stephen Ansolabehere, and Marissa Shih, "Cooperative Election Study Common Content, 2022," Harvard University, 2023, https://dataverse.harvard.edu/dataset.xhtml?persistentId=doi%3A10.7910/DVN/PR4L8P.

demographic and socioeconomic indicators explains a similar share. If adjusting for both racial wokeness *and* religiosity, the gap becomes practically insignificant.

These findings track with a recent study by sociologist George Yancey, who observed that support for race-based activism (which he broadly calls "identity politics") as a means of addressing racial inequality explains nearly the entirety of liberal-conservative differences in mental well-being.[52] Another recent work has replicated the relationships between attitudinal wokeness and poorer mental health outcomes in Finland. In that study, agreement with the statement "If white people have on average a higher income than black people, it is because of racism" shows the strongest correlation with anxiety, depression, and general unhappiness.[53]

Why does this happen? The inverse relationship between "attitudinal wokeness" and mental health may be partly attributable to diminished personal agency. In other words, the prominence of bias-focused explanations of social issues may inadvertently foster a sense of helplessness among the young, reinforcing the notion that life outcomes are mainly shaped by external, uncontrollable forces. This, in turn, exacerbates psychological distress and depressive symptoms.

It could also be the other way around. Reductions in personal agency and heightened feelings of helplessness may have set the stage for the rise in attitudinal wokeness. According to this view, the emerging prominence of woke media narratives might resonate more among those with lower self-esteem and a diminished sense of self-agency, offering an external locus of blame for personal and societal issues. The subsequent embrace of these narratives could have, in turn, perpetuated a cycle of decreased agency, potentially aggravating mental health challenges even further.

The rising trend in recent years of girls self-identifying as liberal may also be intertwined with the dynamics described above. However, political orientations do not exist in isolation. In fact, the relationship may well be bidirectional: While a liberal or left-wing political stance may predispose individuals to experience certain mental health challenges, those experiencing such challenges may also be drawn to left-wing ideologies. Such ideologies, with their focus on attributing societal issues to oppressive "systems" and advocating comprehensive social interventions, may particularly appeal to individuals grappling with mental health issues, allowing them to externalize blame for personal struggles and identify with a broader collective movement that agitates for societal change. However, this externalization and focus on systemic factors, while potentially validating, may also further erode youths' sense of agency and exacerbate feelings of powerlessness or resignation.

Conclusion

In this chapter, I sought to make sense of the relatively recent and abrupt deterioration in youth mental health, particularly the more pronounced decline among young girls and liberals. To this end, I considered what is perhaps the most popular, if not the most compelling, account of this phenomenon—namely, the smartphone and social media boom of the past decade.

In attempting to explain the overall modest negative relationship between social media use and mental health that's found in past research, I propose that the magnitude of this relationship is moderated by individual psychological predispositions—which are more prevalent among girls and liberals than boys and conservatives. Thus, while the overall psychological impact of the digital media revolution may be mildly negative for youth in general, it likely has a more substantial and adverse effect on the psychologically vulnerable.

At the same time, the extent to which social media causally affects mental health remains an open question. The data required to fully test the theory presented in this chapter are not yet sufficiently available. I hope the theory proposed here will guide and inspire future investigations.

Subsequent research should also consider the potential existence of other causal factors, which, although not directly related to technology, may be equally or more relevant in explaining youth mental health trends. These could include long-term cultural shifts, such as declining youth religiosity and increases in overprotective parenting.[54] Such shifts may be inadvertently depriving younger generations of vital psychological resources crucial for managing the stressors that are either inherent in or amplified by our increasingly hyper-connected digital world.

Notes

1. Centers for Disease Control and Prevention, "Youth Risk Behavior Surveillance System (YRBSS)," https://www.cdc.gov/yrbs/index.html.
2. For example, see Jean M. Twenge, *Generations: The Real Differences Between Gen Z, Millennials, Gen X, Boomers, and Silents—and What They Mean for America's Future* (New York: Atria Books, 2023), Figure 6.39.
3. Jay J. Van Bavel et al., "Social Media and Morality," *Annual Review of Psychology* 75 (January 2024): 311–40, https://pubmed.ncbi.nlm.nih.gov/37906950.
4. Daniel Cervone and Lawrence Pervin, *Personality Psychology*, 12th ed. (New York: Wiley, 2013).
5. Jennifer K. Connor-Smith and Celeste Flachsbart, "Relations Between Personality and Coping: A Meta-Analysis," *Journal of Personality and Social Psychology* 93, no. 6 (December 2007): 1080–107, https://pubmed.ncbi.nlm.nih.gov/18072856.
6. Conor Duggan et al., "Neuroticism: A Vulnerability Marker for Depression Evidence from a Family Study," *Journal of Affective Disorders* 35, no. 3 (December 1995): 139–43, https://www.sciencedirect.com/science/article/abs/pii/0165032795000623.
7. Lynne M. Weinstock and Mark A. Whisman, "Neuroticism as a Common Feature of the Depressive and Anxiety Disorders: A Test of the Revised Integrative Hierarchical Model in a National Sample," *Journal of Abnormal Psychology* 115, no. 1 (February 2006): 68–74, https://pubmed.ncbi.nlm.nih.gov/16492097.
8. Stephanie E. Cassin and Kristin M. von Ranson, "Personality and Eating Disorders: A Decade in Review," *Clinical Psychology Review* 25, no. 7 (November 2005): 895–916, https://pubmed.ncbi.nlm.nih.gov/16099563.
9. Melanie J. McGrath et al., "Concept Creepers: Individual Differences in Harm-Related Concepts and Their Correlates," *Personality and Individual Differences* 147 (September 2019): 79–84, https://www.sciencedirect.com/science/article/abs/pii/S0191886919302387.
10. Manfred J. Schmitt, Roland Neumann, and Leo Montada, "Dispositional Sensitivity to Befallen Injustice," *Social Justice Research* 8, no. 4 (December 1995): 385–407, https://www.researchgate.net/publication/227297827_Dispositional_Sensitivity_to_Befallen_Injustice; and Anna Baumert, Mario Gollwitzer, and Manfred Schmitt, "Cognitive Processes Involved in Justice Sensitivity: Selective Information Search," Universität Koblenz-Landau, 2007, https://www.researchgate.net/publication/37367072_Cognitive_Processes_Involved_in_Justice_Sensitivity_Selective_Information_Search.
11. Higher levels of justice sensitivity are associated with lower self-esteem and a variety of mental health issues such as generalized anxiety, depression, social phobia, eating disorders, and intentional self-harm. Rebecca Bondü and Stefan Inerle, "Afraid of Injustice? Justice Sensitivity Is Linked to General Anxiety and Social Phobia Symptoms," *Journal of Affective Disorders* 272 (July 2020): 198–206, https://www.sciencedirect.com/science/article/abs/pii/S0165032719332458; Rebecca Bondü and Birgit Elsner, "Justice Sensitivity in Childhood and Adolescence," *Social Development* 24, no. 2 (May 2015): 420–41, https://onlinelibrary.wiley.com/doi/abs/10.1111/sode.12098; Rebecca Bondü, Ayten Bilgin, and Petra Warschburger, "Justice Sensitivity and

Rejection Sensitivity Predictors and Outcomes of Eating Disorder Pathology: A 5-Year Longitudinal Study," *International Journal of Eating Disorders* 53, no. 6 (June 2020): 926–36, https://pubmed.ncbi.nlm.nih.gov/32270541; and Ayten Bilgin, Rebecca Bondü, and Birgit Elsner, "Longitudinal Associations Between Justice Sensitivity, Nonsuicidal Self-Injury, Substance Use, and Victimization by Peers," *Development and Psychopathology* 34, no. 4 (October 2022): 1560–72, https://pubmed.ncbi.nlm.nih.gov/33910661.

12. William G. Graziano et al., "Agreeableness, Empathy, and Helping: A Person × Situation Perspective," *Journal of Personality and Social Psychology* 93, no. 4 (2007): 583–99, https://psycnet.apa.org/record/2007-13393-006.

13. Gustavo Carlo et al., "The Interplay of Traits and Motives on Volunteering: Agreeableness, Extraversion and Prosocial Value Motivation," *Personality and Individual Differences* 38, no. 6 (April 2005): 1293–305, https://www.sciencedirect.com/science/article/abs/pii/S0191886904002508.

14. Lynn E. O'Connor et al., "Empathy and Depression: The Moral System on Overdrive," in *Empathy in Mental Illness*, ed. Tom F. D. Farrow and Peter W. R. Woodruff (Cambridge, UK: Cambridge University Press, 2009): 49–75, https://www.cambridge.org/core/books/abs/empathy-in-mental-illness/empathy-and-depression-the-moral-system-on-overdrive/E327AF1486C30C32A514BAFF9BB844ED.

15. R. Williams Doherty, "The Emotional Contagion Scale: A Measure of Individual Differences," *Journal of Nonverbal Behavior* 21 (June 1997): 131–54, https://link.springer.com/article/10.1023/A:1024956003661.

16. Robert R. McCrae and Paul T. Costa Jr., "Adding Liebe und Arbeit: The Full Five-Factor Model and Well-Being," *Personality and Social Psychology Bulletin* 17, no. 2 (2021): 227–32, https://journals.sagepub.com/doi/abs/10.1177/014616729101700217.

17. Anne Sophie Bröhl et al., "First Look at the Five-Factor Model Personality Facet Associations with Sensory Processing Sensitivity," *Current Psychology* 41, no. 6 (August 2022): 1–14, https://www.researchgate.net/publication/343772058_First_look_at_the_five-factor_model_personality_facet_associations_with_sensory_processing_sensitivity.

18. Bröhl et al., "First Look at the Five-Factor Model Personality Facet Associations with Sensory Processing Sensitivity."

19. Gabriel Nudelman and Kathleen Otto, "Personal Belief in a Just World and Conscientiousness: A Meta-Analysis, Facet-Level Examination, and Mediation Model," *British Journal of Psychology* 112, no. 1 (February 2021): 92–119, https://bpspsychub.onlinelibrary.wiley.com/doi/10.1111/bjop.12438.

20. Francesco Ruotolo et al., "Psychological Reactions During and After a Lockdown: Self-Efficacy as a Protective Factor of Mental Health," *International Journal of Environmental Research and Public Health* 20, no. 17 (August 2023): 6679, https://pubmed.ncbi.nlm.nih.gov/37681819.

21. Brent Roberts et al., "What Is Conscientiousness and How Can It Be Assessed?," *Developmental Psychology* 50, no. 5 (May 2014): 1315–30, https://pubmed.ncbi.nlm.nih.gov/23276130.

22. Kristin N. Javaras et al., "Conscientiousness Predicts Greater Recovery from Negative Emotion," *Emotion* 12, no. 5 (October 2012): 875, https://www.ncbi.nlm.nih.gov/pmc/articles/PMC3434282.

23. Timothy Allen et al., "Big Five Aspects of Personality Interact to Predict Depression," *Journal of Personality* 86, no. 4 (August 2018): 714–25, https://onlinelibrary.wiley.com/doi/10.1111/jopy.12352.

24. Thomas E. Joiner and Christopher J. Lonigan, "Tripartite Model of Depression and Anxiety in Youth Psychiatric Inpatients: Relations with Diagnostic Status and Future Symptoms," *Journal of Clinical Child Psychology* 29, no. 3 (June 2010): 372–82, https://www.tandfonline.com/doi/epdf/10.1207/S15374424JCCP2903_8.

25. Homero Gil de Zúñiga et al., "Personality Traits and Social Media Use in 20 Countries: How Personality Relates to Frequency of Social Media Use, Social Media News Use, and Social Media Use for Social Interaction," *Cyberpsychology, Behavior, and Social Networking* 20, no. 9 (2017): 540–52, http://www.homerogdz.com/documents/Gil%20de%20Z%C3%BA%C3%B1iga,%20Diehl,%20Huber%20%20and%20Liu%20(2017)%20Cyberpsychology.pdf.

26. Dong Liu and W. Keith Campbell, "The Big Five Personality Traits, Big Two Metatraits and Social Media: A Meta-Analysis," *Journal of Research in Personality* 70 (2017): 229–40, https://psycnet.apa.org/record/2017-43984-022.

27. Alan S. Gerber et al., "Personality Traits and the Consumption of Political Information," *American Politics Research* 39, no. 1 (January 2011): 32–84, https://journals.sagepub.com/doi/abs/10.1177/1532673x10381466.

28. Yeolib Kim and Jae Seon Jeong, "Personality Predictors for the Use of Multiple Internet Functions," *Internet Research* 25, no. 3 (June 2015): 399–415, https://www.emerald.com/insight/content/doi/10.1108/IntR-11-2013-0250/full/html.

29. Thomas Bowden-Green, Joanne Hinds, and Adam Joinson, "How Is Extraversion Related to Social Media Use? A Literature Review," *Personality and Individual Differences* 164 (October 2020), https://www.sciencedirect.com/science/article/abs/pii/S0191886920302294.

30. Yair Amichai-Hamburger and Gideon Vinitzky, "Social Network Use and Personality," *Computers in Human Behavior* 26, no. 6 (November 2010): 1289–95, https://www.sciencedirect.com/science/article/abs/pii/S0747563210000580.

31. Yoram Bachrach et al., "Personality and Patterns of Facebook Usage," in *Proceedings of the 4th Annual ACM Web Science Conference* (New York: Association for Computing Machinery, 2012), 24–32, https://dl.acm.org/doi/10.1145/2380718.2380722.

32. Ha Sung Hwang, "The Influence of Personality Traits on the Facebook Addiction," *KSII Transactions on Internet and Information Systems* 11, no. 2 (February 2017), https://itiis.org/digital-library/21369.

33. Lisa J. Orchard et al., "Individual Differences as Predictors of Social Networking," *Journal of Computer-Mediated Communication* 19, no. 3 (April 2014): 388–402, https://academic.oup.com/jcmc/article/19/3/388/4067527.

34. Laura Marciano, Anne-Linda Camerini, and Peter J. Schulz, "Neuroticism in the Digital Age: A Meta-Analysis," *Computers in Human Behavior Reports* 2 (August–December 2020), https://www.sciencedirect.com/science/article/pii/S2451958820300269.

35. Considering the abbreviated nature of Pew's Big Five battery—wherein most broad domains are represented by just two indicators—the effects observed here could very well understate the magnitudes of the personality domains' true relationships

(while obscuring those of their facets) with affective responses to social media content.

36. Zachary K. Rothschild and Lucas A. Keefer, "Meaningful Outrage: Anger at Injustice Bolsters Meaning for Justice Sensitive Individuals," *European Journal of Social Psychology* 52, no. 1 (February 2022): 124–46, https://onlinelibrary.wiley.com/doi/abs/10.1002/ejsp.2820.

37. To be clear, the implicit assumption in this analysis is not that the reported frequency of encountering emotive social media content in the specific year 2018 influences mental health years later. Rather, the reported frequencies in 2018 are likely to reflect more enduring behavioral tendencies, which are, at least in part, a function of individuals' personality traits.

38. While complicating the models and producing stronger multicollinearity, model fit statistics indicate that including covariates from both the wave of the internalizing symptoms index *and* the wave of the social media emotions indexes (as opposed to one of the two) significantly improves the models' fits.

39. Jennifer S. Lerner and Dacher Keltner, "Beyond Valence: Toward a Model of Emotion-Specific Influences on Judgement and Choice," *Cognition and Emotion* 14, no. 4 (August 2010): 473–93, https://www.tandfonline.com/doi/abs/10.1080/026999300402763.

40. Bhakti Sharma, Susanna S. Lee, and Benjamin K. Johnson, "The Dark at the End of the Tunnel: Doomscrolling on Social Media Newsfeeds," *Technology, Mind, and Behavior* 3, no. 1 (Spring 2022): 1–13, https://tmb.apaopen.org/pub/nn9uaqsz/release/3.

41. Tobias Rothmund, Laurits Bromme, and Flávio Azevedo, "Justice for the People? How Justice Sensitivity Can Foster and Impair Support for Populist Radical-Right Parties and Politicians in the United States and in Germany," *Political Psychology* 41, no. 3 (June 2020): 479–97, https://onlinelibrary.wiley.com/doi/full/10.1111/pops.12632.

42. Hannah B. Waldfogel et al., "Ideology Selectively Shapes Attention to Inequality," *Proceedings of the National Academy of Sciences* 118, no. 14 (April 2021), https://pubmed.ncbi.nlm.nih.gov/33795517.

43. Petri J. Kajonius and John Johnson, "Sex Differences in 30 Facets of the Five Factor Model of Personality in the Large Public (N = 320,128)," *Personality and Individual Differences* 129 (July 2018): 126–30, https://psycnet.apa.org/record/2018-16054-025.

44. Xiaowen Xu, Christopher J. Soto, and Jason E. Plaks, "Beyond Openness to Experience and Conscientiousness: Testing Links Between Lower-Level Personality Traits and American Political Orientation," *Journal of Personality* 89, no. 4 (August 2021): 754–73, https://psycnet.apa.org/record/2021-07716-001.

45. Rothmund, Bromme, and Azevedo, "Justice for the People?"

46. National Addiction & HIV Data Archive Program, "Monitoring the Future (MTF) Public-Use Cross-Sectional Datasets," https://www.icpsr.umich.edu/web/NAHDAP/series/35/studies.

47. Sharon Schumacher et al., "KFF COVID-19 Vaccine Monitor: January 2023," Kaiser Family Foundation, February 7, 2023, https://www.kff.org/report-section/kff-covid-19-vaccine-monitor-january-2023-methodology; Grace Sparks et al., "KFF COVID-19 Vaccine Monitor: March 2023," Kaiser Family Foundation, April 3, 2023, https://www.kff.org/coronavirus-covid-19/poll-finding/kff-covid-19-vaccine-monitor-

march-2023; and Ashley Kirzinger et al., "KFF COVID-19 Vaccine Monitor September 2023: Partisanship Remains Key Predictor of Views of COVID-19, Including Plans to Get Latest COVID-19 Vaccine," Kaiser Family Foundation, September 27, 2023, https://www.kff.org/health-misinformation-and-trust/poll-finding/kff-covid-19-vaccine-monitor-september-2023.

48. David Rozado, "Prejudice and Victimization Themes in *New York Times* Discourse: A Chronological Analysis," *Academic Questions* 33, no. 1 (February 2020): 89–101, https://www.nas.org/academic-questions/33/1/prejudice-and-victimization-themes-in-discourse-a-chronological-analysis.

49. David Rozado, Ruth Hughes, and Jamin Halberstadt, "Longitudinal Analysis of Sentiment and Emotion in News Media Headlines Using Automated Labelling with Transformer Language Models," *PLOS One* 17, no. 10 (October 2022), https://journals.plos.org/plosone/article?id=10.1371/journal.pone.0276367; and David Rozado, "Pessimism in News Media Headlines," Rozado's Visual Analytics, June 1, 2023, https://davidrozado.substack.com/p/pessimism-in-news-media-headlines.

50. The rapid rise in the prominence of woke narratives among today's youth could thus also affect mental health indirectly by galvanizing political engagement and activism. Indeed, an emerging body of work indicates that political engagement, particularly in the current hyperpolarized political climate, can exact a significant psychological cost. Kevin B. Smith, "Politics Is Making Us Sick: The Negative Impact of Political Engagement on Public Health During the Trump Administration," *PLOS One* 17, no. 1 (January 2022), https://pmc.ncbi.nlm.nih.gov/articles/PMC8759681; and Brett Q. Ford et al., "The Political Is Personal: The Costs of Daily Politics," *Journal of Personality and Social Psychology: Attitudes and Social Cognition* (2023), https://www.apa.org/pubs/journals/releases/psp-pspa0000335.pdf. One study found this to be especially true for younger and politically left-aligned individuals, with engagement linked to poorer outcomes across a host of mental well-being indicators such as stress, loss of sleep, and suicidal ideation. Kevin B. Smith, Matthew V. Hibbing, and John R. Hibbing, "Friends, Relatives, Sanity, and Health: The Costs of Politics," *PLOS One* 14, no. 9 (September 2019): e0221870, https://pmc.ncbi.nlm.nih.gov/articles/PMC6760758.

51. Michael T. Schmitt et al., "The Consequences of Perceived Discrimination for Psychological Well-Being: A Meta-Analytic Review," *Psychological Bulletin* 140, no. 4 (July 2014): 921–48, https://pubmed.ncbi.nlm.nih.gov/24547896.

52. George Yancey, "Identity Politics, Political Ideology, and Well-Being: Is Identity Politics Good for Our Well-Being?," *Sociological Forum* 38, no. 4 (December 2023): 1245–65, https://onlinelibrary.wiley.com/doi/10.1111/socf.12966.

53. Oskari Lahtinen, "Construction and Validation of a Scale for Assessing Critical Social Justice Attitudes," *Scandinavian Journal of Psychology* 65, no. 4 (August 2024): 693–705, https://onlinelibrary.wiley.com/doi/10.1111/sjop.13018.

54. Peter Gray, David F. Lancy, and David F. Bjorklund, "Decline in Independent Activity as a Cause of Decline in Children's Mental Well-Being: Summary of the Evidence," *Journal of Pediatrics* 260 (September 2023), https://www.jpeds.com/article/S0022-3476(23)00111-7/abstract.

6

America's Social Experiment with Gender

LEOR SAPIR

When 13-year-old "Ava" came to see Tamara Pietzke, a therapist at the MultiCare health system in Tacoma, Washington, she was a wreck. Ava had been bullied by her schoolmates and kicked out of school on several occasions for threatening to kill others and herself. During therapy sessions, Ava would rock back and forth and communicate with Pietzke by showing her "extremely sadistic and graphic pornographic videos on her phone."[1]

Pietzke quickly discovered that Ava had been sexually abused by her cousin, her mother's ex-boyfriend, and a boy at school. She and her sister grew up in a house in which horror and porn movies were the only ones available. Ava's mother had reportedly practiced bestiality and had tried to kill Ava's sister in front of her. The girls now had a restraining order against their mother and, with their father out of the picture, were being raised by their mother's other former boyfriend.

Ava's difficulty communicating was in part because she had autism. She was also diagnosed with depression, post-traumatic stress disorder, anxiety, and intermittent explosive disorder. Her trauma was so severe that she would occasionally age regress by sucking on a pacifier while watching *Teletubbies*.

Ava had also been "questioning her gender." She told Pietzke about the "xenogenders" she identified with. "It's something autistic people made up," she said. "If you like a food, for instance, there's a gender for it."[2] Ava had been referred to the Gender Health Clinic at Mary Bridge Children's Hospital, which is part of MultiCare. The clinic "affirmed" her as a boy at the first meeting and recommended that she begin testosterone treatment to align her physical appearance with her "gender identity." Ava, however, needed a letter from a mental health provider clearing her of any unaddressed mental health concerns. The clinic's staff instructed Ava to get this letter only from an "affirming" therapist.

Pietzke considers herself an affirming therapist, but she refused to sign. Ava needed more therapy and was in no condition to provide informed consent to life-altering hormones.

Pietzke's colleagues and supervisors disagreed. MultiCare's in-house "gender-affirming care" expert wrote to Pietzke, explaining that "trauma history is not a counterindication of [hormone therapy]" and that "there is not valid, evidence based, peer reviewed research that would indicate that gender dysphoria arises from anything other than gender." Hormones are appropriate where a diagnosis exists, said the expert, and "the diagnosis centers on an incongruence of gender identity and assigned gender at birth."[3] As long as Ava had expressed a "gender identity" that was different from her "assigned gender at birth," she was eligible for hormones.

Due to Pietzke's misgivings, Ava's case was referred to MultiCare's risk management team. This came as a relief to Pietzke, who assumed that an external review by professionals tasked with detecting harmful practices would vindicate her position. But the risk management team concluded that it was actually Pietzke who was a threat to Ava. They reassigned the troubled teen to a therapist who would sign the letter.

Pietzke quit, went public with her concerns, and was promptly targeted with an investigation from Washington state health authorities for, among other things, being insufficiently "affirming."[4]

"Gender-Affirming Care"

Ava's case may be extreme, but it reflects a broader trend that has emerged in Western societies in recent decades. Children and adolescents with some combination of poor mental health, neurocognitive challenges like autism or ADHD, histories of sexual trauma and abuse, and familial instability latch on to "gender" as a catchall explanation for what ails them. Therapists and doctors "affirm" these self-diagnoses and approve young teens for life-altering hormones and surgeries. Once children mention gender, the full complexity of their individual life histories and circumstances is viewed narrowly through that lens. They are assumed to be "trans kids" whose myriad difficulties are due to "minority stress."[5]

Parents who object that "affirming" clinicians are too quick to approve their children for hormones or surgeries are cast as bigots and told that their hesitations will cause their kids to commit suicide. Faced with a choice between a "dead daughter or live transgender son," many relent.

The fifth edition of the Diagnostic and Statistical Manual of Mental Disorders (DSM-5) defines gender dysphoria as distress or difficulty functioning that accompanies the feeling of mismatch between one's sex and one's subjective feeling of being male, female, or other.[6] The World Health Organization's Eleventh International Classification of Diseases requires only the feeling of incongruence.[7] Previous editions of the DSM classified the condition as "gender identity disorder," a term transgender advocates in the mental health fields rejected due to its pathologizing implications.

Transgenderism and gender dysphoria are distinct concepts. "Transgenderism" is currently used as a broad term that encompasses any experience of gender that is different from one's "assigned sex at birth." Across the English-speaking world, the most rapidly rising subcategory under the trans umbrella is "nonbinary," describing one who feels they are neither exclusively male nor exclusively female.[8]

Trans identification skews strongly toward Generation Z and younger millennials. According to the US Census Bureau, "binary" trans identification in 2021 and 2022 was 2.3 percent among Generation Z adults, compared to only 0.1 percent among baby boomers. Nonbinary described just under 1 percent of the respondents among boomers but over 3 percent among Generation Z. There is also a noticeable female skew in Gen Z, with females being at least twice as likely as males to identify as transgender (binary and nonbinary).[9]

The prevalence of transgender identification among US high school students is estimated at 1.4–9.2 percent, depending on how key terms are defined and whether surveys are national or local.[10] Tracking with these new social realities is a sudden and exponential rise in the diagnoses of gender dysphoria in children and teens and in referrals to pediatric gender clinics. In the United Kingdom, referrals to the Gender Identity Development Service (GIDS) rose from 39 in 2009 to 1,497 in 2016, a 38-fold increase. In 2022, GIDS received as many as 5,000 referrals from children under 18.[11] Referrals to GIDS grew steadily between 2009 and 2014, and they accelerated rapidly from 2015 onward.[12]

In the US, 121,882 new diagnoses of gender dysphoria in children age 6–17 were recorded between 2017 and 2021, reflecting a 20 percent increase per year between 2017 and 2020 and a 70 percent increase between 2020 and 2021.[13] National data on referrals to gender clinics are harder to come by, as the US does not have a centralized service like GIDS. But it's telling that the first pediatric gender clinic opened in Boston in 2007, and by 2022 there were more than 100 such clinics across the country.[14]

Individual clinics have reported exponential increases in their caseload. Referrals to the Doernbecher Children's Hospital in Portland, Oregon, rose by 4,500 percent between 2013 and 2021.[15] Mary Bridge Children's Hospital in Tacoma, Washington, documented 59 patients in 2015 and 730 in 2022.[16] The Washington University Transgender Center at the St. Louis Children's Hospital in Missouri took in "four or five" patients per month in 2018. By 2021, it was receiving calls from that number of prospective patients every day.[17]

Once theorized to be a mere "pause button" that allows a young teen time to think about whether to proceed with a full hormonal and surgical "transition," puberty blockers (when used in this context) are now recognized as the first step down the medical pathway.[18] Undergoing full hormonal transition (puberty blockers at Tanner Stage 2 followed by cross-sex hormones) entails lifelong infertility. Other risks may include sexual dysfunction (causing further impairment in quality of life),[19] bone health deficits,[20] lower IQ,[21] cancer,[22] and cardiovascular disease.[23]

At least 17,683 American teens, and potentially many more, were put on puberty blockers or cross-sex hormones between 2017 and 2021.[24] Surgeries, including mastectomies for girls and vaginoplasty for boys, are rarely performed on minors outside the US. In the US they are less common than hormones but have also been on the rise. According to a conservative estimate, at least 3,125 "top surgeries" were performed on adolescents age 12–18 between 2016 and 2020.[25] The youngest of these patients was 12 years old.[26] Genital surgeries on teens are less common, but they do happen. At least 56 such procedures took place between 2019 and 2021.[27] Advocates for "gender-affirming care" assert that these procedures never happen, and when they do recognize their existence, they insist they are so rare their discussion constitutes scare mongering. But the number of teen boys who were surgically castrated and had a pseudo-vagina crafted (in some cases out of intestinal tissue) between 2019 and 2021 is almost triple the number of kids (19) who were killed in school shootings during those years, a problem no one believes is too rare to warrant public concern.[28]

Do the benefits of early medical transition outweigh these risks? To date, every systematic review of the evidence—the gold standard for evaluating the overall state of the research on medical interventions—has found that the evidence for mental health benefits is disturbingly weak.[29] In June 2024, documents unsealed in an Alabama lawsuit revealed that the World Professional Association for Transgender Health (WPATH), the preeminent organization promoting a medical pathway for minors as a "standard of care," suppressed the publication of evidence reviews and misled the public about what is known from research.[30] The documents also revealed that WPATH eliminated age minimums for surgeries under pressure from a transgender official in the Biden administration's Department of Health and Human Services.[31]

Youth gender medicine is "built on shaky foundations," said Hilary Cass,[32] a former president of the UK Royal College of Pediatricians and Child Health, whom England's National Health Service (NHS) tasked with conducting a comprehensive, multiyear review of its gender services for children and adolescents.[33]

In early 2024, NHS banned the routine prescription of puberty blockers for treatment of gender dysphoria.[34] The decision to end Britain's uncontrolled experiment with the notorious drug has enjoyed bipartisan support.[35] The UK joined Denmark,[36] Finland,[37] and Sweden,[38] where youth access to these drugs had already been restricted following systematic reviews of the evidence. Health authorities in France,[39] Germany,[40] and Norway[41] have also issued stern warnings about the lack of evidence for safety and efficacy of puberty blockers and cross-sex hormones.

In the US, as of this writing, major medical associations remain steadfast in their support for the practice and regard skepticism or dissent as evidence of "transphobia."[42] Given cover by left-of-center newspaper editorial boards who see "gender-affirming care" as a nonnegotiable civil right and refuse to fact-check activist narratives, US gender clinicians continue to prescribe hormones virtually on demand—at least in states where these "treatments" aren't banned.

In 2023, Jason Rafferty, author of the American Academy of Pediatrics' policy statement on "gender-affirming care,"[43] explained what he sees as the "main principle" of the affirmative approach: When a child says, "'I'm X,' we operate under the assumption that what they're telling us is their truth, that the child's sense of reality and feeling of who they are is the navigational beacon to sort of orient treatment around."[44]

The true rate of regret and detransition—the effort to reverse the effects of hormonal or surgical body modification—is not currently known.[45] Claims that regret and detransition are extremely rare ("less than 1 percent") rely on studies with high rates of failure to follow up and restrictive definitions of what counts as regret and detransition.[46] Most of the data come from studies on adults who got their procedures done while in their 30s or 40s. Some research suggests a current rate of regret as high as 30 percent,[47] but there are methodological limitations to these assessments. Given the lack of guardrails in the affirmative approach, the actual rate may be higher.

Scarred and faced with a lifetime of medical problems, including infertility, some "detransitioners" are demanding to know how the professionals to whom they entrusted their health failed them so miserably.

What Explains the Youth Transgender Phenomenon?

Transgender advocates argue that all humans have an innate "gender identity" that likely has a biological basis. They attribute the explosion in transgender identification among teens to "broader acceptance and destigmatization of gender diversity in some parts of the world (with increasing media visibility)."[48] In this telling, trans-identified kids are "born that way" and have always existed at these rates, but only now they are feeling comfortable coming out as their true selves.

The epidemiological data call this explanation into question. First, even if growing social acceptance could explain *some* of the rise, it could not explain a surge this dramatic and this rapid. Nor could it explain why the surge is concentrated in Gen Z or among teen girls and young women in particular.

Second, whereas in the past most people referred to gender clinics were adult men who suffered for many years and wished to live as women, nowadays the main clinical presentation of gender dysphoria is adolescent girls with no prepubertal history of gender dysphoria and high rates of psychiatric and neurocognitive challenges. Gender clinics did see children in the past, but these were mainly prepubertal boys, and over two-thirds of them desisted (that is, came to terms with their sex) by adulthood. Most turned out to be gay, which led gender clinicians at the time to conclude that early gender incongruence was far more predictive of homosexuality than of lifelong suffering on account of being male.[49]

The high rates of psychiatric diagnoses, neurocognitive challenges, and traumatic histories seen in the new patient cohort by the mid-2010s led clinicians, first in Finland and then elsewhere,[50] to question the practice of youth transition. In the UK, co-occurrence of gender dysphoria and autism in GIDS-referred youth rose from 6.8 percent in 2015 to 16.6 percent in 2021, a percentage far higher than the average rate in the age-matched general population (approximately 3 percent).[51] Teens seen at GIDS were almost nine times more likely than their age-matched peers to have been involved in the foster care system.[52] A US study from 2018 found that more than two-thirds of adolescents referred to gender clinics in California and Georgia had preexisting mental health diagnoses.[53]

"Minority Stress"

Advocates of youth gender transition argue that the poor mental health of trans-identified kids is because of minority stress, or the negative psychological impacts that come from living in a society that is hostile to transgender people.[54] Setting aside the obvious tension with the social acceptance narrative, minority stress is unpersuasive as an explanation for the co-occurrence of gender issues and other psychiatric problems.

First, it's not clear how the combination of trans identity and minority stress can cause neurocognitive conditions like autism, though some gender clinicians argue that it does.[55] Second, minority stress ignores evidence that gender issues arise after other psychiatric problems in most clinic-referred adolescents. Third, minority stress cannot explain the lack of credible evidence that medical transition improves mental health. Nor can it explain why medical transition does not seem to affect suicide rates, which, research has shown, is better explained by the presence of comorbid conditions.[56]

Fourth and perhaps most important, minority stress ignores the wider context in which the youth transgender phenomenon has emerged: a collapse of youth mental health. Gen Z reports alarmingly high rates of loneliness, pessimism, anxiety, and depression. Teens of this generation spend less time building friendships face-to-face and more time on their phones. They sleep less (likely as a result of phone use), are gaining more weight, engage more in self-harm, and commit suicide at higher rates than previous generations.[57] In April 2023, US Surgeon General Vivek Murthy called youth mental health "the defining public health crisis of our time."[58]

These trends have little to do with societal hostility, real or imagined, toward trans identity. Rather, they have to do with what New York University psychologist Jonathan Haidt has called "the great rewiring": Teens, and girls in particular, are disengaging from the activities that promote psychological independence and emotional resilience and becoming ever more enmeshed in online pseudo-communities. Other causes of the youth mental health crisis are "gentle parenting" and its scholastic expression, "social-emotional learning," which encourages students to see themselves as fragile and constantly ruminate about their negative feelings.[59]

In 2018, physician and researcher Lisa Littman introduced the term "rapid-onset gender dysphoria" into the clinical literature. Using data gleaned from interviews with 256 parents of adolescents and young adults who experienced distress over their sex, Littman hypothesized that the new presentation of gender dysphoria could be a maladaptive coping mechanism for underlying mental health problems (62.5 percent of the sample) or influenced by peer group pressures (70 percent) and social media exposure (65 percent).[60] In a later study on detransitioners, also by Littman, 38 percent of respondents said "their gender dysphoria was caused by . . . trauma, abuse, or a mental health condition." Almost a quarter cited "difficulty accepting themselves as lesbian, gay, or bisexual" as a contributing factor.[61]

Puberty is a time of great psychological and emotional upheaval for most adolescents. The difference between Gen Z and previous generations is how puberty is now conceived. The logic of de-pathologizing transgender identity requires the pathologizing of puberty as a condition to be cured, rather than a rite of passage to be endured. "The surrounding culture," writes Edward Shorter in *From Paralysis to Fatigue: A History of Psychosomatic Illness in the Modern Era*, "provides our unconscious minds with templates, or models, of [psychic] illness." These templates "constitute a symptom pool—the culture's collective memory of how to behave when ill."[62]

"It is the norm that all experiences of health and illness are understood through the norms and beliefs of an individual's trusted social group," writes Cass in her report to the NHS. "Thus, it is more likely that bodily discomfort, mental distress or perceived differences from peers may be interpreted through this cultural lens."[63]

A young teen girl who sees body fat emerging in awkward places and who becomes the object of unwanted male sexual desire might come to see her body as alien to her "true self." Transgender identity allows her to interpret her feelings of alienation as evidence that she was "assigned the wrong sex at birth." A "trans boy" identity beckons, promising a protective cocoon. (And why not enjoy "male privilege"?) The prohibition against "deadnaming" (any reference to aspects of one's pre-transition identity) assures a rebirth, an opportunity to start afresh. "Transition" is redemption, bringing elevated social status.

Pathologizing puberty implies that puberty is a treatable condition. From here it is a short step to the belief that adolescents have a moral and legal right not to be forced to go through the "wrong puberty." As the World Professional Association for Transgender Health once put it, "Neither puberty suppression nor allowing puberty to occur is a neutral act."[64]

Concept Creep

A final reason to doubt the social acceptance explanation has to do with changes in the meaning of four key terms: gender identity, sex, transgender, and gender dysphoria. Coined by the sexologist Robert Stoller in the 1960s, gender identity used to mean one's understanding of being male or female. Now it means one's "internal sense" of gender, which is in principle distinct from one's "assigned sex at birth." Sex is no longer understood as a binary of male or female, determined at conception and defined by the organization of the body toward the production of large or small gametes, but as a social construct.[65] "Assigning sex at birth" means arbitrarily picking out some traits (genitals) and ignoring others (gender identity).

The term "transgender" entered academic and activist parlance in the 1990s and gradually replaced "transsexual," which used to refer to people—typically adult men—who undergo medical procedures to make themselves appear as the other sex. "Transgender" reflects a far wider range of expression, ideas, and experiences.

As the evolutionary biologist Colin Wright shows in his op-ed "Every Tomboy Is Tagged 'Transgender,'" major institutions in American society now equate "gender nonconforming" with "transgender." The American Psychological Association defines transgender as "an umbrella term for persons whose gender identity, gender expression or behavior does not conform to that typically associated with the sex to which they were assigned at birth." The Centers for Disease Control and Prevention defines it as "an umbrella term for persons whose gender identity or expression (masculine, feminine, other) is different from their sex (male, female) at birth."[66] Under these definitions, any person whose subjective feelings about gender are in any way at odds with his or her "assigned sex" is or can be transgender. In other words, the critical distinction between gender nonconformity and transgender has collapsed.

A teacher training module conducted by the British transgender activist group Mermaids nicely illustrates how the new definition of transgender can encourage teens to interpret their puberty-related angst or run-of-the-mill gender nonconformity as evidence of being transgender. One of the group's training slides[67] features 12 stick figures side by side, with a female on the far left, a male on the far right, and 10 figures shading from female to male in between. The far left (female) figure appears above a Barbie doll, and the far right (male) figure above a G.I. Joe. Teachers are urged to ask their students, "Where on a spectrum might your gender identity be?"[68] If you're female but don't feel like a Barbie doll, or male but don't feel like G.I. Joe, then you're probably not a girl or a boy, respectively, but something else—perhaps "nonbinary."

For good reason, feminists have wondered how in a few short years progressive politics has come to embrace an ideology built on regressive and demeaning sex stereotypes.[69] Yesterday's stereotype-defying tomboy is today's stereotype-confirming trans boy.

The School-to-Clinic Pipeline

Any assessment of how the social acceptance theory entered the mainstream must look at how it's being propagated in schools, even from an early age. Not only are schools frequently teaching new theories about sex and gender, but they are also helping funnel students into highly invasive medical interventions, often while keeping parents in the dark.

Most of us remember elementary school as a time for learning math basics like addition and subtraction, doing fun science experiments with static electricity, crowding around the cage of our class's pet gerbil, and hanging from the monkey bars at recess. Elementary school kids still do these things today, but they're also being introduced to radical ideas about sex and gender.

In Evanston-Skokie School District 65, near Chicago, teachers encouraged kids to question whether the sex they were "assigned at birth" matched their gender identity and introduced them to novel pronouns like "they/them" or "ze/zir."[70] A school district in Edmonds, Washington, reportedly gave elementary students a handout telling them that they can identify as a boy, a girl, "neither or both," and recommending a book that introduces readers "to the nonbinary experience."[71] In Portland, Oregon, students were asked to situate themselves along an "infinite gender spectrum."[72]

In 2023, the New York State Department of Education issued a document offering guidance to schools on how they should support "transgender and gender expansive students" as part of their legal obligation to offer "health education." K–12 teachers, the document stated, "should consult the National Sex Education Standards,"[73] a guidebook written by advocacy groups that recommends students be able to explain the "role of hormone blockers on young people who identify as transgender" by the end of fifth grade and define "anal sex" by the end of eighth grade.[74]

A 2023 report on 18- to 20-year-olds nationwide by researchers Zach Goldberg and Eric Kaufmann found that 31 percent were taught in school that "gender is an identity choice," regardless of the biological sex you were born into, and 20 percent "heard [this idea] from an adult at school." (Respondents had the option of choosing both answers.) An additional 9 percent said they weren't sure if they'd been exposed to gender identity concepts. Twenty-five percent of respondents said they were taught "there are many genders." Although students in Democratic-leaning regions were more likely to be exposed than students in Republican-leaning states, one-third of the latter nevertheless reported being taught gender identity concepts.

Only one-third of students who were exposed to these ideas were taught that there were "respectable" counterarguments, and 27 percent were not even exposed to these. Two-thirds of Democrat-leaning students said they feared sanctions if they voiced controversial opinions on sex and gender. Among independents, 56 percent feared being punished, shamed, or expelled. And among Republican-leaning students, three-fourths were too afraid to speak their minds.[75]

Many US schools have policies designed to facilitate on-demand gender transition at school, often without parents' knowledge or consent. Students of whatever age who wish to embark on their "gender journey" can decide on a new name and pronouns, which school personnel must use. Many schools have policies that prohibit school staff from notifying or seeking approval from parents before using students' preferred names and pronouns. According to Parents Defending Education, an organization advocating for parental rights, as of May 2024 there were at least 1,062 school districts, serving almost 11 million students, that had parental-secrecy policies.[76]

Advocates of parental-secrecy policies claim that using a child's preferred name and pronouns is nothing more than a sign of respect and expression of inclusivity. A second claim, somewhat at odds with the first, is that creating an "affirming" environment is essential to the mental health of "gender diverse and transgender" students. When it comes to notifying parents, advocates argue that schools should do so only if the student gives permission, as some parents may be "abusive" toward their children. They define "abuse" to mean not just parents inflicting emotional or physical harm on their children but also being skeptical that going along with their child's gendered self-definition is in his or her best interest.

The notion that using a child's preferred name and pronouns is merely a sign of respect is unfounded. In reality, it constitutes what is known as social transition. Drawing on decades of research and clinical experience, the Cass Review notes that "it is important to view [social transition] as an active intervention because it may have significant effects on the child or young person in terms of their psychological functioning and longer-term outcomes."[77] For this reason, the Cass Review recommends that clinicians be involved and that parents direct the process. "Outcomes for children and adolescents are best if they are in a supportive relationship with their family."[78]

Are these interventions beneficial for all students who want them? Are they beneficial for some? The only existing systematic review of evidence for social transition to date has found that there is no reliable evidence for or against social transition, at least in terms of short-term mental health impacts.[79]

Are schools accommodating trans-identified kids or creating them? Does social transition merely acknowledge the reality of a child's true self, or does it create that reality? Recognizing that the research is inconclusive, the Cass Review reports that social transition may interfere with the natural resolution of gender incongruence and lock in a temporary state of identity confusion.[80] In 2022, the American Academy of Pediatrics' flagship journal, *Pediatrics*, published a study that has become a Rorschach test for how Americans think about these questions.[81]

A team of psychologists at Princeton University followed children with an assumed transgender identity for five years. By the end of the follow-up period, the researchers found that 94 percent still identified as the opposite sex while 3.5 percent identified as nonbinary. Only 2.5 percent had desisted. For the authors, who are supporters of the "gender affirming" approach, the findings were good news. Their study seemed to contradict five decades of research showing that more than two-thirds of gender dysphoric kids desist (i.e., come to terms with their sex), with the majority turning out to be gay.[82] That research is cited in support of an approach called "watchful waiting," in which children are neither "affirmed" in their declared gender nor talked down from it but are allowed to mature and figure things out for themselves. The Princeton study, in contrast, seemed to suggest that trans-identified kids know who they are and will continue living as their "authentic" gender if affirmed and given support by adults in their lives.

But there is another interpretation. In contrast to previous studies on gender dysphoria desistence, where it was the norm, the kids in the Princeton study had been socially transitioned. It's possible that the kids in this study had failed to come to terms with their sex after five years because social transition itself caused their cross-sex feelings and beliefs to persist. By "affirming" the children, adults interfered with the developmental process that would likely have resolved their gender incongruence.

If this second interpretation is correct, critics of early social transition are right to be worried: The majority of the kids in the Princeton study had medically transitioned by the end of the follow-up period.

In May 2024, the Biden administration issued new rules under Title IX—the 1972 law that prohibits discrimination "on the basis of sex" in education—that effectively require schools to facilitate gender transition for students on demand, regardless of age, mental health status, or familial circumstances. The rules instruct schools to defer to students about whether and when to notify their parents. Gone is the presumption that parents are well-intentioned and most invested in their children's health and safety.

Laura Edwards-Leeper, a psychologist who helped found the first pediatric gender clinic in Boston, told *On Point*'s Meghna Chakrabarti in a show on the Cass Review,

> What I have seen over and over in my clinical practice is how withholding information from parents is really very rarely in the child's best interest. Because 99% of the time, these young people have significant mental health issues and so by not sharing the gender distress with parents, it also often means not sharing the rest of the mental health picture.
>
> And it ends up tearing families apart.[83]

Conclusion

Youth gender medicine originated in a small-scale experiment in the Netherlands. Before the results were in, it quickly expanded under the aegis of a new human rights cause to other countries, where all eligibility criteria were relaxed and critics were silenced. "Gender-affirming care" did not grow out of the youth mental health crisis, but that crisis and its associated sociocultural factors were responsible for accelerating the demand for hormones and surgeries.

The case of Ava, discussed at the beginning of this chapter, may be a shocking example of the logical endpoint of this experiment, but it is hardly unique. Across the country, thousands of young teens have been subjected to experimental hormonal treatments and undergone life-altering surgeries on the belief that they were "born in the wrong body." Children as young as 3 are trusted to have innate and infallible knowledge of their true selves—selves that will presumably endure into adulthood. The role of adults is to recognize and celebrate this authentic selfhood, using superficial analogies to gay acceptance as a means of appeasing any doubts that arise, as they inevitably must, from centuries of experience with child-rearing. When historians look back at the first decades of the 21st century, they are likely to greet youth gender medicine with a mixture of fascination and horror.

Notes

1. Leor Sapir, "What Happened at MultiCare?," *City Journal*, February 16, 2024, https://www.city-journal.org/article/what-happened-at-multicare.
2. Sapir, "What Happened at MultiCare?"
3. Sapir, "What Happened at MultiCare?"
4. Tamara Pietzke, "I Was Told to Approve All Teen Gender Transitions. I Refused.," Free Press, February 5, 2024, https://www.thefp.com/p/i-refused-to-approve-all-teen-gender-transitions; and Sapir, "What Happened at MultiCare?"
5. Michael L. Hendricks and Ryan J. Testa, "A Conceptual Framework for Clinical Work with Transgender and Gender Nonconforming Clients: An Adaptation of the Minority Stress Model," *Professional Psychology: Research and Practice* 43, no. 5 (October 2012): 460–67, https://psycnet.apa.org/record/2012-21304-001?doi=1; Ilan H. Meyer, "Prejudice, Social Stress, and Mental Health in Lesbian, Gay, and Bisexual Populations: Conceptual Issues and Research Evidence," *Psychological Bulletin* 129, no. 5

(September 2003): 674–97, https://psycnet.apa.org/record/2003-99991-002?doi=1; and Rylan J. Testa et al., "Development of the Gender Minority Stress and Resilience Measure," *Psychology of Sexual Orientation and Gender Diversity* 2, no. 1 (March 2015): 65–77, https://psycnet.apa.org/record/2014-57149-001?doi=1.

6. American Psychiatric Association, *Diagnostic and Statistical Manual of Mental Disorders*, 5th ed. (Arlington, VA: American Psychiatric Association Publishing, 2013).

7. ICD-11 for Mortality and Morbidity Statistics, "HA60 Gender Incongruence of Adolescence or Adulthood," January 2024, https://icd.who.int/browse/2024-01/mms/en#90875286.

8. Hilary Cass, *Independent Review of Gender Identity Services for Children and Young People: Final Report*, Cass Review, April 2024, 90, https://cass.independent-review.uk/home/publications/final-report.

9. Jean M. Twenge, *Generations: the Real Differences Between Gen Z, Millennials, Gen X, Boomers, and Silents—and What They Mean for America's Future* (New York: Atria Books, 2023), 354–55.

10. Abbie E. Goldberg, *The Impact of Anti-DEI Legislation on LGBTQ+ Faculty in Higher Education*, University of California, Los Angeles, School of Law, Williams Institute, May 2024, https://williamsinstitute.law.ucla.edu/publications/anti-dei-laws-higher-ed; and Kacie M. Kidd et al., "Prevalence of Gender-Diverse Youth in an Urban School District," *Pediatrics* 147, no. 6 (Summer 2021), https://publications.aap.org/pediatrics/article/147/6/e2020049823/180292/Prevalence-of-Gender-Diverse-Youth-in-an-Urban.

11. Due to a limitation in the data, it's possible there was some double counting of referrals. Cass, *Independent Review of Gender Identity Services for Children and Young People*, 85.

12. Cass, *Independent Review of Gender Identity Services for Children and Young People*, Appendix 5.

13. Chad Terhune, Robin Respaut, and Michelle Conlin, "As More Transgender Children Seek Medical Care, Families Confront Many Unknowns," Reuters Investigates, October 6, 2022, https://www.reuters.com/investigates/special-report/usa-transyouth-care.

14. Terhune, Respaut, and Conlin, "As More Transgender Children Seek Medical Care, Families Confront Many Unknowns."

15. Terhune, Respaut, and Conlin, "As More Transgender Children Seek Medical Care, Families Confront Many Unknowns."

16. Sapir, "What Happened at MultiCare?"

17. Jamie Reed, "I Thought I Was Saving Trans Kids. Now I'm Blowing the Whistle," Free Press, February 9, 2023, https://www.thefp.com/p/i-thought-i-was-saving-trans-kids; and Jamie Reed, "Affidavit of Jamie Reed" (affidavit, St. Louis, Missouri, 2023), https://ago.mo.gov/wp-content/uploads/2-07-2023-reed-affidavit-signed.pdf.

18. Cass, *Independent Review of Gender Identity Services for Children and Young People*, 176.

19. Abigail Shirer, "Top Trans Doctors Blow the Whistle on 'Sloppy' Care," Free Press, October 4, 2021, https://www.thefp.com/p/top-trans-doctors-blow-the-whistle.

20. Daniel Klink et al., "Bone Mass in Young Adulthood Following Gonadotropin-Releasing Hormone Analog Treatment and Cross-Sex Hormone Treatment in Adolescents with Gender Dysphoria," *Journal of Clinical Endocrinology & Metabolism* 100, no. 2 (February 2015): E270–75, https://academic.oup.com/jcem/article/100/2/E270/2814818.

21. Sallie Baxendale, "The Impact of Suppressing Puberty on Neuropsychological Function," Authorea, February 7, 2024, https://www.authorea.com/users/713322/articles/697715-the-impact-of-suppressing-puberty-on-neuropsychological-function.

22. Christel J. M. de Blok et al., "Breast Cancer Risk in Transgender People Receiving Hormone Treatment: Nationwide Cohort Study in the Netherlands," *BMJ* 365 (2019): 1652, https://www.bmj.com/content/365/bmj.l1652.

23. Darios Getahun et al., "Cross-Sex Hormones and Acute Cardiovascular Events in Transgender Persons: A Cohort Study," *Annals of Internal Medicine* 169, no. 4 (May 2024): 205–13, https://www.acpjournals.org/doi/abs/10.7326/m17-2785.

24. Terhune, Respaut, and Conlin, "As More Transgender Children Seek Medical Care, Families Confront Many Unknowns."

25. Jason D. Wright et al., "National Estimates of Gender-Affirming Surgery in the US," *Jama Network Open* 6, no. 8 (2023): e2330348, https://jamanetwork.com/journals/jamanetworkopen/fullarticle/2808707.

26. Annie Tang et al., "Gender-Affirming Mastectomy Trends and Surgical Outcomes in Adolescents," *Annals of Plastic Surgery* 88, no. 4 (May 2022): 325–31, https://journals.lww.com/annalsplasticsurgery/fulltext/2022/05004/gender_affirming_mastectomy_trends_and_surgical.4.aspx.

27. Terhune, Respaut, and Conlin, "As More Transgender Children Seek Medical Care, Families Confront Many Unknowns."

28. *Education Week*, "School Shootings over Time: Incidents, Injuries, and Deaths," June 15, 2023, https://www.edweek.org/leadership/school-shootings-over-time-incidents-injuries-and-deaths.

29. Iris Pasternack et al., "Lääketieteelliset menetelmät sukupuolivariaatioihin liittyvän dysforian hoidossa. Systemaattinen katsaus" [Medical Approach to Treatment of Dysphoria Related to Gender Variations], SummaryX, May 15, 2019, https://app.box.com/s/y9u791np8v9gsunwgpr2kqn8swd9vdtx; Kellan E. Baker et al., "Hormone Therapy, Mental Health, and Quality of Life Among Transgender People: A Systematic Review," *Journal of the Endocrine Society* 5, no. 4 (April 2021): bvab011, https://academic.oup.com/jes/article/5/4/bvab011/6126016; National Institute for Health and Care Excellence, "Evidence Review: Gonadotrophin Releasing Hormone Analogues for Children and Adolescents with Gender Dysphoria," Cass Review, October 2020, https://cass.independent-review.uk/nice-evidence-reviews; National Institute for Health and Care Excellence, "Evidence Review: Gender-Affirming Hormones for Children and Adolescents with Gender Dysphoria," Cass Review, October 2020, https://cass.independent-review.uk/nice-evidence-reviews; Jonas F. Ludvigsson et al., "A Systematic Review of Hormone Treatment for Children with Gender Dysphoria and Recommendations for Research," *Acta Paediatrica* 112, no. 11 (November 2023): 2279–92, https://onlinelibrary.wiley.com/doi/10.1111/apa.16791; Florian D. Zepf et al., "Beyond NICE: Aktualisierte Systematische Übersicht Zur Evidenzlage Der Pubertätsblockade und Hormongabe Bei Minderjährigen mit Geschlechtsdysphorie" [Beyond

NICE: Updated Systematic Review on the Current Evidence of Using Puberty Blocking Pharmacological Agents and Cross-Sex-Hormones in Minors with Gender Dysphoria], *Zeitschrift für Kinder und Jugendpsychiatrie und Psychotherapie* 52, no. 3 (May 2024): 167–87, https://pubmed.ncbi.nlm.nih.gov/38410090/; Jo Taylor et al., "Interventions to Suppress Puberty in Adolescents Experiencing Gender Dysphoria or Incongruence: A Systematic Review," *Archives of Disease in Childhood* (2024): 1–15, https://adc.bmj.com/content/archdischild/early/2024/04/09/archdischild-2023-326669.full.pdf; and Romina Brignardello-Petersen, "Effects of Gender Affirming Therapies in People with Gender Dysphoria: Evaluation of the Best Available Evidence," Florida Agency for Health Care Administration, https://t.co/WrZ64Sgtlg.

30. *The Economist*, "Research into Trans Medicine Has Been Manipulated," June 27, 2024, https://www.economist.com/united-states/2024/06/27/research-into-trans-medicine-has-been-manipulated.

31. Benjamin Ryan, "'Damning' Information About Trans Medical Group Expected to Reach Supreme Court, as Justices Consider Challenge to Ban on Gender Treatments for Minors," New York Sun, July 10, 2024, https://www.nysun.com/article/damning-information-about-trans-medical-group-expected-to-reach-supreme-court-as-justices-consider-challenge-to-ban-on-gender-treatments-for-minors.

32. Hilary Cass, "Gender Medicine for Children and Young People Is Built on Shaky Foundations. Here Is How We Strengthen Services," BMJ, April 9, 2024, https://www.bmj.com/content/385/bmj.q814.

33. Cass, *Independent Review of Gender Identity Services for Children and Young People*.

34. Adrian O'Dowd, "NHS Services in England Are Told to Stop Routine Prescribing of Puberty Blockers," BMJ, March 14, 2024, https://www.bmj.com/content/384/bmj.q660.

35. Ben Quinn and Peter Walker, "Wes Streeting Expected to Tell Parliament Why He Backs Puberty Blockers Ban," *The Guardian*, July 15, 2024, https://www.theguardian.com/politics/article/2024/jul/15/wes-streeting-defends-puberty-blocker-ban-decision-after-labour-criticism.

36. Society for Evidence-Based Gender Medicine, "Denmark Joins the List of Countries That Have Sharply Restricted Youth Gender Transitions," August 17, 2023, https://segm.org/Denmark-sharply-restricts-youth-gender-transitions.

37. Society for Evidence-Based Gender Medicine, "One Year Since Finland Broke with WPATH 'Standards of Care,'" July 2, 2021, https://segm.org/Finland_deviates_from_WPATH_prioritizing_psychotherapy_no_surgery_for_minors.

38. Society for Evidence-Based Gender Medicine, "Sweden's Karolinska Ends All Use of Puberty Blockers and Cross-Sex Hormones for Minors Outside of Clinical Studies," May 5, 2021, https://segm.org/Sweden_ends_use_of_Dutch_protocol.

39. Society for Evidence-Based Gender Medicine, "National Academy of Medicine in France Advises Caution in Pediatric Gender Transition," March 3, 2022, https://segm.org/France-cautions-regarding-puberty-blockers-and-cross-sex-hormones-for-youth.

40. Society for Evidence-Based Gender Medicine, "The German Medical Assembly Passes a Resolution to Restrict Youth Gender Transitions to Controlled Research Settings," May 10, 2024, https://segm.org/German-resolution-restricts-youth-gender-transitions-2024.

41. Jennifer Block, "Norway's Guidance on Paediatric Gender Treatment Is Unsafe, Says Review," BMJ, March 23, 2023, https://www.bmj.com/content/380/bmj.p697.

42. Moira Szilagyi, "Academy of Pediatrics Responds on Trans Treatment for Kids," *Wall Street Journal*, August 21, 2022, https://www.wsj.com/articles/trans-gender-pediatric-aap-kids-children-care-surgery-affirm-treatment-11660942086; and World Professional Association for Transgender Health and US Professional Association for Transgender Health, "WPATH and USPATH Comment on the Cass Review," May 17, 2024, https://www.wpath.org/media/cms/Documents/Public%20Policies/2024/17.05.24%20Response%20Cass%20Review%20FINAL%20with%20ed%20note.pdf.

43. Jason Rafferty et al., "Ensuring Comprehensive Care and Support for Transgender and Gender-Diverse Children and Adolescents," *Pediatrics* 142, no. 4 (October 2018): 2018-62, https://publications.aap.org/pediatrics/article/142/4/e20182162/37381/Ensuring-Comprehensive-Care-and-Support-for.

44. Jennifer Block, "Youth Gender Medicine Has Become a Hall of Mirrors," *Boston Globe*, November 7, 2023, https://www.bostonglobe.com/2023/11/07/opinion/gender-affirming-care-trans-kids.

45. J. Cohn, "The Detransition Rate Is Unknown," *Archives of Sexual Behavior* 52 (June 2023): 1937–52, https://link.springer.com/article/10.1007/s10508-023-02623-5.

46. Pablo Exposito-Campos and Roberto D'Angelo, "Letter to the Editor: Regret After Gender-Affirmation Surgery: A Systematic Review and Meta-Analysis of Prevalence," *Plastic and Reconstructive Surgery-Global Open* 9, no. 11 (November 2021): 3951, https://journals.lww.com/prsgo/fulltext/2021/11000/letter_to_the_editor__regret_after.29.aspx.

47. Christina M. Roberts et al., "Continuation of Gender-Affirming Hormones Among Transgender Adolescents and Adults," *Journal of Clinical Endocrinology & Metabolism* 107, no. 9 (September 2022): e3937–43, https://academic.oup.com/jcem/article/107/9/e3937/6572526.

48. Stephen M. Rosenthal, "Challenges in the Care of Transgender and Gender-Diverse Youth: An Endocrinologist's View," *Nature Reviews Endocrinology* 17 (August 2021): 581–91, https://www.nature.com/articles/s41574-021-00535-9.

49. Cass, *Independent Review of Gender Identity Services for Children and Young People*, 84–105; Michael Biggs, "The Dutch Protocol for Juvenile Transsexuals: Origins and Evidence," *Journal of Sex & Marital Therapy* 49, no. 4 (September 2023): 348–68, https://www.tandfonline.com/doi/full/10.1080/0092623X.2022.2121238; James M. Cantor, "Transgender and Gender Diverse Children and Adolescents: Fact-Checking of AAP Policy," *Journal of Sex and Marital Therapy* 46, no. 4 (2020): 307–13, https://pubmed.ncbi.nlm.nih.gov/31838960; Julia Temple Newhook et al. "A Critical Commentary on Follow-Up Studies and 'Desistance' Theories About Transgender and Gender-Nonconforming Children," *International Journal of Transgenderism* 19, no. 2 (2018): 212–24, https://www.tandfonline.com/doi/abs/10.1080/15532739.2018.1456390; and Kenneth J. Zucker, "The Myth of Persistence: Response to 'A Critical Commentary on Follow-Up Studies and "Desistance" Theories About Transgender and Gender Non-conforming Children' by Temple Newhook et al. (2018)," *International Journal of Transgenderism* 19, no. 2 (2018): 231–45, https://www.tandfonline.com/doi/citedby/10.1080/15532739.2018.1468293.

50. Riittakerttu Kaltiala-Heino et al., "Two Years of Gender Identity Service for Minors: Overrepresentation of Natal Girls with Severe Problems in Adolescent Development," *Child and Adolescent Psychiatry and Mental Health* 9, no. 9 (April 2015), https://capmh.biomedcentral.com/articles/10.1186/s13034-015-0042-y.

51. Elizabeth O'Nions et al., "Autism in England: Assessing Underdiagnosis in a Population-Based Cohort Study of Prospectively Collected Primary Care Data," *Lancet Regional Health* 29 (April 2023): 100626, https://www.thelancet.com/journals/lanepe/article/PIIS2666-7762(23)00045-5/fulltext.

52. Tom Matthews, "Gender Dysphoria in Looked-After and Adopted Young People in a Gender Identity Development Service," *Clinical Child Psychology and Psychiatry* 24, no. 1 (August 2018): 112–28, https://pubmed.ncbi.nlm.nih.gov/30101601/.

53. Tracy A. Becerra-Culqui et al., "Metal Health of Transgender and Gender Nonconforming Youth Compared with Their Peers," *Pediatrics* 141, no. 5 (May 2018): e20173845, https://publications.aap.org/pediatrics/article-abstract/141/5/e20173845/37843/Mental-Health-of-Transgender-and-Gender.

54. Rylan J. Testa et al., "Development of the Gender Minority Stress and Resilience Measure," *Psychology of Sexual Orientation and Gender Diversity* 2, no. 1 (2015): 65–77, https://psycnet.apa.org/doiLanding?doi=10.1037%2Fsgd0000081.

55. Diane Ehrensaft, *The Gender Creative Child* (New York: The Experiment, 2016), 103–4.

56. Sami-Matti Ruuska et al., "All-Cause and Suicide Mortalities Among Adolescents and Young Adults Who Contacted Specialised Gender Identity Services in Finland in 1996–2019: A Register Study," *BMJ Mental Health* 27, no. 1 (February 2024): e300940, https://mentalhealth.bmj.com/content/27/1/e300940.long.

57. Jonathan Haidt, *The Anxious Generation: How the Great Rewiring of Childhood Is Causing an Epidemic of Mental Illness* (New York: Penguin Press, 2024); and Twenge, *Generations*.

58. Caitlynn Peetz, "Kids' Declining Mental Health Is the 'Crisis of Our Time,' Surgeon General Says," *Education Week*, April 25, 2023, https://www.edweek.org/leadership/kids-declining-mental-health-is-the-crisis-of-our-time-surgeon-general-says/2023/04.

59. Abigail Shrier, *Bad Therapy: Why the Kids Aren't Growing Up* (New York: Sentinel, 2024).

60. Lisa Littman, "Parent Reports of Adolescents and Young Adults Perceived to Show Signs of a Rapid Onset of Gender Dysphoria," *PLOS One* 14, no. 3 (August 2018): e0214157, https://journals.plos.org/plosone/article?id=10.1371/journal.pone.0202330. There have been several criticisms of Littman's rapid-onset gender dysphoria hypothesis in academic literature, but these fall short for various reasons. See, for example, Arjee Javellana Restar, "Methodological Critique of Littman's (2018) Parental-Respondents Accounts of 'Rapid-Onset Gender Dysphoria,'" *Archives of Sexual Behavior* 49 (April 2019): 61–66, https://link.springer.com/article/10.1007/s10508-019-1453-2; Lisa Littman, "The Use of Methodologies in Littman (2018) Is Consistent with the Use of Methodologies in Other Studies Contributing to the Field of Gender Dysphoria Research: Response to Restar (2019)," *Archives of Sexual Behavior* 49 (January 2020): 67–77, https://link.springer.com/article/10.1007/s10508-020-01631-z; Jack L. Turban, "Age of Realization and Disclosure of Gender Identity Among Transgender Adults,"

Journal of Adolescent Health 72, no. 6 (June 2023): 852–59, https://www.sciencedirect.com/science/article/abs/pii/S1054139X23000708; and Leor Sapir, Lisa Littman, and Michael Biggs, "The US Transgender Survey of 2015 Supports Rapid-Onset Gender Dysphoria: Revisiting the 'Age of Realization and Disclosure of Gender Identity Among Transgender Adults,'" *Archives of Sexual Behavior* 53 (December 2023): 863–68, https://link.springer.com/article/10.1007/s10508-023-02754-9.

61. Lisa Littman, "Individuals Treated for Gender Dysphoria with Medical and/or Surgical Translation Who Subsequently Detransitioned: A Survey of 100 Detransitioners," *Archives of Sexual Behavior* 50 (October 2021): 3353–69, https://link.springer.com/article/10.1007/s10508-021-02163-w.

62. Edward Shorter, *From Paralysis to Fatigue: A History of Psychosomatic Illness in the Modern Era* (New York: Free Press, 1992), 2.

63. Cass, *Independent Review of Gender Identity Services for Children and Young People*.

64. E. Coleman et al., "Standards of Care for the Health of Transsexual, Transgender, and Gender-Nonconforming People, Version 7," *International Journal of Transgenderism* 13, no. 4 (August 2012): 178, https://www.tandfonline.com/doi/abs/10.1080/15532739.2011.700873.

65. Alex Byrne, *Trouble with Gender: Sex Facts, Gender Fictions* (Cambridge, UK: Polity Press, 2024).

66. Colin Wright, "Every Tomboy Is Tagged 'Transgender,'" *Wall Street Journal*, September 22, 2022, https://www.wsj.com/articles/every-tomboy-is-tagged-transgender-transsexual-gender-dysphoria-children-hormones-clinic-terminology-expectations-11663872092.

67. Madeleine Kearns, "Don't Tell the Parents," *The Spectator*, October 6, 2018, https://www.spectator.co.uk/article/don-t-tell-the-parents.

68. Transgender Trend, "What Questions Should a School Be Asking About Mermaids Training for Teachers?," September 9, 2019, https://www.transgendertrend.com/questions-school-mermaids-training-teachers.

69. Kathleen Stock, *Material Girls: Why Reality Matters for Feminism* (London: Fleet, 2021); Helen Joyce, *Trans: When Ideology Meets Reality* (London: Oneworld Publications, 2022); and Rebecca Reilly-Cooper, "Gender Is Not a Spectrum," Aeon, June 28, 2016, https://aeon.co/essays/the-idea-that-gender-is-a-spectrum-is-a-new-gender-prison.

70. Christopher F. Rufo, "Radical Gender Lessons for Young Children," *City Journal*, April 21, 2022, https://www.city-journal.org/article/radical-gender-lessons-for-young-children.

71. Jason Rantz, "Edmonds School District Tells 7-Year-Olds That Gender Doesn't Exist, Asked for Their Pronouns," 770 KTTH Conservative. Talk Radio., March 27, 2022, https://mynorthwest.com/3409243/rantz-edmonds-school-district-gender-pronouns.

72. Nate Hochman, "Oregon's Inverted Political Priorities," *National Review*, January 10, 2023, https://www.nationalreview.com/corner/oregons-inverted-political-priorities.

73. University of the State of New York, "Creating a Safe, Supportive, and Affirming School Environment for Transgender and Gender Expansive Students: 2023

Legal Update and Best Practices," New York State Education Department, 2023, https://www.nysed.gov/sites/default/files/programs/student-support-services/creating-a-safe-supportive-and-affirming-school-environment-for-transgender-and-gender-expansive-students.pdf.

74. Future of Sex Education Initiative, *National Sex Education Standards: Core Content and Skills, K–12*, 2nd ed., SIECUS, 2020, https://siecus.org/resource/national-sex-ed-standards-second-edition.

75. Zach Goldberg and Eric Kaufmann, "School Choice Is Not Enough: The Impact of Critical Social Justice Ideology in American Education," Manhattan Institute, February 23, 2023, https://manhattan.institute/article/school-choice-is-not-enough-the-impact-of-critical-social-justice-ideology-in-american-education.

76. Parents Defending Education, "List of School District Transgender-Gender Nonconforming Student Policies," March 7, 2023, https://defendinged.org/investigations/list-of-school-district-transgender-gender-nonconforming-student-policies.

77. Cass, *Independent Review of Gender Identity Services for Children and Young People*.

78. Cass, *Independent Review of Gender Identity Services for Children and Young People*, 164.

79. Ruth Hall et al., "Impact of Social Transition in Relation to Gender for Children and Adolescents: A Systematic Review," *Archives of Disease in Childhood* (April 2024), https://adc.bmj.com/content/early/2024/04/09/archdischild-2023-326112.

80. Cass, *Independent Review of Gender Identity Services for Children and Young People*, 162–63.

81. Kristina R. Olson et al., "Gender Identity 5 Years After Social Transition," *Pediatrics* 150, no. 2 (August 2022): e2021056082, https://publications.aap.org/pediatrics/article/150/2/e2021056082/186992/Gender-Identity-5-Years-After-Social-Transition.

82. Zucker, "The Myth of Persistence."

83. Dorey Scheimer, Meghna Chakrabarti, and Tim Skoog, "'Cass Review' Author: More 'Caution' Advised for Gender-Affirming Care for Youth," WBUR, May 8, 2024, https://www.wbur.org/onpoint/2024/05/08/hilary-cass-review-caution-nhs-gender-affirming-care-youth.

7

Cannabis, Psychosis, and the Teen Brain

KEN C. WINTERS AND HOLLY B. WALDRON

The changes in Katrina were at first subtle, but her dad eventually began to sense something was not right. He knew that teenage years could be rocky for any adolescent, and he had expected the usual teen angst. But what he was seeing did not comport with his anticipation. There was the usual pushback against parental rules and expectations, but there was also a bigger issue: Katrina had shifted from her health-first attitude and begun experimenting with weed at age 15.

Her parents saw signs she was using regularly, sometimes before school. When confronted, Katrina would get defensive and dismissive. Not long before, she had shunned the idea of using drugs and was a high achiever—an excellent student-athlete and multitalented in art and dance. But within a year her social life seemed to center on using cannabis, and to make matters worse, her older boyfriend appeared to be a dealer.

For a trained psychiatrist who had previously seen a happy and well-adjusted youth, Katrina's dad was blindsided by his daughter's unusual thoughts and atypical behaviors that coincided with her heavy cannabis use. She complained that her friends were not treating her well and that others were controlling some of her thoughts. She altered her appearance several times, saying she was seeking "a better self." Once an honor roll student, Katrina became so disengaged with school that she was barely passing her classes.

Things got to the point that she was using daily and mixing cannabis with other drugs. On several occasions, her parents tried to get her medical help, but her low interest in sticking with any treatment plan led to many relapses. A recent conversation with her father provided a cautiously hopeful view that remission periods might be longer and that medication could prevent Katrina's delusional thinking and poor motivation, which had often gotten her fired from work. And he was hopeful that she would stop using cannabis for good.

Katrina's devastating case is not all that rare. The vast body of scientific research now points to the main intoxicant in the cannabis plant, THC (also known as Delta-9), as a possible trigger of or aggravating factor for psychosis, including schizophrenia. As a result, the connection between cannabis use and psychosis, particularly among young people, is becoming a more prominent public health concern. But for years, favorable attitudes toward cannabis use and a widespread push for legalization led to its increased availability. Despite its harmful effects on young people like Katrina, a wide segment of the public considers cannabis largely harmless and normal.

How did that come to be?

The Normalization of Cannabis in the US

THC is among the most frequently used "illicit" psychoactive substances in the US.[1] In a national survey of substance use, nearly 20 percent of those age 18 or older reported using cannabis at least once in 2021.[2] The prevalence of cannabis use disorder (CUD) has concurrently increased in recent years. Past-year CUD among Americans age 18–25 spiked significantly, from 4.9 percent in 2014 to 5.9 percent in 2018.[3] The lifetime likelihood of having a CUD among cannabis users is estimated to range between 9 percent and 30 percent.[4] Daily cannabis users now surpass daily drinkers.[5]

Drug treatment systems are also witnessing cannabis becoming more common. In a national study of individuals seeking treatment at state-funded substance abuse facilities, cannabis ranked third (behind alcohol and opioids) as the substance abused most by people 12 years and older. It was overwhelmingly the most common substance abused by adolescents—which is especially concerning.[6] Experts generally agree that two major factors contribute to this risk: the use of high-potency cannabis and initiating cannabis use during adolescence.[7]

Despite its risks, Americans of all age groups tend to favor legalization, although younger and more politically liberal individuals express a more favorable view than older and politically conservative ones. According to a

2022 Pew Research Center survey, 59 percent of US adults favor legalizing cannabis for commercial sales, and nearly all favor medical legalization.[8] As of June 2024, the commercial sale of cannabis is legal in 24 states and the District of Columbia. An additional 23 states allow the medicinal use of at least some cannabis compounds, and many states have enacted reduced penalties for possession and other decriminalization features.

With legalization, cannabis products have changed, and varieties of the product—edibles, liquids, and topicals, for example—are now widely available. Moreover, cannabis potency has increased dramatically. In the 1960s, THC levels averaged around 3 percent; today, the typical street product averages THC levels of around 15 percent. Concentrated products commonly sold in dispensaries can have up to 90 percent potency.[9]

In this context of increased popularity and permissible legislation, cannabis has been misleadingly spun as a harmless drug, which has emboldened many to no longer hide personal use. To take one cultural marker, our society has gone from one presidential candidate (Bill Clinton in 1992) claiming, "I did not inhale," to another (Kamala Harris during a CNN interview in 2019) being comfortable joking about cannabis use on the campaign trail.[10] During state legislative hearings, one of this chapter's authors witnessed how many representatives trivialized the matter by claiming things like "cannabis is not addictive," "cannabis helps its user's mental health," and "driving high on cannabis is like driving high on cough syrup."

The shift in attitudes and increased use of cannabis came about for complex reasons. Aggressive pro-cannabis campaigns have argued that cannabis is safer than nicotine and alcohol, that use and addiction would not increase significantly if it is legalized, and that legalization would not contribute to greater underage use or social and health problems. Proponents of legalization also argue that black market activity and legal system burdens would decrease.

Two other interrelated factors appear to be driving the recent pro-cannabis swing. Reasonable people can debate the extent to which compounds in the cannabis plant are effective treatments for numerous ailments and disorders. However, the widespread view that cannabis is a source of wellness has enabled the legalization of the plant for all adults. The "medicalization of cannabis" is now part of the 47 states that have some form of a medical cannabis program.

Moreover, some business interests are supporting legalization. Like Big Tobacco before it, so-called Big Cannabis is exerting its influence on several fronts, including through political donations, legislative lobbying, and media support. In several states, cannabis industry representatives are allowed to sit on rulemaking bodies. It's no surprise that the narrative that legalizing cannabis will address many social problems has been compelling to much of the general public.[11]

Youth Vulnerability to THC Exposure

The concern that teens are particularly vulnerable to the effects of cannabis is justifiably receiving public health attention. After all, mounting evidence shows adolescents are more susceptible to the various harmful effects of cannabis than adults are. Consider three recent studies.

First, officials from the National Institute on Drug Abuse concluded with a medium level of confidence that cannabis use alters brain development. They also claimed with a high level of confidence that adolescents who use cannabis are at a great risk of addiction and diminished academic achievement compared with nonusers and those who begin use during adulthood.[12] Similarly, in a National Academy of Sciences report on the health effects of cannabis use, the authors concluded that a moderate to substantial amount of evidence links adolescent onset of cannabis use with elevated risk of addiction and mental health problems.[13] Lastly, an international panel of cannabis researchers cited a moderate grade of evidence that "initiation of cannabis use should be delayed until after late adolescence, or the completion of puberty, to reduce development-related vulnerabilities for harm."[14]

According to a combination of studies that followed young cannabis users from New Zealand, Switzerland, and the US, those who start using in adolescence develop numerous negative outcomes compared with their non-using peers. These deleterious impacts include declines in IQ, greater likelihood of mental disorders, poorer social functioning, more criminal involvement, more polydrug use, downward socioeconomic mobility, and diminished life satisfaction.[15]

Animal and human clinical studies based on brain imaging data and studies involving neurocognitive measures provide clues to why adolescent onset triggers such negative effects. Early exposure to cannabis use is associated with altered neurodevelopment, particularly in the regions of the brain that are associated with decision-making and emotional regulation. These effects are most prominent among very heavy and dependent users of high-potency THC cannabis products.[16] Moreover, research supports the notion that adolescent exposure to cannabis use differs from adult exposure in that adolescent users display a greater activation of THC-sensitive brain receptors (known as cannabinoid receptors) that populate multiple brain regions. This heightened sensitivity to the effects of THC may underlie the greater functional deficits in adolescent cannabis users compared with those who initiate use during adulthood.[17]

David: A Case of Cannabis-Induced Psychosis

David began using cannabis in his mid-teens for reasons that are likely common among youth. "It seemed he did it for social acceptance and to fit in," said his mother. But David's parents did not want to convey that cannabis use was acceptable. They made it clear to him that they disapproved and often cited the risk that anyone could get addicted to it. Yet as a willful teen, David readily pushed back from these views that he thought were outdated and "just wrong."[18]

After graduating from high school, David decided to move out and live independently. The move initially gave his parents hope that their son was getting serious about adulthood. David even founded a streetwear fashion company and obtained a real estate license. He talked about his goals and about being a productive grown-up.

But in retrospect, his parents think David's move was the beginning of his downfall. That's because he moved to Colorado, a state where high-potency cannabis was readily available.

David obtained a medical marijuana card, although it was not needed given the weak guardrails that made it easy for the 19-year-old to purchase cannabis at dispensaries illegally. He began using daily, including blunts and concentrates with 50 percent greater potency levels of THC. His life centered on using and getting cannabis, and his social circles included only those who shared this habit.

Later, when his parents got access to David's laptop, they saw how he was detaching from reality. He was convinced that he was on the verge of becoming a rap star, even though he had never been interested in music. More distressing was the paranoia. As his mother recalls, "He thought the FBI was tracking him through his phone and laptop and that the mob was coming after the whole family." Along with these psychotic-like symptoms, his cannabis use escalated.[19]

David did not make it past his 21st birthday. Text messages to his parents showed a despair that eventually hit rock bottom. He admitted that he could not easily quit using cannabis even though he felt the drug made him "crazy." He also confessed to frustrating his parents by not staying in drug treatment for more than a few days.[20]

Perhaps the emotional downward spiral—made worse by addiction to cannabis—was too much for him. David's final text to his parents the day before his fatal opioid overdose asked that they forgive him for being a "disappointment."[21]

The Cannabis-Psychosis Link: A Look at the Research

Whereas psychotic disorders frequently occur alongside other substance-use disorders, the co-occurrence of psychosis and a CUD is common, occurring in up to 43 percent of people with schizophrenia.[22] The relationship between psychosis and cannabis is complex, and it can be affected by many factors: genetics, family environment, trauma and stress, and community characteristics. Many studies have sought to figure out the ins and outs of this relationship, including by taking into account a person's social context, new research on brain circuitry, and longitudinal research on the development of schizophrenia and other psychotic disorders.

Some of the best evidence available to study the link between cannabis and psychosis comes from meta-analyses. In essence, meta-analyses assess and synthesize findings across multiple previous research studies to reach conclusions about that large body of research. In particular, two recent meta-analyses—one led by Theresa H. M. Moore of the University of Bristol and another by Arianna Marconi of King's College London—have addressed the potential THC-psychosis link.

Moore's and Marconi's Meta-Analyses. Moore and her coauthors located eight studies from numerous literature research services that reported longitudinal data about cannabis use and psychosis.[23] The studies differed about how broadly they defined psychotic disorders, but all cases met the criteria for the presence of psychotic symptoms with concurrent evidence of impaired functioning. All the studies adjusted for other drug use, although two did not adjust for alcohol use.

Pooling data across all eight studies, Moore found that any use of cannabis was associated with an increased risk of psychotic outcomes, and she estimated that about 14 percent of psychotic outcomes would not have occurred if cannabis had not been consumed. Six of the eight studies examined the relationship of cannabis use frequency, and all six reported a dose-response effect: Higher-frequency users were about twice as likely to have psychosis.[24]

Marconi's research group focused on the association between the degree of cannabis consumption and psychosis.[25] Eighteen published studies, comprising 66,816 individuals, were included because they reported these two key variables: intensity of cannabis use before the onset of psychosis and psychosis-related outcomes. The results indicated that the intensity of cannabis use (frequency and quantity) was consistently associated with increased risk for psychosis in all 18 studies. Thus, the heaviest users were at the most elevated risk. In fact, the pooled analysis for these 18 studies showed about a fourfold elevated risk of psychosis-related outcomes (including schizophrenia) among the heaviest cannabis users compared with nonusers.[26] The authors concluded:

> Current evidence shows that high levels of cannabis use increase the risk of psychotic outcomes and confirms a dose-response relationship between the level of use and the risk for psychosis. Although a causal link cannot be unequivocally established, there is sufficient evidence to justify harm reduction prevention programs.[27]

Though Moore's and Marconi's meta-analyses support the hypothesis that there is a causal link between THC and psychosis, they don't explain whether cannabis use influences rates of psychotic disorder at a *population level*. It may be that they primarily reflect phenomena in smaller, localized environments.

Fortunately, separate research teams in Europe have now published such population-based data that further inform the nexus of THC and psychosis.

EU Multicenter Study. Led by Marta Di Forti of King's College London, a multicenter, case-control study across 11 cities—10 in Europe and one in Brazil—examined the relationship between cannabis use and the likelihood of developing a psychotic disorder by comparing individuals with and without psychosis.[28] The investigators recruited 1,237 patients age 18–64 years who presented with first-episode psychosis to psychiatric services in participating sites and recruited 901 control participants representative of the local populations. The researchers also assessed the frequency of cannabis use and tapped Europe-wide and national data on the expected concentration of THC in the different types of cannabis available across the sites. This procedure resulted in various groupings of patients based on patterns of use—ranging from rare to daily use—and on the THC intensity of cannabis used by participants.

Among the EU group, the strongest predictors for developing a psychotic disorder were the combination of daily cannabis use and the use of a high-potency variant. Compared with those who had never used the drug, participants who used high-potency cannabis daily were four times more likely to develop a psychotic disorder. If they began using cannabis before age 16, there was an additional but modest increase in the odds of developing a psychotic disorder. However, early-onset users who were not daily users and did not use high-potency products did not show an elevated risk.[29]

The study results regarding THC potency are particularly striking. Cities where high-potency cannabis (common potency levels well above 10 percent) was widely available—such as Amsterdam, London, and Paris—were associated with the highest likelihood of psychotic disorder. By contrast, cities with low availability of high-potency cannabis—such as Barcelona, Bologna, and Cambridge—had lower risks. The authors also speculated on the effect of high-potency cannabis being unavailable. If high-potency cannabis were not available, 12 percent of cases of first-episode psychosis could be prevented across Europe, with the preventive effect estimated at 30 percent in London and 50 percent in Amsterdam.

Not only does the EU study replicate previous findings, but it also provides—with a very large sample across a range of countries where different types of cannabis were available—the first direct evidence of a dose-response link between cannabis use and psychosis.[30] Moreover, evidence indicates that cannabis use affects variation in the incidence of psychotic disorders.

Danish Studies. Two recent publications from Denmark also provide an illuminating view of the nexus of THC and psychosis. In both cases, researchers were interested in figuring out whether an increase in the proportion of schizophrenia cases could be attributable to cannabis use. Because the health system in Denmark relies on a nationwide, historical health database of its citizens, researchers managed to conduct a cohort study of all people in Denmark who were (1) born before December 31, 2000, and (2) alive and at least 16 years old at some point from January 1, 1972, to December 31, 2016.[31]

Though any registry-based study encounters limitations (e.g., data available are necessarily limited, and possible variation exists concerning how data are obtained and recorded), the Danish studies provide a unique opportunity to examine the cannabis-schizophrenia connection with population-wide data. Moreover, the studies particularly examine a country with the increased availability and presumably greater normalization of cannabis use and a marketplace of high-potency cannabis.

As reported in one of the studies, published in 2021, Denmark's incidence of new schizophrenia cases steadily increased from 2.8 per 100,000 persons in 2006 to 6.1 per 100,000 persons in 2016.[32] Also during this period, the proportion of these new cases of schizophrenia with a coexisting CUD steadily rose from less than 5 percent in 2006 to nearly 20 percent in 2016.

To further pinpoint the extent to which CUD played a role in the escalation of schizophrenia incidences, the authors used a statistical strategy known as a population attributable risk fraction (PARF). PARF is an estimate of the proportion of cases of a disorder (in this case, schizophrenia) that occur by virtue of exposure to a presumed causal agent (in this case, meeting criteria for a CUD). PARF assumes—but does not confirm—a causal association between a disorder and risk agent. Assuming that the association between having a CUD and schizophrenia may be causal, the schizophrenia PARF for CUD increased threefold to fourfold over the past two decades, paralleling the increases in the use and potency of cannabis.[33] Put another way, if there had been no increases in the use and potency of cannabis in Denmark from 2000 to 2016, and thus no increases in the incidence of CUD, one could assume that Denmark would have seen 30–40 percent fewer cases of schizophrenia.

Brain Imaging and Effects on the Brain. During the fetal stage, cannabinoid receptors are important for brain development and may have extended developmental influence during adolescence.[34] Also, THC stimulates neurotransmitters in the brain's reward system that signal the release of the neurochemical dopamine, which can be viewed as the natural appetite brain chemical. Like with most other drugs that people misuse, surges of dopamine from THC ingestion "teach" the brain to repeat the rewarding behavior, helping account for THC's addictive properties.

Advances in brain imaging technology have revealed that THC's chemical structure resembles cannabinoid receptors in the brain and, less densely, in the lungs, liver, and kidneys. Powerful and omnipresent cannabinoid receptors are in many brain regions that influence thinking, memory, learning, pleasure, movement, physical coordination, sensory and time perception, and immune functioning.[35] In short: The widespread location of cannabinoid receptors and THC's similarity to these receptors helps explain the numerous effects of this drug on the user.

It is instructive to distinguish moderate and short-term use of cannabis from chronic, long-term use. On one hand, "THC can bend the brain" when it is used occasionally and its effects are transient. On the other, "THC can break the brain" when it is used at chronic levels over an extended period, contributing to profound and lasting effects. Thus, THC may have a range of harmful effects on brain functions, resulting in transitory symptoms at one end and chronic disruptions in mood, perception, and decision-making at the other. This continuum is a function of the intensity and duration of THC exposure and a host of biopsychosocial risk factors.

For the occasional user, the disruptions are likely to be transient, and such effects will pass as the person uses less or stops altogether. Cannabis users commonly report experiencing an altered sense of vision, hearing, and time, as well as difficulty with thinking and problem-solving. In experimental studies of healthy individuals with no history of psychosis who were administered THC, temporary psychosis-like symptoms (e.g., disorganized thinking, distorted sensory perceptions, and increased anxiety) are often reported.[36] Moreover, brain imaging studies show alterations in regions of the brain that control social cognitions, emotion processing, and decision-making.[37] These human clinical and laboratory studies suggest that, although many individuals experience relaxation and less anxiety after THC use, THC can produce a broad range of transient symptoms, behaviors, and cognitive deficits in healthy individuals that resemble some features of psychotic disorders.

THC Potency and Youth Risk

Several epidemiological studies reviewed here offer a strong case that heavy cannabis use can significantly elevate the risk of developing a chronic, persistent psychosis disorder, particularly if high-potency THC products (e.g., greater than 15 percent THC potency) are used around adolescence.[38] The effects of THC on the disrupting neurotransmitter activity in brain regions linked to regulating thinking, sensory information, and mood are consistent with symptoms of psychotic disorders.[39] Animal studies also show a link between THC exposure and its impact on learning and disruptions in brain receptor activity linked to psychosis.[40] As Anissa Bara of the Icahn School of Medicine concluded, "The causal disturbances of neural processes in adulthood by early cannabinoid exposure are linked to behavioural phenotypes predictive of psychiatric and addiction risk."[41]

A compounding factor of THC's potential causal role in psychosis is that cannabis is addictive.[42] That is, the brain adapts to large amounts of the drug by reducing the production of and its sensitivity to its own brain chemicals. As a result, a person feels withdrawal symptoms when not taking the drug. Addiction or dependence on THC occurs more readily with the use of contemporary products whose potency levels have steadily increased in recent decades. The National Institute on Drug Abuse estimates that up to 30 percent of cannabis users meet official diagnostic criteria for a CUD.[43] The addiction process triggers THC-enabled derailment of normal brain functions and advances a vicious cycle in which the person compulsively continues cannabis use while the onset of a psychotic disorder concurrently accelerates.

Psychotic disorders are most certainly linked to multiple risk factors that stem from biological, environmental, psychological, and social influences. Preexisting risk factors and exposure to THC interact in complex ways. Yet a question remains: Does THC contribute to the onset of a psychotic disorder in a person *absent or with a minimal level of* preexisting psychosis risk factors? That is, can an individual with virtually no risk factors develop psychosis after heavy and chronic use of high-potency THC?

Some data provide provocative but inconclusive support in the affirmative. Most relevant are the population-based studies from the US, Denmark, and Europe, in which studies collectively show or infer an association between new cases (incident rates) of psychosis and recent use and greater accessibility to cannabis.[44] Yet none of them offer insights as to participants' preexisting risk factors before cannabis use, and only the Europe investigators collected and measured THC products that study participants likely used. To clarify this issue, future research is needed that examines the association of varying exposure levels to cannabis across groups of youth ranging from no to multiple risk factors for psychosis.[45]

Nevertheless, the numerous studies reviewed in this chapter suggest that the link between cannabis and psychosis is partially causal.[46] By now, researchers are right to posit that cannabis use has a significant causal role in psychosis that persists beyond transient intoxication. Moreover, higher-potency cannabis and early use worsen the incidence of psychotic disorders. Whereas some have claimed that research has not identified an unsafe consumption level, abstaining from cannabis during adolescence seems to help, especially those with a family history of psychosis. Also, for an adolescent to limit the use of high-potency cannabis products, decreased use has an obvious harm-reduction benefit, regardless of their proneness to psychosis.

Will the toxic effects of high-concentration cannabis products and its links to serious mental disorders, including psychosis, get more attention from the public and policymakers? The dramatic expansion of legalized cannabis products for adults throughout the US poses a great challenge since the expansion seems to be enabled by cultural misperceptions that cannabis is a relatively harmless and effective medicine. Claims that legalization will effectively address social ills dominate when health risks are minimized.

Yet recent history affirms that bipartisan policies and legislative momentum can be garnered to address health issues. As with restrictions on nicotine access and the local response to COVID-19, both policymakers and the public at large have used public health information to tackle a persistent concern. So it can be with cannabis.

Notes

1. Carsten Hjorthøj et al., "Association Between Cannabis Use Disorder and Schizophrenia Stronger in Young Males Than in Females," *Psychological Medicine* 53, no. 15 (November 2023): 7322–28, https://www.cambridge.org/core/journals/psychological-medicine/article/association-between-cannabis-use-disorder-and-schizophrenia-stronger-in-young-males-than-in-females/E1F8F0E09C6541CB8529A326C3641A68.

2. US Department of Health and Human Services, Substance Abuse and Mental Health Services Administration, "2021 NSDHU Detailed Tables," January 4, 2023, https://www.samhsa.gov/data/report/2021-nsduh-detailed-tables.

3. Hjorthøj et al., "Association Between Cannabis Use Disorder and Schizophrenia Stronger in Young Males Than in Females."

4. Deborah S. Hasin et al., "Prevalence of Marijuana Use Disorders in the United States Between 2001–2002 and 2012–2013," *JAMA Psychiatry* 72, no. 12 (December 2015): 1235–42, https://jamanetwork.com/journals/jamapsychiatry/fullarticle/2464591.

5. Jonathan P. Caulkins, "Changes in Self-Reported Cannabis Use in the United States from 1979 to 2022," *Addiction*, May 22, 2024, https://onlinelibrary.wiley.com/doi/10.1111/add.16519.

6. Deborah S. Hasin et al., "Prevalence and Correlates of DSM-5 Cannabis Use Disorder, 2012–2013: Findings from the National Epidemiologic Survey on Alcohol and Related Conditions—III," *American Journal of Psychiatry* 173, no. 6 (March 2016): 588–99, https://psychiatryonline.org/doi/10.1176/appi.ajp.2015.15070907.

7. Ken C. Winters and Kevin A. Sabet, "Marijuana and Health," *Journal of Drug Abuse* 3, no. 1 (2017): 1–4, https://www.primescholars.com/articles/marijuana-and-health-107133.html.

8. Ted Van Green, "Americans Overwhelmingly Say Marijuana Should Be Legal for Medical or Recreational Use," Pew Research Center, November 22, 2022, https://www.pewresearch.org/short-reads/2022/11/22/americans-overwhelmingly-say-marijuana-should-be-legal-for-medical-or-recreational-use.

9. Mahmoud A. ElSohly et al., "A Comprehensive Review of Cannabis Potency in the United States in the Last Decade," *Biological Psychiatry: Cognitive Neuroscience and Neuroimaging* 6, no. 6 (June 2021): 603–6, https://www.sciencedirect.com/science/article/abs/pii/S2451902221000227.

10. Devan Cole, "Harris Says She Has Smoked Pot and Supports Marijuana Legalization," CNN, February 11, 2019, https://www.cnn.com/2019/02/11/politics/kamala-harris-marijuana-legalization/index.html.

11. Smart Approaches to Marijuana, *Impact Report 2023–2024: Lessons Learned from State Marijuana Legalization*, https://learnaboutsam.org/wp-content/uploads/2023/04/2023-Report.pdf.

12. Nora D. Volkow et al., "Adverse Health Effects of Marijuana Use," *New England Journal of Medicine* 370, no. 23 (June 5, 2014): 2219–27, https://www.nejm.org/doi/10.1056/NEJMra1402309.

13. National Academies of Sciences, Engineering, and Medicine, *The Health Effects of Cannabis and Cannabinoids: The Current State of Evidence and Recommendations for Research* (Washington, DC: National Academies Press, 2017), https://nap.nationalacademies.org/read/24625/chapter/1.

14. Benedikt Fischer et al., "Lower-Risk Cannabis Use Guidelines (LRCUG) for Reducing Health Harms from Non-Medical Cannabis Use: A Comprehensive Evidence and Recommendations Update," *International Journal of Drug Policy* 99 (January 2022): 1–21, https://www.sciencedirect.com/science/article/pii/S0955395921002863.

15. William E. Copeland, Sherika N. Hill, and Lilly Shanahan, "Adult Psychiatric, Substance, and Functional Outcomes of Different Definitions of Early Cannabis Use," *Journal of the American Academy of Child & Adolescent Psychiatry* 61, no. 4 (April 2022): 533–43, https://www.jaacap.org/article/S0890-8567(21)01350-2/abstract; Madeline H. Meier et al., "Persistent Cannabis Users Show Neuropsychological Decline from Childhood to Midlife," *Psychological and Cognitive Sciences* 109, no. 40 (August 27, 2012): E2657–64, https://www.pnas.org/doi/full/10.1073/pnas.1206820109; Madeline H. Meier et al., "Long-Term Cannabis Use and Cognitive Reserves and Hippocampal Volume in Midlife," *American Journal of Psychiatry* 179, no. 5 (May 2022): 362–74, https://psychiatryonline.org/doi/10.1176/appi.ajp.2021.21060664; and Lilly Shanahan et al., "Frequent Teenage Cannabis Use: Prevalence Across Adolescence and Associations with Young Adult Psychopathology and Functional Well-Being in an Urban Cohort," *Drug and Alcohol Dependence* 228 (2021): 1–9, https://www.sciencedirect.com/science/article/abs/pii/S0376871621005585.

16. Matthew D. Albaugh et al., "Association of Cannabis Use During Adolescence with Neurodevelopment," *JAMA Psychiatry* 78, no. 9 (June 2021): 1031–40, https://jamanetwork.com/journals/jamapsychiatry/fullarticle/2781289; and Claire Gorey et al., "Age-Related Differences in the Impact of Cannabis Use on the Brain and Cognition: A Systematic Review," *European Archives of Psychiatry and Clinical Neuroscience* 269, no. 1 (January 2019): 37–58, https://link.springer.com/article/10.1007/s00406-019-00981-7.

17. Matthew D. Albaugh et al., "Association of Cannabis Use During Adolescence with Neurodevelopment," *JAMA Psychiatry* 78, no. 9 (September 2021): 1031–40, https://jamanetwork.com/journals/jamapsychiatry/fullarticle/2781289.
18. David's mother, interview with Ken C. Winters, February 2021.
19. David's mother, interview.
20. David's mother, interview.
21. David's mother, interview.
22. Saeed Ahmed et al., "The Impact of THC and CBD in Schizophrenia: A Systematic Review," *Frontiers in Psychiatry* 12 (2021): 1–16, https://www.frontiersin.org/journals/psychiatry/articles/10.3389/fpsyt.2021.694394/full.
23. Theresa H. M. Moore et al., "Cannabis Use and Risk of Psychotic or Affective Mental Health Outcomes: A Systematic Review," *The Lancet* 370, no. 9584 (July 2007): 319–28, https://www.thelancet.com/journals/lancet/article/PIIS0140-6736(07)61162-3/abstract.
24. Moore et al., "Cannabis Use and Risk of Psychotic or Affective Mental Health Outcomes."
25. Arianna Marconi et al., "Meta-Analysis of the Association Between the Level of Cannabis Use and Risk of Psychosis," *Schizophrenia Bulletin* 42, no. 5 (September 2016): 1262–69, https://academic.oup.com/schizophreniabulletin/article/42/5/1262/2413827.
26. Marconi et al., "Meta-Analysis of the Association Between the Level of Cannabis Use and Risk of Psychosis," 1265.
27. Marconi et al., "Meta-Analysis of the Association Between the Level of Cannabis Use and Risk of Psychosis," 1262.
28. Marta Di Forti et al., "The Contribution of Cannabis Use to Variation in the Incidence of Psychotic Disorder Across Europe (EU-DEI): A Multicentre Case-Control Study," *Lancet Psychiatry* 6, no. 5 (May 2019): 427–36, https://www.thelancet.com/journals/lanpsy/article/PIIS2215-0366(19)30048-3/fulltext.
29. Di Forti et al., "The Contribution of Cannabis Use to Variation in the Incidence of Psychotic Disorder Across Europe."
30. Di Forti et al., "The Contribution of Cannabis Use to Variation in the Incidence of Psychotic Disorder Across Europe."
31. Carsten Hjorthøj, Christine Merrild Posselt, and Merete Nordentoft, "Development over Time of the Population-Attributable Risk Fraction for Cannabis Use Disorder in Schizophrenia in Denmark," *JAMA Psychiatry* 78, no. 9 (September 2021): 1013–19, https://jamanetwork.com/journals/jamapsychiatry/fullarticle/2782160; and Hjorthøj et al., "Association Between Cannabis Use Disorder and Schizophrenia Stronger in Young Males Than in Females."
32. Hjorthøj, Posselt, and Nordentoft, "Development over Time of the Population-Attributable Risk Fraction for Cannabis Use Disorder in Schizophrenia in Denmark."
33. Hjorthøj, Posselt, and Nordentoft, "Development over Time of the Population-Attributable Risk Fraction for Cannabis Use Disorder in Schizophrenia in Denmark."
34. Joanna Jacobus and Susan F. Tapert, "Effects of Cannabis on the Adolescent Brain," *Current Pharmaceutical Design* 20, no. 13 (2014): 2186–93, https://www.ncbi.nlm.nih.gov/pmc/articles/PMC3930618.

35. Ty Brumback et al., "Effects of Marijuana Use on Brain Structure and Function: Neuroimaging Findings from a Neurodevelopmental Perspective," *International Review of Neurobiology* 129 (2016): 33–65, https://www.ncbi.nlm.nih.gov/pmc/articles/PMC5094349.

36. Moore et al., "Cannabis Use and Risk of Psychotic or Affective Mental Health Outcomes."

37. Christopher J. Hammond et al., "A Meta-Analysis of fMRI Studies of Youth Cannabis Use: Alterations in Executive Control, Social Cognition/Emotion Processing, and Reward Processing in Cannabis Using Youth," *Brain Sciences* 12, no. 10 (October 2022): 1281, https://www.mdpi.com/2076-3425/12/10/1281.

38. Di Forti et al., "The Contribution of Cannabis Use to Variation in the Incidence of Psychotic Disorder Across Europe."

39. Nicola Black et al., "Cannabinoids for the Treatment of Mental Disorders and Symptoms of Mental Disorders: A Systematic Review and Meta-Analysis," *Lancet Psychiatry* 6, no. 12 (December 2019): 995–1010, https://www.thelancet.com/journals/lanpsy/article/PIIS2215-0366(19)30401-8/abstract; and Moore et al., "Cannabis Use and Risk of Psychotic or Affective Mental Health Outcomes."

40. Marie-Odile Krebs, Oussama Kebir, and Therese M. Jay, "Exposure to Cannabinoids Can Lead to Persistent Cognitive and Psychiatric Disorders," *European Journal of Pain* 23, no. 7 (August 2019): 1225–33, https://onlinelibrary.wiley.com/doi/10.1002/ejp.1377.

41. Anissa Bara et al., "Cannabis and Synaptic Reprogramming of the Developing Brain," *Nature Reviews Neuroscience* 22, no. 7 (July 2021): 423–38, https://www.ncbi.nlm.nih.gov/pmc/articles/PMC8445589.

42. Nora D. Volkow et al., "Effects of Cannabis Use on Human Behavior, Including Cognition, Motivation, and Psychosis: A Review," *JAMA Psychiatry* 73, no. 3 (March 2016): 292–97, https://jamanetwork.com/journals/jamapsychiatry/article-abstract/2488041.

43. US Department of Health and Human Services, National Institutes of Health, National Institute on Drug Abuse, "Cannabis (Marijuana) DrugFacts," December 2019, https://nida.nih.gov/publications/drugfacts/cannabis-marijuana.

44. Ofir Livne et al., "Association of Cannabis Use–Related Predictor Variables and Self-Reported Psychotic Disorders: U.S. Adults, 2001–2002 and 2012–2013," *American Journal of Psychiatry* 179, no. 1 (January 2022): 36–45, https://psychiatryonline.org/doi/10.1176/appi.ajp.2021.21010073; Hjorthøj, Posselt, and Nordentoft, "Development over Time of the Population-Attributable Risk Fraction for Cannabis Use Disorder in Schizophrenia in Denmark"; and Di Forti et al., "The Contribution of Cannabis Use to Variation in the Incidence of Psychotic Disorder Across Europe."

45. Olga Santesteban-Echarri et al., "Cannabis Use and Attenuated Positive and Negative Symptoms in Youth at Clinical High Risk for Psychosis," *Schizophrenia Research* 248 (October 2022): 114–21, https://www.sciencedirect.com/science/article/abs/pii/S0920996422003073.

46. Hjorthøj, Posselt, and Nordentoft, "Development over Time of the Population-Attributable Risk Fraction for Cannabis Use Disorder in Schizophrenia in Denmark."

8

Help Kids Resist the Lure of Screens

PAUL E. WEIGLE

In my 20 years as a child psychiatrist, I have witnessed an ever-growing preoccupation with screen media among my patients. They, their parents, and I all worry that screens and their related technologies crowd out other ambitions and threaten to dominate their thoughts and efforts. Though they offer immediate pleasures, screens stunt and displace habits and behaviors that support kids' health, development, and goals.

It's easy to forget that things have not always been this way. Since 2000, screen entertainment has become progressively more accessible, personalized, and engaging. The worldwide video game industry has ballooned from $35 billion in annual sales to well over $200 billion.[1] National surveys indicate the average time American youth age 10–14 spend on screens nearly doubled during the COVID-19 pandemic to an average of eight hours per day.[2] For older, minority, and low-income teens, the numbers are even higher.[3] Many young people spend more time entertaining themselves with these technologies than participating in any other activity (except possibly sleep). Over a year, youth age 8–18 spend more than twice the amount of time on screens than they do in school.[4]

The explosion in screen engagement is no accident. Gaming, social media, and streaming services are so alluring precisely because they are designed to be. These technologies boast increasingly sophisticated visual stimuli, intuitive controls, rewarding feedback, and advanced features to entice us to engage and stay engaged. While screen time varies among demographic groups (boys spend double the time playing video games, and girls devote more attention to social media) and individuals (some youth spend little time in front of screens, while others dedicate nearly all their waking hours), technology has often managed to exploit human psychology to command and hold the attention of today's youth.[5]

My patients who are most enamored with video games, streaming, or social media are those most in need of external limits—and most inclined to resist them. If we want to help them, it's important to begin by understanding how screens of various kinds affect their psychology.

Online Habits and Youth Health

Teens' engagement in daily entertainment screen media has been steadily increasing for decades. However, it was not until around 2007—coinciding with the launch of the iPhone and prevalent social media use—that their rates of serious mental health conditions began to rise. Since then, rates of depression, anxiety, self-harm, and suicide among adolescents have all steadily gone up. These trends worsened during and after the COVID-19 pandemic quarantine, as average screen media engagement increased dramatically, with the biggest increases in online gaming and social media.[6] Simultaneous increases in daily screen media engagement and mental illness among youth have led many to suspect a causal relationship.[7]

The relationship between online habits and mental health is complex. Many studies have found a small but significant correlation between time spent engaging in screen media and mental health problems in general. Screen time has been strongly linked to depression in dozens of studies, with more modest links to behavior problems, low self-esteem, and poor physical fitness in hundreds of others.[8] The relational nature of most studies makes it difficult to differentiate cause and effect, but mounting evidence demonstrates how screen media engagement seems to cause mental health problems. For example, one longitudinal study in children found every daily hour of screen media use was associated with a progressively increased risk of suicidal thinking two years later.[9]

Most screen media experiences do not appear psychologically harmful in a direct, overt fashion. In fact, more screen time seems to have benefited the health and well-being of today's youth in several ways. Children engaged on screens are generally physically safe and require less immediate parental attention, almost as if screens act as a virtual babysitter. Significant declines in unplanned pregnancy, motor vehicle deaths, violent crime, and drug and alcohol abuse among adolescents correspond with increases in screen engagement.[10] Social media can even help young people connect with like-minded or diverse peers they may not have met in person—a particularly welcome by-product for marginalized or minority youth.

Nevertheless, the most significant screen-related health drawbacks appear to be related to displacement. In other words, the more time young people spend streaming, playing video games, and on social media, the less they engage in a healthy balance of daily activities: socializing, exercising, having regular meals, developing hobbies with academic or artistic value, and especially sleeping.

Generational research shows that today's young people socialize less in person than previous generations and that they are turning to online platforms to connect. The obesity rate among adolescents rose from 10.5 percent between 1988 and 1994 to 20.6 percent in 2013–14. Obesity is most likely for those whose excessive screen habits displace physical activities and tend to accompany a junk-food diet.[11] Youth whose daily routines are dominated by screens necessarily dedicate less time to healthier hobbies and activities, including sports, music, extracurriculars, household chores, art, and reading. For example, the steady rise of screen habits among teens has seen the percentage of teens who read books, newspapers, or magazines daily plummet from 60 percent in the late 1970s to less than 20 percent by 2016.[12]

Perhaps the most vital routine disrupted by the screen habits of American youth is sleep. Young people routinely stay up late on screens, with a great majority of teens now failing to sleep even seven hours most days (far less than the eight to 10 hours their bodies require).[13] This results in a sleep deficit that stunts the learning process, weakens the immune system, and increases the risk of obesity. Insomnia leads to and exacerbates depression, anxiety, and suicidal tendencies.[14]

Screens in the bedroom only make this problem worse. Many young people end up going to sleep later because they are using screen media late into the night. Video games and social media increase physiological arousal, which delays sleep onset and impairs sleep quality long after screens are turned off. The blue light emitted by screens disrupts the already-sensitive circadian rhythms (i.e., internal clock) of children and teens, essentially fooling their brains into functioning at night as if it were daytime. When young people retreat to their bedrooms during the day to be on their phones, tablets, or video game consoles, they reinforce a psychological disconnect between the bedroom and sleep in a process called deconditioning.[15] Finally, adolescents experiencing "FOMO" (fear of missing out) are compelled to check social media periodically through the night.

Many of my patients privately admit to playing video games or streaming videos in the middle of the night when their parents believe them to be asleep. As a result of screen disruption, they are chronically sleep-deprived and typically feel unhappy, unfocused, and unmotivated, with related depression and failure at school. They resist getting up in the morning to go to school due to these symptoms and have developed a maladaptive coping skill of napping after school, which only exacerbates nighttime insomnia. It's a vicious cycle. The disruption of healthy sleep habits may be the most detrimental effect of increased screen use and a major contributor to mental illness—and therefore one of the primary causes of young people's current mental health crisis.[16]

More and more screens in the lives of America's youth seem to have disrupted many habits of healthy living. But how exactly do particular technologies affect their minds? Let's examine two of the most common ones: video games and social media.

The Video Game Compulsion Loop

Like other forms of screen media, video games command and hold many young minds by satisfying three universal psychological needs: autonomy, competence, and relatedness.

Video games grant players an amazing degree of autonomy, giving them far more control than other recreational activities like reading or watching TV. Far from early *Pac-Man* iterations, contemporary video games present vast virtual worlds that offer players innumerable choices and challenges, including customizable avatars and intricate paths to unlocking achievements. The typical video game controller features dozens of different inputs to direct play. Serious gamers typically perform five button presses per second, which, multiplied by the number of possible inputs, allows for millions of possible inputs every second of play.[17] This degree of autonomy sucks in the player.

Humans have a psychological need for competence, defined as a desire to deal effectively with our environment. Again, video games meet this need. They typically challenge players to an optimal degree, requiring some ability yet nevertheless ensuring a path to success. These conditions produce a state of flow—one in which players are wholly mentally engaged in the task of gaming. As a player's skill improves, video games increase in difficulty by adding enough challenges (but not too many) to maintain that state of flow. When I ask my patients what they're good at, the most prevalent response is "video games." Many even aspire to become professional gamers in adulthood.

The third psychological need met by video games is relatedness. Human beings are a social species, and cooperation is an evolutionary marker of success as a species. A significant portion of our brain is dedicated to social interactions, and we share a psychological need to feel connected to others. One might imagine that the last thing a young person playing video games would feel is socially connected, but many children and teens regularly game socially with school peers or online acquaintances. Games such as *Fortnite* and *Call of Duty* instantly introduce a player to dozens of others. They chat with one another, often with aggressive trash talk or cooperative planning, which may lead to online friendships. Interacting with computer-controlled characters simulates social interactions, which may make players feel less lonely. The real-life friendships of children and teens, especially boys, are often based on shared interests. Many boys in my practice play video games primarily to connect with school peers, or they may watch streaming videos of gameplay to be able to discuss games they cannot play. It seems as though video games help fulfill our psychological need for relatedness.

At least they do at first. While video games gratify the genuine desire for autonomy, competence, and relatedness, they are far less fulfilling in the long term. For those who spend the most time playing video games, who play excessively to the detriment of hobbies and functioning, the result is typically negative: They feel less competent in real-world skills, less socially connected, and as though they have less meaning in their lives. Despite their initial lure, video games are ultimately counterproductive for those who over-engage.

Overexposure also affects an essential developmental task of youth—namely, play. Universal to mankind and most other mammals, play enables the young to practice roles and situations anticipated in adulthood. This fosters vital psychological readiness for dealing with these circumstances when later encountered. Though traditional play relies heavily on imagination and cooperation between playmates, video games are creeping into or replacing imaginative play for many American youth. Children, particularly boys, have role-played fighting and war games since time immemorial, but they now often build their fantasy world around video game characters and stories, reenacting scenarios from *Minecraft* or *Sonic the Hedgehog*. The narrow scripts involved in playing video games lack the breadth, creative expression, and social skill building found in imaginative play. Ultimately, video games do little to prepare our youth for a responsible and productive adulthood.

But they do serve as vehicles for escapism. Children on average feel modestly competent and successful in social, athletic, and academic endeavors; in video games, they often feel exceptional. Video games cast them as protagonists in a story where they overcome seemingly insurmountable odds along a personalized hero's journey, becoming progressively powerful and saving the world. Success in the game is ultimately inevitable, given the requisite amount of effort and focus these games command and the paper-tiger nature of computer-controlled opposition. More than once a young male patient has confided to me, "I am no good at life, but I am good at video games." Video games make young people feel effective and powerful, often a welcome relief in stark contrast to their perceived place in the real world.

Unlike traditional forms of entertainment, though, video games lack stopping cues. Traditional games—be they athletic contests or card games—require a manageable time frame to complete, ranging from several minutes to a couple of hours. Television programs and movies are similarly timed. Video games, by contrast, can be played in perpetuity with no discernible ending or one that takes dozens of hours to reach.

Playing video games often involves what psychologists refer to as a "compulsion loop."[18] For example, in an adventure game, a player will work toward earning enough in-game currency to purchase a more effective weapon. After the requisite duration of play, the player invariably achieves this goal and is awarded the improved item. But despite having reached the goal, the player is not then inclined to end play. The player is instead motivated to experiment with the new weapon, discover how best to use it, and enjoy the results. In doing so, the player makes progress toward other goals and is driven to complete them, renewing another cycle of the compulsion loop.

Parents attempting to moderate their kids' gaming habits often face a daunting, thankless task. Youth who enjoy games the most typically have the most difficult time disengaging, often delaying or resisting when asked to end the game and becoming dysregulated when forced to stop. It's not unusual for a child compelled to turn off their video game to throw a tantrum, use profanity, and lash out verbally (or even physically) toward parents in response. Those in greatest need of parental limits are unfortunately those who respond most poorly to those limits being set.

The Itches Social Media Scratches

Following Facebook's launch in 2004, social media rapidly became central to most adolescents' everyday lives, transforming the way they interact with each other. The adolescent mind is developmentally primed to evaluate peer feedback and magnify its significance. Social media exploits this vulnerability to entice teens to log on regularly—and often excessively.

Interacting via social media is in some ways like doing so in person, but important distinctions exist. Social media interactions are much more immediately available, enabling teens to contact most of the peers they know—and a great many they have never met—at any moment. Social media interactions are asynchronous, allowing young people ample time to craft an ideal response and avoid feeling put on the spot, a feature that socially anxious youth greatly prefer. Online exchanges grant more explicit quantitative and qualitative feedback, which means youth can compare themselves to peers over the number of "friends" they have or the number of responses they receive for a post. Social media interactions are largely public and permanent, greatly raising the stakes when compared to in-person exchanges. This can turn a well-timed insight into a viral sensation or a minor faux pas into a consequential humiliation.

Like other forms of screen media, social media is linked to poor mental health. For example, one study documented significant declines in mental health on college campuses following the introduction of Facebook.[19] Most youth appear more susceptible to mental health problems with increasing time spent on social media. A meta-analysis of 12 studies found a significant relationship between self-reported social media use and depressive symptoms.[20] This may be especially true for low-income students, students who are bullied, those who engage in extremely negative content (e.g., posts about self-harm and suicide), and those who primarily converse with strangers rather than school peers. Social media also facilitates social comparison. Viewing the idealized online profiles of peers makes adolescents, especially girls, more likely to feel dissatisfied with their own appearance and can lead to pathological behaviors like eating disorders.[21]

Adolescents suffering from depression value social media more than their peers as a place to garner social support, share their own experiences, and be inspired.[22] However, the same teens are more likely to experience negative consequences of their social media posts, including negative peer feedback. Depressed teens are also particularly sensitive to such negative feedback, further exacerbating their distress. For many, excessive social media use leads to depression, which in turn leads to greater reliance on social media—again, resulting in a destructive cycle.

In my practice, many depressed teen girls spend their after-school hours lying in bed scrolling social media and feeling progressively worse about themselves and their relationships. They typically fear separation from social media, but when forced to abstain, following a period of withdrawal, they often show relief and insight into what problems it had caused in their lives.

Screens and Sexually Explicit Content

The internet has made pornography access affordable, anonymous, and readily available, especially for those with access to a smartphone. It shouldn't be surprising, therefore, that pornography engagement by children and teens has greatly increased in recent decades. Research indicates that teens have typically seen far more porn than their parents believe they have and a greater amount and variety than their parents have. One study of 614 teen-parent pairs found parents consistently underestimated their child's exposure to porn and its impact.[23] Adolescents viewing the most pornography are typically older boys and those with poor supervision, depression, or same-sex attraction.[24]

Though many young people consider it to be the best way to learn about sex, pornography risks teaching many of the wrong lessons. Porn typically features actors with unrealistic bodies engaging in aggressive, condom-less sex, during which a male dominates and an objectified female strives to please. Such videos show no evidence of care, intimacy, or an ongoing relationship. Videos that would have been considered extreme in previous generations—such as those featuring group sex, incest, bondage, sadism, and sexual assault—are just as available and popular as more traditional forms.

Porn has been shown to shape the sexual beliefs and behaviors of youth, who fail to distinguish theater from reality. Teens internalize scripts seen in pornographic videos and frequently attempt to replicate these acts in their real-world relationships.

Some of the most heartbreaking stories from my practice deal with children who have been affected by early exposure to pornography. In one case, an 8-year-old boy with no history of abuse watched videos featuring anal intercourse and subsequently reenacted it with his 5-year-old brother. Teenage girls have confided to me that their boyfriends assumed slapping or choking during sex would be pleasurable to a female partner because it appeared that way in pornography videos. Viewing porn has also been associated with later perpetration of sexual harassment and assault among teens, although causality remains unproven.[25] Among young women, pornography use is a key predictor of sexual victimization, although causality is unproven and may be bidirectional.[26]

Exposure to pornography has also been shown to decrease interest in real-world romantic relationships. It has been linked to dissatisfaction with existing relationships, dissatisfaction with sex, and sexual dysfunction.[27] For many, this effect can create a vicious cycle: The more pornography they consume, the less exciting real-world romance seems, and the less they pursue it, the more daunting it seems, leading to a greater reliance on pornography. Boys in my practice today are far more familiar with pornography than with relationships. Much like video games, pornography has negative displacing effects for them, including crowding out dates with female peers. Some religious young men, concerned about the immorality of their pornography addiction, have come to me seeking treatment, typically with related depression, social anxiety, and problematic gaming habits.

Sexting—often defined as sending or receiving nude pictures via text or social media—is an increasingly common behavior among teens. Studies of college students indicate that roughly half admit to engaging in sexting before age 18.[28] Curiously, teens report positive, neutral, and negative consequences of sexting in roughly equal measure. Teens who send nude pictures in the context of a preexisting relationship are most likely to report positive or neutral consequences. Younger and LGBT teens are more likely to sext outside of a preexisting relationship and experience negative consequences, including harassment or having pictures shared without their consent. In some cases, this can lead to strong feelings of shame and regret—particularly when exacerbated by related social rejection from classmates—and even lead to a mental health crisis such as suicidal behavior. Girls frequently experience significant pressure in the form of digital pestering or coercion to share sexts, but those who give in often regret doing so.

How Parents Can Monitor Screen Time

Who will ultimately guard kids from excessive screen use? Different institutions have different roles in this effort. Schools should ban smartphones from the classroom, include healthy screen media habits in health curricula, and perhaps even offer lessons for parents to understand parental control software and other ways to create a screen-free environment. Companies could create video games, streaming, and social media platforms that encourage more moderate use. For example, video game rewards could diminish after the game is played for more than three hours in a single day, and social media platforms could eliminate the endless scroll or autopay functions and remind users to take a break after hours of use. Legislators should promote means to regulate access to social media for kids (e.g., effective age verification), aiming to strike a balance between parents' right to care for their children, technological innovation, and children's mental well-being.

Given the near-ubiquitous nature of screen media in the lives of America's youth, it ultimately falls on parents to limit the content children and adolescents engage with and the extent to which they engage with it and to guide them toward a moderate, healthy use of age-appropriate content. This is particularly challenging for parents who came of age in a world without the social media, video streaming, and sophisticated video games that captivate their "digital native" children.

There are many things parents can do to help their kids navigate the risks of the online world and form better screen habits. Parents should strive to provide a daily structure that safeguards sufficient time for sleep, homework, exercise, extracurriculars, sit-down meals, and face-to-face interaction with friends and family. Only the remaining time should be allotted for entertainment screen use (e.g., two hours on weekdays and three on weekends). To this end, families must typically maintain involvement in structured activities, like household chores and sports leagues, and establish screen-free times (e.g., mealtime and bedtime) and zones (e.g., the bedroom and the bathroom).

It is vital for parents to model a healthy relationship with screen media, including by moderating their own use. Children tend to follow their parents' examples, and parents distracted by screen media are typically ineffective in supervising their children. Parents should understand the media their children consume and allow access to only age-appropriate material. (For example, children should not be permitted unrestricted access to YouTube or graphic games such as *Call of Duty* or *Grand Theft Auto*.) And in addition to assigning daily chores, parents should enforce "Grandma's rule" for screens: No screen time allowed until homework and chores are complete.

Managing youth screen time can be quite challenging, particularly for those who need limits the most. In my experience, parents are most successful when they can understand and accept the child's perspective while maintaining high expectations (i.e., an authoritative parenting style), which has been associated with a number of positive psychological outcomes and academic achievement. Research backs this up too.[29]

Parental controls, such as those on gaming consoles or smartphones, may be tricky to navigate, but they can be enormously helpful. These controls should be used extensively for younger children, with restrictions easing as the child demonstrates competence and responsibility. Yet because savvy youth can circumvent them, these controls should be used as a complement to, not a substitute for, traditional direct supervision. Devices should be removed from bedrooms, where they disrupt sleep and cannot be adequately supervised. Wi-Fi routers should be disabled at night in the homes of youth who are tempted to surreptitiously go online when parents think they are sleeping.

As children age and show maturity, their parents' role in encouraging a healthy relationship with screen media should transition to be more like a guide and less like a cop. Mature youth should have more say in negotiating family rules around screen use. Parents should maintain open dialogue with children about technology use, incorporating a curious and nonjudgmental stance to help them moderate their screen habits. In these conversations, parents should refrain from expressing negative emotions or solving the child's online problems whenever possible, instead demonstrating calm interest and confidence in the child's ability to do so themselves.

It is helpful for parents to routinely enjoy screen media activities with their children: streaming videos, playing video games, and walking a child through their first social media experiences. Shared media experiences serve as common reference points that stimulate valuable conversations. Parental supervision and guidance regarding screen media activities can be challenging and often thankless, but it's ultimately rewarding and strongly protective against the most common types of mental illness.

If parents feel unable to control their child's media habits or if they believe their child's screen activities are harming their health or functioning, they should consult their child's pediatrician or a qualified mental health professional. Excessive, unsafe, and even obsessive engagement with video games, social media, and streaming are often related to other mental health problems, including ADHD, behavior disorders, depression, and social anxiety. It is frequently necessary to reestablish healthy screen habits to best alleviate concurrent mental health conditions, although treating those conditions is regularly helpful in addressing problematic screen use as well. Individual and family counseling, and at times even medication, can be effective for not only psychiatric conditions but related problematic screen media habits.

Afterword

In a memorable passage from the Greek epic *The Odyssey*, Homer narrates how Odysseus's crew lost interest in returning to their native land of Ithaca after eating the lotus fruit. Despite spending years away during the Trojan War, Odysseus's crew "had no longer any wish to bring back word or to return" to their families; the lotus fruit made them "forgetful of their homeward way."[30] To snap them out of their stupor, Odysseus ultimately dragged them back to their ship, despite their supplications to the contrary.

The story resonates with my experiences as a child and adolescent psychiatrist in the digital age. I often find myself at odds with those I serve. In preparation for independence and adulthood, the children and adolescents I treat typically recognize the importance of friendships, academic success, family harmony, physical fitness, and mental health. However, many are constantly sidetracked by the immediate gratification that screen entertainment offers.

Only after a painful withdrawal from the lotus fruit did Odysseus's crew return to their senses and rededicate themselves to their quest of returning home. Like Odysseus, those who care for children and teens are faced with the unenviable task of forcibly dragging them away from the object of their obsession or leaving them to languish. Parents, teachers, counselors, and medical professionals must steer today's youth away from the lure of constant screen media engagement to achieve a healthy life balance. Although the challenges are considerable, so are the stakes.

Notes

1. Grand View Research, *Video Game Market Size, Share & Trends Analysis Report by Device (Console, Mobile, Computer), by Type (Online, Offline), by Region (Asia Pacific, North America, Europe), and Segment Forecasts, 2023–2030*, August 22, 2023, https://www.grandviewresearch.com/industry-analysis/video-game-market.

2. Jason M. Nagata et al., "Screen Time Use Among US Adolescents During the COVID-19 Pandemic: Findings from the Adolescent Brain Cognitive Development (ABCD) Study," *JAMA Pediatrics* 176, no. 1 (November 2021): 94–96, https://jamanetwork.com/journals/jamapediatrics/fullarticle/2785686.

3. Nagata et al., "Screen Time Use Among US Adolescents During the COVID-19 Pandemic"; and Victoria Rideout and Michael B. Robb, *The Common Sense Census: Media Use by Tweens and Teens, 2019*, Common Sense Media, 2019, https://www.commonsensemedia.org/sites/default/files/research/report/2019-census-8-to-18-full-report-updated.pdf.

4. Rideout et al., *The Common Sense Census*.

5. Rideout et al., *The Common Sense Census*.

6. Rideout et al., *The Common Sense Census*.

7. Vaishnavi S. Nakshine et al., "Increased Screen Time as a Cause of Declining Physical, Psychological Health, and Sleep Patterns: A Literary Review," *Cureus* 14, no. 10 (October 2022): e30051, https://www.cureus.com/articles/112862; and Jean M. Twenge, *Generations: The Real Differences Between Gen Z, Millennials, Gen X, Boomers, and Silents—and What They Mean for America's Future* (New York: Atria Books, 2023).

8. Nagata et al., "Screen Time Use Among US Adolescents During the COVID-19 Pandemic"; Liqing Li et al., "Screen Time and Depression: A Meta-Analysis of Cohort Studies," *Frontiers in Psychiatry* 13 (December 2022): 1058572, https://www.frontiersin.org/journals/psychiatry/articles/10.3389/fpsyt.2022.1058572/full; and Stefanie Braig et al., "Screen Time, Physical Activity and Self-Esteem in Children: The Ulm Birth Cohort Study," *International Journal of Environmental Research and Public Health* 15, no. 6 (June 2018): 1275, https://www.mdpi.com/1660-4601/15/6/1275.

9. Jonathan Chu et al., "Screen Time and Suicidal Behaviors Among U.S. Children 9–11 Years Old: A Prospective Cohort Study," *Preventive Medicine* 169 (April 2023): 107452, https://www.sciencedirect.com/science/article/pii/S0091743523000324.

10. Richard A. Miech et al., *Monitoring the Future National Survey Results on Drug Use, 1975–2022: Secondary School Students*, University of Michigan Institute for Social Research, June 2023, https://monitoringthefuture.org/wp-content/uploads/2022/12/mtf2022.pdf; Alexandria K. Mickler and Jessica Tollestrup, *Teen Birth Trends: In Brief*, Congressional Research Service, September 1, 2022, https://crsreports.congress.gov/product/pdf/R/R45184; Sally C. Curtin and Betzaida Tejada-Vera, "Motor Vehicle Traffic Death Rates Among Adolescents and Young Adults Aged 15–24, by Urbanicity: United States, 2000–2018," Centers for Disease Control and Prevention, October 2020, https://stacks.cdc.gov/view/cdc/95231; and Liz Ryan and Nancy La Vigne, "Juvenile Justice Statistics National Report Series Fact Sheet," US Department of Justice, Office of Justice Programs, August 2022, https://ojjdp.ojp.gov/publications/trends-in-youth-arrests.pdf.

11. Cynthia L. Ogden et al., "Trends in Obesity Prevalence Among Children and Adolescents in the United States, 1988–1994 Through 2013–2014," *JAMA* 315, no. 21 (June 2016): 2292–99, https://jamanetwork.com/journals/jama/fullarticle/2526638; and Thomas N. Robinson et al., "Screen Media Exposure and Obesity in Children and Adolescents," *Pediatrics* 140, no. 2 (November 2017): S97–101, https://publications.aap.org/pediatrics/article/140/Supplement_2/S97/34162/Screen-Media-Exposure-and-Obesity-in-Children-and.

12. Jean M. Twenge, Gabrielle N. Martin, and Brian Spitzberg, "Trends in U.S. Adolescents' Media Use, 1976–2016: The Rise of Digital Media, the Decline of TV, and the (Near) Demise of Print," *Psychology of Popular Media Culture* 8, no. 4 (August 2018): 329–45, https://psycnet.apa.org/doiLanding?doi=10.1037%2Fppm0000203.

13. Centers for Disease Control and Prevention, "Sleep in Middle and High School Students," https://www.cdc.gov/healthyschools/features/students-sleep.htm.

14. Alexander J. Scott et al., "Improving Sleep Quality Leads to Better Mental Health: A Meta-Analysis of Randomised Controlled Trials," *Sleep Medicine Reviews* 60 (December 2021): 101556, https://www.sciencedirect.com/science/article/pii/S1087079221001416.

15. Vijay Rajput and Steven M. Bromley, "Chronic Insomnia: A Practical Review," *American Family Physician* 60, no. 5 (October 1999): 1431–42, https://www.aafp.org/pubs/afp/issues/1999/1001/p1431.html.

16. Xian Li et al., "Sleep Mediates the Association Between Adolescent Screen Time and Depressive Symptoms," *Sleep Medicine* 57 (May 2019): 51–60, https://www.sciencedirect.com/science/article/abs/pii/S1389945718305975.

17. Umut Ziya Kocak, "Are eSports More Than Just Sitting? A Study Comparing Energy Expenditure," *Journal of Comparative Effectiveness Research* 11, no. 1 (2022): 39–45, https://becarispublishing.com/doi/10.2217/cer-2021-0223.

18. John Hopson, "Behavioral Game Design," Game Developer, April 27, 2001, https://www.gamedeveloper.com/design/behavioral-game-design.

19. Luca Braghieri, Ro'ee Levy, and Alexey Makarin, "Social Media and Mental Health," *American Economic Review* 112, no. 11 (November 2022): 3660–93, https://www.aeaweb.org/articles?id=10.1257/aer.20211218.

20. Elizabeth J. Ivie et al., "A Meta-Analysis of the Association Between Adolescent Social Media Use and Depressive Symptoms," *Journal of Affective Disorders* 275 (October 2020): 165–74, https://www.sciencedirect.com/science/article/abs/pii/S0165032720323727.

21. Pilar Aparicio-Martinez et al., "Social Media, Thin-Ideal, Body Dissatisfaction and Disordered Eating Attitudes: An Exploratory Analysis," *International Journal of Environmental Research and Public Health* 16, no. 21 (October 2019): 4177, https://www.mdpi.com/1660-4601/16/21/4177.

22. Victoria Rideout and Susannah Fox, "Digital Health Practices, Social Media Use, and Mental Well-Being Among Teens and Young Adults in the U.S.," *Providence Digital Commons* (Summer 2018), https://digitalcommons.providence.org/publications/1093.

23. Paul J. Wright et al., "Parents Underestimate Their Children's Pornography Use and Learning," *Archives of Sexual Behavior* 52 (October 2022): 373–83, https://link.springer.com/article/10.1007/s10508-022-02449-7.

24. Gail Hornor, "Child and Adolescent Pornography Exposure," *Journal of Pediatric Health Care* 34, no. 2 (March 2020): 191–99, https://www.jpedhc.org/article/S0891-5245(19)30384-0/fulltext.

25. Emily A. Waterman et al., "Prospective Associations Between Pornography Viewing and Sexual Aggression Among Adolescents" *Journal of Research on Adolescence* 32, no. 4 (December 2022): 1612–25, https://doi.org/10.1111/jora.12745.

26. Brooke de Heer et al., "Women's Pornography Consumption, Alcohol Use, and Sexual Victimization," *Violence Against Women* 27, no. 10 (August 2021): 1678–95, https://journals.sagepub.com/doi/10.1177/1077801220945035.

27. Aleksandra Diana Dwulit and Piort Rzymski, "The Potential Associations of Pornography Use with Sexual Dysfunctions: An Integrative Literature Review of Observational Studies," *Journal of Clinical Medicine* 8, no. 7 (June 2019): 914, https://www.mdpi.com/2077-0383/8/7/914.

28. Heidi Strohmaier, Megan Murphy, and David DeMatteo, "Youth Sexting: Prevalence Rates, Driving Motivations, and the Deterrent Effect of Legal Consequences," *Sexuality Research and Social Policy* 11, no. 3 (September 2014): 245–55, https://link.springer.com/article/10.1007/s13178-014-0162-9.

29. Diana Baumrind, "The Influence of Parenting Style on Adolescent Competence and Substance Abuse," *Journal of Early Adolescence* 11, no. 1 (February 1991): 56–95, https://journals.sagepub.com/doi/abs/10.1177/0272431691111004; and Susie D. Lamborn et al., "Patterns of Competence and Adjustment Among Adolescents from Authoritative, Authoritarian, Indulgent, and Neglectful Families," *Child Development* 62, no. 5 (October 1991): 1049–65, https://www.jstor.org/stable/1131151.

30. Homer, *The Odyssey with an English Translation by A. T. Murray*, trans. A. T. Murray (Cambridge, MA: Harvard University Press, 1995), Book 9, lines 94–99, https://www.perseus.tufts.edu/hopper/text?doc=Perseus:text:1999.01.0136.

9

The Benefits of Religious Optimism

MICHELLE SHAIN

The great psychologists of the 20th century disagreed vehemently about the relationship between religion and mental health. Sigmund Freud called religion a "universal obsessional neurosis," a delusion that harms psychological functioning.[1] On the other end of the spectrum, William James believed that religion encourages psychological health and a deep sense of optimism—in his words, a "sky-blue tint."[2]

A century later, we can confidently say Freud was wrong about religion. Researchers have conducted thousands of studies examining the relationship between religion and mental health, and there are dozens of meta-analyses that evaluate and summarize that research. Religious people are less likely to suffer from anxiety or depression, commit suicide, or abuse alcohol or other drugs. They tend to be more confident, happy, optimistic, and generally satisfied with their lives than their nonreligious peers are.[3]

At the same time, the number of religious people in America is falling fast. In 1972, 90 percent of American adults reported they were Christians, and only 5 percent had no religion. In the half century since, millions of people who were raised with a religion left it behind. By 2020, the number of Americans without a religion had risen to almost 30 percent. If current trends continue, half of Americans will not have a religion by 2070.[4]

What will this retreat from religion mean for the mental health of America's youth?

The Religious Optimism of Teens and Young Adults

To understand the move away from religion, consider the millennial generation, those born between 1981 and 1996. Their adolescence was marked by the Columbine school shooting and the 9/11 terror attacks. When they

Table 1. Religious Trajectory of Millennials, 2002–12

	2002 Age 13–17	2012 Age 23–27
Conservative Protestant	31%	23%
Catholic	27%	17%
Black Protestant	11%	7%
Mainline Protestant	11%	6%
Other	8%	8%
Not Religious	12%	40%

Note: Percentages may not add to 100 due to rounding.
Source: Author's analysis based on Association of Religion Data Archives, National Study of Youth and Religion, https://www.thearda.com/data-archive/browse-category?cid=C-A-A-F.

were teens, almost 90 percent of them identified as part of a religious tradition, and four in five attended religious services at least sometimes. Then, as they grew into young adulthood—amid the war in Afghanistan, the Great Recession, the explosion of social media, and the launch of the iPhone—they moved away from religion. The proportion with no religion almost tripled, and all major Christian groups lost millennial adherents between 2002 and 2012, according to the National Study of Youth and Religion from the University of Notre Dame (Table 1).[5]

Most up-to-date studies on the youth mental health crisis do not examine religion at all, so it's difficult to say precisely how America's retreat from religion affects the health of young people today.[6] But we do know religion was a powerful predictor of mental health for millennial teens. Two-thirds of the teens who attended religious services weekly had William James's "sky-blue tint," saying they rarely or never felt depressed. By contrast, only half of the teens who never attended religious services said the same (Table 2). Similarly, teens who said they felt very close to God also reported feeling depressed less often than teens who felt distant from God or who didn't believe in God at all.

What explains the optimism religious young people report feeling? Responses from the American Families of Faith Project, led by Brigham Young University professors David C. Dollahite and Loren D. Marks, shed

Table 2. How Often Millennial Teens Felt Depressed, by Religious Service Attendance (2002)

	Never Attend Religious Services	Attend Religious Services Less Than Weekly	Attend Religious Services Weekly or More
Usually or Always Feel Depressed	9%	7%	7%
Sometimes Feel Depressed	38%	31%	26%
Rarely or Never Feel Depressed	53%	63%	67%

Source: Author's analysis based on Association of Religion Data Archives, National Study of Youth and Religion, https://www.thearda.com/data-archive/browse-category?cid=C-A-A-F.

light on this question. When asked about their faith, some religious young people describe it as a tool to stay calm in the face of stress, such as the stress of schoolwork and exams. A 20-year-old Muslim woman, for example, said, "And just whatever worry I have, and I pray for it, then I feel a sense of relaxation. I just have control over myself, when I do that."[7]

Other religious young people describe their religious experience as akin to emotional support. In the words of a 15-year-old Catholic boy, "Being religious is kind of like you have another friend. It's God and Jesus, you feel like you're able to lean back on someone, if the going's tough."[8]

Moreover, an 18-year-old Baptist woman shared that sense of being supported by God:

> I'm so happy that I have some place where I can go and God loves us unconditionally. And no matter what I do He's always there, and He always loves me. And just thinking that you know the creator of the universe; thinking that God actually loves me is just amazing.[9]

And a 17-year-old Jewish girl who described herself as "still figuring out" her religious beliefs agreed that the idea of God makes her feel less alone: "I do believe in like some sort of higher faith, higher being, higher power. It would be very lonely, if it turned out there wasn't one."[10]

These young people believe that religion acts as a positive force in their lives. But might religion simply attract people who *already* have good mental health and push away those who are struggling? Does going to church alleviate depression, or do people who feel depressed simply stop going to church?

There is no definitive answer to this cause-and-effect question. Longitudinal studies that follow the same individuals over time have shown that changes in religiosity usually *precede* changes in mental health, suggesting that people who become more religious subsequently show improved mental health, not the reverse.[11] However, other unknown factors may cause both improved mental health and increased religiosity. Furthermore, the finding that mental health changes follow changes in religiosity is necessarily based on only people who change their religious beliefs or practice over time, and those people may be fundamentally different from people who remain religious throughout their lives.

Some experiments have shown that introducing religion into treatment for mental health disorders leads to better outcomes. Many of these experiments involved randomly assigning patients to either traditional cognitive behavioral therapy or religiously integrated cognitive behavioral therapy, which includes elements like prayer and memorizing passages from a religious text. Results of these randomized control trials indicate that incorporating religious elements into treatment does improve mood disorders, at least for people who had enough affinity for religion that they could participate sincerely in the experiment.[12] But no experiment, of course, can randomly assign nonbelievers to have faith.

The beliefs humans hold about life, the universe, and God are deep and complex. Religion cannot be prescribed like a pill, and it can't and shouldn't be instrumentalized as a remedy for America's mental health crisis. At the same time, thinking about *how* religion protects against mental illness might suggest ways to support young people in a complicated and fast-changing world—even outside the context of a faith community.

The Social Benefits of Religious Belief

How, then, might religion help protect against mental illness? In particular, three social benefits of religion stand out.

First, religion supports healthy families. Young people have better mental health when they grow up in a positive, caring family environment. Those who grow up surrounded by frequent conflict, stress, and negative interactions are more likely to have emotional and behavioral problems, including suffering from OCD and anxiety disorder. Parental divorce or separation in particular are associated with poor family functioning.[13]

In most religious traditions, families are sacred, and marriage and child-rearing are core values. Religious adults are more likely to marry rather than live together without marrying; once married, they have happier marriages and lower divorce rates. Religious parents also engage in more activities with their children, show more affection, provide more supervision, and—for better or worse—are stronger disciplinarians. As adolescents, children from more religious homes have closer, more positive relationships with their parents.[14]

When millennials were in their teens, those who regularly attended worship services spoke to their mothers more often about personal subjects, such as friendships, dating, and drinking. The percentage of teens who never or rarely had those discussions was twice as high among those who never attended worship services compared to those who attended regularly (Table 3).

Shared activities and rituals help nurture this familial closeness. For religious families, some shared activities might include attending worship services, celebrating holidays, and praying together. Many religious traditions also set aside sacred time for family togetherness—for example, Jews observe the Sabbath and Latter-day Saints have Family Home Evening. These practices help families remain happy and stable. A 15-year-old Christian and Missionary Alliance girl who spoke to Dollahite and Marks about going to church with her family described the experience as follows:

Table 3. How Often Millennial Teens Spoke with Their Mothers About Personal Subjects, by Religious Service Attendance (2002)

	Never Attend Religious Services	Attend Religious Services Less Than Weekly	Attend Religious Services Weekly or More
Talk to Mom Very or Fairly Often	46%	55%	56%
Sometimes Talk to Mom	28%	28%	31%
Rarely or Never Talk to Mom	26%	17%	13%

Source: Author's analysis based on Association of Religion Data Archives, National Study of Youth and Religion, https://www.thearda.com/data-archive/browse-category?cid=C-A-A-F.

It's a break in the week. It's something that's consistent, that we do every week together. We get in the car and go to church and come home. And it's nice to sort of step back from the busyness of everything and just have something that we all do together.[15]

Second, religion offers community. Even beyond the immediate family, positive relationships with others are key to mental health. A community that offers emotional support and practical help reduces depression and anxiety, while social isolation exacerbates these mental health conditions.[16] A religious community centered around a church, synagogue, or other house of worship can be a powerful source of social support. Members have a place to belong and meet like-minded people who can become caring friends.[17] Young adults who attend religious services regularly are far less likely to feel alone (Table 4).

One 20-year-old Lutheran woman explained the feeling of worshipping with her community: "There's a lot of strength that I draw from being able to share communion with other believers and the reminder and the forgiveness that comes through that is definitely, I guess strengthening."[18]

The social support of religious communities takes another form as well. People in religious communities develop what sociologists refer

Table 4. How Often Millennial Adults Felt Alone and Misunderstood, by Religious Service Attendance (2007)

	Never Attend Religious Services	Attend Religious Services Less Than Weekly	Attend Religious Services Weekly or More
Feel Alone a Lot	8%	7%	4%
Feel Alone Some	25%	20%	16%
Feel Alone a Little	31%	35%	33%
Never Feel Alone	37%	38%	48%

Note: Percentages may not add to 100 due to rounding.
Source: Author's analysis based on Association of Religion Data Archives, National Study of Youth and Religion, https://www.thearda.com/data-archive/browse-category?cid=C-A-A-F.

to as "weak ties"—ties between people who know each other but spend very little time together and whose interactions are pleasant but often superficial. Yet these weak ties are important. People with a lot of weak ties have a lot of friends of friends, and these friends of friends provide access to valuable social resources, such as job opportunities, childcare, and medical services.[19] There is power in the coffee hour after church, where congregants can get help and information. People who are embedded in these large social networks full of weak ties are less depressed than their peers whose social networks consist of smaller numbers of intertwined friends and family.[20]

Third, religion provides opportunities to help others. Young people who help and support those around them—for example, by volunteering— become more resilient, more optimistic, and less likely to experience depression or abuse alcohol or drugs. They appreciate the opportunity to make a meaningful contribution and be recognized for it.[21] Religious people also give and volunteer at higher rates than nonreligious people. People who attend religious services regularly give three times as much money to charitable causes as those who do not attend regularly.[22] In a 2016 study by the Pew Research Center, 45 percent of Americans who pray and attend religious services regularly reported volunteering in the past week, compared to 28 percent of other Americans.[23] As one 14-year-old Catholic girl explained to Dollahite and Marks, "I just like serving the church. It makes me feel good that I'm serving the community."[24] And religious people do not limit their help to religious organizations and causes—they have higher rates of giving and volunteering for *nonreligious* organizations and causes as well.[25]

How does religion facilitate giving and volunteerism? It may be that faith communities simply provide a structure for giving and volunteering and social pressure to do so. It may also be that religious beliefs and teachings inculcate generosity, forgiveness, and selflessness. In psychological experiments, when people are "primed" to think about religion—for example, by answering questions about their religious beliefs or sitting in view of a religious building—they subsequently score higher on tests of ethical, cooperative, and generous behaviors.[26]

Though religion appears to strengthen families, build communities, and offer service opportunities, these social benefits are not inextricable from the content of religious belief. Many nonreligious people form close-knit families and robust communities, give generously, and volunteer regularly. Many organizations can provide opportunities for generosity and caring, and all of these efforts could reap tremendous benefits for America's struggling youth.

Yet even still, something critical is missing from all these endeavors—something transcendent, something above and independent of the universe—in short, something *religious*.

The Religious Pull

Humans have a deep, abiding need to understand the world and find meaning in it. Who am I? Why am I here? What should I do? We need a sense of purpose and direction, a feeling that we are part of something greater than ourselves.[27]

Religion is a powerful framework for fulfilling this need. It provides answers to existential questions about the meaning of life and death. It offers ways to understand stressful events and gives believers a sense of control over their destinies. Perhaps most importantly, believers have a sense of cosmic significance, assurance that they matter in the grand scheme of things.[28] As St. Augustine, who famously addressed God in his *Confessions*, put it, "Our heart is restless until it rests in you."[29]

Religious young people often describe their sense of purpose in contrast to the aimlessness they perceive in their nonreligious peers. In the words of a 17-year-old Muslim girl:

> I see many other people in school, that they, they're lost, you know, in their lives. Or they don't even know they're lost. And the way that they lead their lives, it's, you know, very hectic, chaotic, and there's so much negative influence on them all the time, and they don't even, they don't realize that there is a better way.[30]

Similarly, an 18-year-old Catholic young man described a sense of calm that comes from following church standards of behavior, even when it involves some personal sacrifice:

> I think in the end it's rewarding. I don't mean like "heaven points" or something like that. I just mean you feel better about yourself. I mean it's helpful. I think it kind of puts you at ease, like peace of mind.[31]

Many religious young people also have a sense of certainty about right and wrong that they believe nonreligious people lack. An 18-year-old Baptist woman, for example, recalled:

> I just remember sitting in English class last year and we were discussing a lot of things and I just remember sitting there thinking how confused I'd be on this earth if I didn't have the Bible and God's standard and morality to live by.[32]

An 18-year-old Baptist man echoed the idea that religion provides clear guidance and directs behavior: "You're not going to be all wishy-washy and say you know, just do whatever's right for you. . . . There's a right answer."[33]

But beyond calm and certainty, religion can also give young people a sense of permanence. An 18-year-old Muslim woman who spoke to Dollahite and Marks about her beliefs remarked that the purpose of life is to attain paradise in the hereafter:

> Anything in this earth can go away. Toys can get broken, people can die . . . but when you have something that is for an afterlife, it's not something that can go away. It's not something that can be taken away. It's something that you strive for and it's there for good, you know, it's not something that's disposable or something.[34]

Religious young people share similar sentiments regardless of specific faith traditions. Some religious groups—such as Latter-day Saints, Orthodox Jews, and Protestants in the evangelical and historically black traditions—reap greater psychological benefits simply by virtue of their higher levels of commitment and participation. However, most Americans find meaning in the general idea of a benevolent, engaged God rather than specific theological doctrines and tenets of their professed faith.[35]

Of course, nonreligious individuals can and do construct frameworks of meaning separate from God, which may involve self-knowledge, freedom, challenge, comfort, community, or love. Nevertheless, religious people are more likely than others to feel that their lives have purpose and meaning.[36] Once millennials passed their college years, those who never attended worship services as teens were significantly more likely to feel that life is meaningless (Table 5).

When nonreligious people find themselves facing existential uncertainty and the anxiety associated with it, they search for meaning in other groups and identities. Today, this trend is perhaps most visible in what historian Emilio Gentile calls the "sacralization of politics."[37] Many young Americans are now imbuing their political convictions with the sort of meaning often ascribed to religion. Increasingly, our politics define how we understand the world, leading to partisan fervor and entrenchment. Ironically, evidence is accumulating that this deeply polarized political climate is itself causing significant stress and anxiety.[38]

Table 5. "How Often, If Ever, Does Life Feel Meaningless to You?" by Religious Service Attendance as Teens (Millennial Adults, 2012)

	Never Attend Religious Services	Attend Religious Services Less Than Weekly	Attend Religious Services Weekly or More
Life Very or Fairly Often Feels Meaningless	14%	9%	9%
Life Sometimes Feels Meaningless	25%	24%	19%
Life Rarely or Never Feels Meaningless	61%	68%	73%

Note: Percentages may not add to 100 due to rounding.
Source: Author's analysis based on Association of Religion Data Archives, National Study of Youth and Religion, https://www.thearda.com/data-archive/browse-category?cid=C-A-A-F.

The positive relationship between religion and mental health should not be a cause for triumphalism by religious people. Success does not equal superiority. A strong focus on family can be painful and isolating for individuals who are unmarried or childless; a close-knit community can be suffocating. In all things, what is true for humanity writ large is still false for some individuals.

Nevertheless, religion clearly protects the mental health of young people. As America's move away from religion shows no signs of abating, we must find ways to capture the protective benefits of religion outside the context of a faith community. We must grow the webs of human connection that work as a buffer against depression, anxiety, and existential malaise. Perhaps most importantly, we must help young adults find purpose, a way to know their lives matter. A framework of meaning is also a framework for psychological wellness.

Notes

1. Sigmund Freud, "Obsessive Actions and Religious Practices," in *The Standard Edition of the Complete Psychological Works of Sigmund Freud* (1907; London: Hogarth Press and the Institute of Psycho-analysis, 1981), 9:115–28.

2. William James, *The Varieties of Religious Experience: A Study in Human Nature* (New York: Longmans, Green and Co., 1905), 80.

3. Bert Garssen, Anja Visser, and Grieteke Pool, "Does Spirituality or Religion Positively Affect Mental Health? Meta-Analysis of Longitudinal Studies," *International Journal for the Psychology of Religion* 31, no. 1 (2021): 4–20, https://www.tandfonline.com/doi/full/10.1080/10508619.2020.1729570; Charles H. Hackney and Glenn S. Sanders, "Religiosity and Mental Health: A Meta-Analysis of Recent Studies," *Journal for the Scientific Study of Religion* 42, no. 1 (2003): 43–55, https://onlinelibrary.wiley.com/doi/10.1111/1468-5906.t01-1-00160; Harold G. Koenig and David B. Larson, "Religion and Mental Health: Evidence for an Association," *International Review of Psychiatry* 13, no. 2 (May 2001): 67–78, https://www.tandfonline.com/doi/abs/10.1080/09540260124661; Harold George Koenig et al., *Handbook of Religion and Health* (New York: Oxford University Press, 2001); and Giancarlo Lucchetti, Harold G. Koenig, and Alessandra Lamas Granero Lucchetti, "Spirituality, Religiousness, and Mental Health: A Review of the Current Scientific Evidence," *World Journal of Clinical Cases* 9, no. 26 (September 2021): 7620–31, https://www.wjgnet.com/2307-8960/full/v9/i26/7620.htm.

4. Pew Research Center, "Modeling the Future of Religion in America," September 13, 2022, https://www.pewresearch.org/religion/2022/09/13/modeling-the-future-of-religion-in-america.

5. The National Study of Youth and Religion, https://youthandreligion.nd.edu, whose data were used by permission here, was generously funded by Lilly Endowment Inc., under the direction of Christian Smith, of the Department of Sociology at the University of Notre Dame.

6. Questions about religion are absent from the Centers for Disease Control and Prevention's (CDC) 2021 Adolescent Behaviors and Experiences Survey; the CDC's ongoing Youth Risk Behavior Surveillance System; the National Survey on Drug Use and Health, sponsored by the US Department of Health and Human Services; and the CDC's ongoing National Health Interview Survey.

7. All quotations from young people are drawn from the American Families of Faith Project led by David C. Dollahite and Loren D. Marks at Brigham Young University. Emily Layton, Sam A. Hardy, and David C. Dollahite, "Religious Exploration Among Highly Religious American Adolescents," *Identity* 12, no. 2 (April 2012): 172, https://www.tandfonline.com/doi/abs/10.1080/15283488.2012.668728.

8. Emily Layton, David C. Dollahite, and Sam A. Hardy, "Anchors of Religious Commitment in Adolescents," *Journal of Adolescent Research* 26, no. 3 (May 2011): 395–96, https://journals.sagepub.com/doi/10.1177/0743558410391260.

9. Layton, Dollahite, and Hardy, "Anchors of Religious Commitment in Adolescents," 396.

10. Layton, Hardy, and Dollahite, "Religious Exploration Among Highly Religious American Adolescents," 178.

11. Garssen, Visser, and Pool, "Does Spirituality or Religion Positively Affect Mental Health?"; and Tyler J. VanderWeele, John W. Jackson, and Shanshan Li, "Causal Inference and Longitudinal Data: A Case Study of Religion and Mental Health," *Social Psychiatry and Psychiatric Epidemiology* 51, no. 11 (November 2016): 1457–66, https://link.springer.com/article/10.1007/s00127-016-1281-9.

12. Adilson Marques et al., "Religious-Based Interventions for Depression: A Systematic Review and Meta-Analysis of Experimental Studies," *Journal of Affective Disorders* 309 (July 2022): 289–96, https://www.sciencedirect.com/science/article/abs/pii/S0165032722004700; Naomi Anderson et al., "Faith-Adapted Psychological Therapies for Depression and Anxiety: Systematic Review and Meta-Analysis," *Journal of Affective Disorders* 176 (May 2015): 183–96, https://www.sciencedirect.com/science/article/abs/pii/S0165032715000233; and J. P. B. Gonçalves et al., "Religious and Spiritual Interventions in Mental Health Care: A Systematic Review and Meta-Analysis of Randomized Controlled Clinical Trials," *Psychological Medicine* 45, no. 14 (October 2015): 2937–49, https://doi.org/10.1017/S0033291715001166.

13. Claudia Scully, Jacintha McLaughlin, and Amanda Fitzgerald, "The Relationship Between Adverse Childhood Experiences, Family Functioning, and Mental Health Problems Among Children and Adolescents: A Systematic Review," *Journal of Family Therapy* 42, no. 2 (April 2020): 291–316, https://onlinelibrary.wiley.com/doi/10.1111/1467-6427.12263.

14. Christopher G. Ellison and Xiaohe Xu, "Religion and Families," in *The Wiley Blackwell Companion to the Sociology of Families* (Hoboken, NJ: John Wiley & Sons, 2014), 277–99; Annette Mahoney, "Religion in Families, 1999–2009: A Relational Spirituality Framework," *Journal of Marriage and Family* 72, no. 4 (August 2010): 805–27, https://www.researchgate.net/publication/51816882_Religion_in_Families_1999-2009_A_Relational_Spirituality_Framework; and Annette Mahoney et al., "Religion in the Home in the 1980s and 1990s: A Meta-Analytic Review and Conceptual Analysis of Links Between Religion, Marriage, and Parenting," *Journal of Family Psychology* 15, no. 4 (2001): 559–96, https://pubmed.ncbi.nlm.nih.gov/11770466.

15. Layton, Dollahite, and Hardy, "Anchors of Religious Commitment in Adolescents," 394.

16. Ziggi Ivan Santini et al., "The Association Between Social Relationships and Depression: A Systematic Review," *Journal of Affective Disorders* 175 (April 1, 2015): 53–65, https://www.sciencedirect.com/science/article/abs/pii/S0165032714008350; and Alan R. Teo, Robert Lerrigo, and Mary A. M. Rogers, "The Role of Social Isolation in Social Anxiety Disorder: A Systematic Review and Meta-Analysis," *Journal of Anxiety Disorders* 27, no. 4 (May 2013): 353–64, https://www.sciencedirect.com/science/article/abs/pii/S0887618513000571.

17. R. David Hayward and Neal Krause, "Religion, Mental Health, and Well-Being: Social Aspects," in *Religion, Personality, and Social Behavior* (New York: Psychology Press, 2014), 255–80.

18. Layton, Dollahite, and Hardy, "Anchors of Religious Commitment in Adolescents," 401.

19. Mark S. Granovetter, "The Strength of Weak Ties," *American Journal of Sociology* 78, no. 6 (May 1973): 1360–80, https://snap.stanford.edu/class/cs224w-readings/

granovetter73weakties.pdf; and Mark Granovetter, "The Strength of Weak Ties: A Network Theory Revisited," *Sociological Theory* 1 (1983): 201–33, https://www.jstor.org/stable/202051.

20. Santini et al., "The Association Between Social Relationships and Depression"; and Teo, Lerrigo, and Rogers, "The Role of Social Isolation in Social Anxiety Disorder."

21. Saima Hirani et al., "Understanding the Role of Prosocial Behavior in Youth Mental Health: Findings from a Scoping Review," *Adolescents* 2, no. 3 (2022): 358, https://www.mdpi.com/2673-7051/2/3/28; and Christine I. Celio, Joseph Durlak, and Allison Dymnicki, "A Meta-Analysis of the Impact of Service-Learning on Students," *Journal of Experiential Education* 34, no. 2 (September 2011): 164–81, https://www.mdpi.com/2673-7051/2/3/28.

22. David Eagle, Lisa A. Keister, and Jen'nan Ghazal Read, "Household Charitable Giving at the Intersection of Gender, Marital Status, and Religion," *Nonprofit and Voluntary Sector Quarterly* 47, no. 1 (February 2018): 185–205, https://journals.sagepub.com/doi/10.1177/0899764017734650.

23. Pew Research Center, "Religion in Everyday Life," April 12, 2016, https://www.pewresearch.org/religion/2016/04/12/religion-in-everyday-life.

24. Layton, Dollahite, and Hardy, "Anchors of Religious Commitment in Adolescents," 401.

25. Kidist Ibrie Yasin, Anita Graeser Adams, and David P. King, "How Does Religion Affect Giving to Outgroups and Secular Organizations? A Systematic Literature Review," *Religions* 11, no. 8 (August 2020): 405, https://www.mdpi.com/2077-1444/11/8/405. See also Luke W. Galen, "Does Religious Belief Promote Prosociality? A Critical Examination," *Psychological Bulletin* 138, no. 5 (September 2012): 876–906, https://psycnet.apa.org/doiLanding?doi=10.1037%2Fa0028251.

26. Azim F. Shariff et al., "Religious Priming: A Meta-Analysis with a Focus on Prosociality," *Personality and Social Psychology Review* 20, no. 1 (February 2016): 27–48, https://journals.sagepub.com/doi/10.1177/1088868314568811.

27. A. H. Maslow, "A Theory of Human Motivation," *Psychological Review* 50, no. 4 (July 1943): 370–96, https://psycnet.apa.org/doiLanding?doi=10.1037%2Fh0054346; Abraham H. Maslow, "The Farther Reaches of Human Nature," *Journal of Transpersonal Psychology* 1 (1969): 1–9; and Viktor E. Frankl, *Man's Search for Meaning* (1946; New York: Beacon Press, 2006).

28. Michael Prinzing, Patty Van Cappellen, and Barbara L. Fredrickson, "More Than a Momentary Blip in the Universe? Investigating the Link Between Religiousness and Perceived Meaning in Life," *Personality and Social Psychology Bulletin* 49, no. 2 (February 2023): 180–96, https://journals.sagepub.com/doi/10.1177/01461672211060136.

29. Augustine of Hippo, *Confessions*, trans. Henry Chadwick (Oxford, UK: Oxford University Press, 2009).

30. Layton, Hardy, and Dollahite, "Religious Exploration Among Highly Religious American Adolescents," 172–73.

31. David C. Dollahite et al., "Giving Up Something Good for Something Better: Sacred Sacrifices Made by Religious Youth," *Journal of Adolescent Research* 24, no. 6 (2009): 714, https://journals.sagepub.com/doi/10.1177/0743558409343463.

32. Layton, Hardy, and Dollahite, "Religious Exploration Among Highly Religious American Adolescents," 175.

33. Layton, Hardy, and Dollahite, "Religious Exploration Among Highly Religious American Adolescents," 171.

34. Dollahite et al., "Giving Up Something Good for Something Better," 712.

35. Rodney Stark, *What Americans Really Believe: New Findings from the Baylor Surveys of Religion* (Waco, TX: Baylor University Press, 2008).

36. Koenig and Larson, "Religion and Mental Health"; Crystal L. Park, "Religion and Meaning," in *Handbook of the Psychology of Religion and Spirituality*, ed. Raymond F. Paloutzian and Crystal L. Park (New York: Guilford Publications, 2013), 357–79; Hayward and Krause, "Religion, Mental Health, and Well-Being"; and Kenneth I. Pargament et al., "The Religious Dimension of Coping," in *Handbook of the Psychology of Religion and Spirituality*, ed. Raymond F. Paloutzian and Crystal L. Park, 2nd ed. (New York: Guilford Press, 2013), 560–79.

37. Emilio Gentile, *Politics as Religion*, trans. George Staunton (Princeton, NJ: Princeton University Press, 2006).

38. Timothy Fraser et al., "The Harmful Effects of Partisan Polarization on Health," *PNAS Nexus* 1, no. 1 (March 2022): 11, https://academic.oup.com/pnasnexus/article/1/1/pgac011/6545770; and Brett Q. Ford et al., "The Political Is Personal: The Costs of Daily Politics," *Journal of Personality and Social Psychology* 125, no. 1 (July 2023): 1–28, https://supp.apa.org/psycarticles/supplemental/pspa0000335/pspa0000335_supp.html.

10

Let Kids Do More on Their Own

CAMILO ORTIZ AND LENORE SKENAZY

One of our colleagues in suburban Kentucky lets his 12-year-old daughter walk two houses down to her friend's place. At the end of each playdate, however, the other girl's mom walks his daughter home. "Just to be safe," our colleague tells us.[1]

Such excessive caution is hardly unusual. Over the past several decades, children have become less and less independent. Instead of running outside to play after school or riding their bikes around *Stranger Things* style, they're more likely to be indoors on social media or in adult-run classes and organized sports. Or, like our colleague's daughter, they're protected from a danger that's all but nonexistent. (Today's crime rate may feel high, but in fact, "the violent-crime rate in 2023 was near its lowest level in more than 50 years," according to the *New York Times*.[2])

Nonetheless, parents across the economic spectrum today believe that the more supervised and structured their kids' activities are, the safer and better-off their kids will be.[3] A 2023 survey of 1,000 parents by the University of Michigan's C. S. Mott Children's Hospital concluded that most parents

> endorse the idea that children benefit from free time without parent supervision, and say they allow their child to do things themselves. But parents' description of what their child does independently suggests a sizable gap between parent attitudes and actions.[4]

How sizable? The study found that less than a quarter of parents with kids age 5–8 let them prepare their own snacks. Most parents of 9- to 11-year-olds were unwilling to let them walk to a friend's home, wait briefly in the car by themselves, or play in the park with a friend. Just 15 percent said they would let their kids trick-or-treat without adult supervision. While their chief fear was safety, only 17 percent said they live in a neighborhood where it's not safe for a child to be alone. Perhaps most shockingly, half of the parents would not even let their children find an item at the store while they shopped in another aisle.[5] Parents certainly recognize that independence is healthy for kids. They truly want to provide it; they just can't bring themselves to let go.

By now, it should be clear that this excess supervision has the opposite of its intended effect. Instead of kids being happier and better off, the stats on childhood anxiety and depression are alarming. In perhaps the most avoidable and heartbreaking instance of a self-fulfilling prophecy, these constant parental interventions are making children less persistent, flexible, and creative. Over-parenting is depriving kids of the opportunity to solve problems, making them more likely to crumble when faced with hardship. Seeing their kids so needy just confirms parents' belief that they must be even more involved, and the cycle repeats itself. In extreme situations, children can even experience a "failure to launch"—the inability of young adults to leave their childhood home because they lack the skills or wherewithal to live independently.

How did we get here?

The Rise of Over-Parenting

It wasn't always this way. A parenting book from 1979, for example, listed the things almost every neurotypical first grader could do, including telling their right hand from their left and counting eight to 10 pennies correctly. At that age, the book says, a first grader should be able to "travel alone in the neighborhood (four to eight blocks) to store, school, playground, or to a friend's home." (Not just a few aisles away!) Kids went to the store, shopped, and returned home by themselves by age 6.[6]

There are many reasons for today's clampdown on kids. In the 1980s, cable TV suddenly took hold, bringing us the 24-hour news cycle. This evolved into round-the-clock internet news alerts, bringing parents a stream of scary stories.[7] A gradual increase in homework also started in the '80s, thanks to the fear that American kids were falling behind their international counterparts.[8] As the years went by, parents growing wary of a winner-takes-all economy also focused ever more on getting their kids into college. They sprang for things like tutors and travel teams, giving their kids a more curated, less autonomous childhood.[9] Many parents and teachers came to view free time and, in particular, free play as a waste of time.

But as kids' freedom fell, their anxiety rose.[10] Vivek Murthy, the surgeon general of the United States, has declared worsening mental health among children to be the "crisis of our time."[11] As a society, we've been trying seemingly everything to keep kids from shrinking from life, from breathing exercises to therapeutic horse grooming.[12]

Individual parents often react to their kids' anxiety by increasing what psychologists call "parental accommodations." These attempts aim to allay children's fears, including by stepping in to do the things kids find uncomfortable, difficult, or too scary to do themselves. But the effect is the same as with other kinds of over-parenting. The intervention deprives kids of the experience of tolerating discomfort, distress, disappointment, and mild danger (or, as we call them, "the four D's"). The upshot is pretty straightforward: Kids are growing up so overprotected that they're scared of the world.

Is there a solution that would be equally straightforward? We think there is.

The Mind of an Anxious Child

Over the past 15 years, the two of us have been dedicated to studying childhood independence and mental health. One of us started a national nonprofit promoting childhood autonomy and resilience. The other is a psychologist who trains clinicians and treats child patients struggling with anxiety. Both of us have witnessed worsening trends in childhood independence and anxiety in recent years.

Lenore Skenazy is a New York writer who let her 9-year-old ride the subway alone in 2008, wrote a column about it, and got labeled "America's worst mom."[13] From that odd launching pad, she started the Free-Range Kids movement, which grew into Let Grow, a national nonprofit promoting childhood independence and resilience.[14] She has been monitoring the landscape of American childhood, talking to parents, teachers, and kids—including teens who've never been allowed to go to the park without an adult, run an errand, or even cut their own meat. One 17-year-old told her he'd love to get pulled over for going 10 miles over the speed limit. That, at least, would be on *him*. Alone, without parental help, he'd have to deal with the cop.

Camilo Ortiz is a psychology professor who researches treating kids with cognitive behavioral therapy. He also uses it in his practice and has witnessed firsthand the increase in children's anxiety since he started treating them 20 years ago. The data back up his observations.

Consider a study by Katharine Parodi and colleagues in *Social Psychiatry and Psychiatric Epidemiology*. The study screened a diverse sample of 37,360 children age 14 to 18 in 2012, 2015, and 2018 for anxiety symptoms. It showed a rise in clinical levels of anxiety from 34.1 percent in 2012 to 44 percent in 2018.[15]

While psychologists typically treat people with a diagnosis, subclinical or garden-variety anxiety has also unquestionably increased. The difference between the two is principally that diagnosable anxiety affects functioning more. For kids, that might entail refusing to go to school, having trouble sleeping in their own beds, struggling with significant insomnia, or avoiding speaking with others.

The available evidence suggests that constant supervision and intervention could be hurting kids' chances to become brave and resilient. As Peter Gray, who recently wrote a piece on the importance of childhood free play and independence in the *Journal of Pediatrics*, says:

> Children who have more opportunities for independent activities are not only happier in the short run, because the activities engender happiness and a sense of trustworthiness and competence, but also happier in the long run, because independent activities promote the growth of mental capacities for coping effectively with life's inevitable stressors.[16]

What's missing today isn't just the thrill of climbing trees or playing flashlight tag. Rather, it's having more time independent of adult supervision. When an adult is always present—in person or electronically—kids never really get to see what they're made of. Kids should have a loving and secure relationship with their parents, of course. But if you think back to a time you were alone as a child and got lost or fell off your bike, you probably still remember what happened next. You limped home or asked a stranger for help. You managed. And that was a milestone.

Kids need a lot of those experiences. They are anxiety busters. How would muddling through something a little daunting or difficult inoculate against later anxiety? A closer look at the minds of anxious children helps answer this question.

Kids with clinical anxiety tend to be different from non-anxious kids in important ways, though there is much overlap between the groups. Anxious kids are very intolerant of uncertainty. Not knowing what will happen next deeply unsettles them. Psychologists call this "anxiety sensitivity." Because they find these feelings uncomfortable and naturally want them to go away, kids task their parents with being anxiety erasers. Increasingly, parents have been tasking *themselves* with removing not just anxiety from their children's experiences but also all kinds of discomfort. This idea that good parenting equals ever-present (emotionally and physically) parenting has been called "intensive parenting ideology."[17] It is destructive and unsustainable.

When kids faced minor challenges in the past, more parents would tell them to figure it out. Now that the definition of good parenting has shifted, many parents are rushing in to save the day. That's when avoidance creates its own feedback loop.

For instance, say you're a kid who's scared of birthday parties. You beg your parents not to make you go. They say, "Just try it." But now you're crying. You're shaking with fear and pain. Your parents hate seeing you this upset, so at the apex of your agony, they relent. You're flooded with relief. Now you associate avoiding parties with this wonderful, safe feeling. But it's fleeting. If you'd gone to the party, you probably would have discovered it's not so bad—and maybe even great.

Avoidance robs people of skills, experiences, and joy. For kids, it robs them of the growth that comes from facing something daunting, doing it, and experiencing "corrective learning"—that is, breaking the avoidance feedback loop. Traditional cognitive behavioral therapy asks kids—or anyone—to stop avoiding the thing they're afraid of. Go to the party. Start a conversation with someone you don't know. Pet the scary dog. The problem is that anxious kids don't want to do these things, and their parents tend to think that pushing them equals bad parenting. Under those circumstances, therapy can become distressing for all involved, including the therapist. Everyone's focusing on what the kid hates most.

But what if instead of having to face their specific fears, anxious kids could simply start doing other, seemingly unrelated independent activities that sounded pretty fun to them? What if tackling these new things made them see themselves as capable? Could independence, in other words, turn into a new kind of therapy?

Let Grow

The Let Grow Experience is a do-it-yourself version of anxiety mitigation.[18] It's a bravery-building exercise that Let Grow developed for schoolchildren—all of them, not just the ones with anxiety. The main feature of the Let Grow Experience is a homework assignment we recommend teachers or school counselors give students so they can learn to tackle more things on their own. The instructions tell the kids to go home and do something new *with* their parents' permission but *without* their parents, such as walk the dog, run an errand, or make the family breakfast—something they feel ready to do but haven't done yet. Kids in grades K–12 can do their Let Grow projects by themselves or with a friend.

Teachers and parents have told us that kids' confidence starts climbing when they participate. For instance, a seventh-grade boy pushed himself to go on a ride at Disney World, something he'd been too scared to do before. After he braved the child-friendly Slinky Dog Dash, there was no stopping him—he went on ride after ride.

Another seventh grader, a girl who was afraid to try out for the swim team, decided to start by walking to church by herself. That made her feel very grown-up. Then she got her ears pierced (with her parents' permission). Soon after, she started doing CVS runs for her mom, which made her feel responsible. The errands also made her feel closer to her mom. She finally realized how much her mom had been doing for her all along and how boring and thankless it was. And yes, the girl eventually tried out for the swim team—and made it.

Sometimes the impact is a little goofier. Ever since her elementary school started doing the Let Grow Experience, one principal told Skenazy, "Fewer kids are sticking their feet out."

"They'd been tripping each other?" Skenazy asked.

No, said the principal. "Fewer kids are asking their teacher to tie their shoes."

And here's what one girl at a Las Vegas elementary school wrote. (The spelling is all hers.)

> This is my fist let gow project. I canpleted my project on September 11, 2023. I went shoping by my self. The materials I needed were a phone to tack a picksher a list to know what to get and mony to pay. I handle it weel but the ceckout was a little hard but it was fun to do. I learnd that I am brave and can go shop by my self. I loved my porject.

That girl is a fifth grader in special ed, but now she is also the kid whose parents trusted her with a grown-up task. The kid who went on a hero's journey. The kid who discovered she is brave.

We suspect her parents are braver now too.

Parents witnessing their kids' growth have their own new feedback loop: By letting their kids go, they get to experience the intense satisfaction of seeing how much they can do. Fear and worry are replaced by pride and joy. A little push is all either generation really needs for great growth.

Independence Therapy

Of course, as the saying goes, the plural of "anecdote" is not "data." But psychological research corroborates these success stories.

Ortiz had heard about the Let Grow Experience and offered to test independence as therapy in a clinical setting. He was already practicing exposure therapy, which has clients confront their fears, but this was a radical reconceptualization of the treatment. Instead of saying, "I hear you're afraid to sleep in your own bed—how about trying that tonight?" now he would ask, "What cool things would you like to do on your own?"

Using this technique, he and his doctoral student Matt Fastman (now Dr. Fastman) employed an intensive methodology called a multiple-baseline design to closely examine the effect of their treatment on four patients (a white girl, a white boy, an Asian girl, and a Latino boy), age 9 to 14, who were diagnosed with an anxiety disorder. This research methodology differs dramatically from the typical before-and-after approach to testing the effectiveness of interventions. Instead, it measures effects daily, almost like a stock ticker, across the entire time patients are treated. It also randomly begins patients' treatment at different times, so only the treatment can reasonably have caused any improvement.

The intervention required five office (or Zoom) visits with the parents and child. The first visit was with only the parents, who discussed their child's particular anxieties with Ortiz. The four family visits focused solely on independence. The kids each did about 10–20 new things on their own. Fastman took daily ratings of the kids' anxiety: how confident they were that they could do things without help from parents, how confident they were that they could handle situations when something went wrong, and the quality of their relationship with their parents. He also asked parents daily how much they intervened to reduce their kids' anxiety and how confident they were that their child could do things on their own.

The results were incredibly encouraging. Published in the prestigious *Journal of Anxiety Disorders*,[19] the results showed that despite the kids' worries, there were many things they wanted to try alone, like going to the grocery store or taking the local bus. One patient wanted to take his little brother to a carnival. All four children went from saying they felt worried most of the time to saying they felt worried only a little bit of the time. The other questions also showed surprising improvement for such a short treatment. Parents reported that anxiety had been a problem for all four children for years, making these changes even more impressive.

Statistically, this independence therapy worked better than drugs—and faster than cognitive behavioral therapy. Most of all, the treatment gave kids confidence to try new challenges.

For instance, one patient, a 10-year-old, was afraid even to go up or down stairs at home by himself. For one of his independence activities, he decided to walk home from school. His mother was so worried that she took the day off work. But walk he did. Then he walked home every day. For another activity, he rode the local commuter train.

Two months later, on the boy's first day of middle school, the school permitted students to bring their parents to help find their homerooms and get oriented. Most did. But this boy—who'd been too scared to go upstairs in his own home—told his parents, "I got this." He later revealed he was one of the only kids who did *not* bring a mom or dad that day.

Another patient, also age 10, was afraid to sleep in her own bed. For some of her independence activities, she sold bracelets at school and went to the local grocery store by herself. Her dad told Ortiz it took every ounce of self-control for him not to trail her to the store to make sure she was safe. He ended up peeking through the blinds from the moment she left until she returned. But as far as his daughter knew, he trusted her on her own.

That's when she decided to take the local city bus by herself to school. While on her journey, however, something went wrong with her phone. She couldn't pull up the map. How was she going to know where to get off? Or when?

As upset as she was, she managed to talk to the woman next to her, a stranger, who helped her figure out the route. The worst had happened—the girl was lost, away from home, with a nonworking phone, surrounded by strangers—and nevertheless, she was able to handle the situation.

While this might seem like a bad outcome because things didn't go as planned and the girl certainly felt stressed, it was actually the best outcome. Had her trip been uneventful, she would have ended the journey a little more independent at best. Instead, this more stressful experience taught her far more valuable lessons. In particular, three lessons—which are more applicable to anxious than non-anxious kids—stand out.

First, she learned she can be flexible in responding to unanticipated things. Psychological flexibility has been shown to be predictive of just about every positive outcome related to well-being.[20] Second, she learned she is capable. For all the talk about increasing children's self-esteem, seeing her own capabilities—not endless self-affirmation—is the most helpful. The way to increase self-esteem is by allowing children to persevere through difficulty. Third, she learned that people are generally good and helpful. Children get bombarded with messages that people are evil and dangerous. This feeds unhelpful avoidance. While dangerous people are out there, most are kind and helpful, and kids miss out on learning experiences when they are constantly protected from strangers.

After this difficult but successful experience, the girl came home, brimming with pride. That night, without saying a word to anyone, she brushed her teeth, got in her pajamas, and slept in her own bed for the first time in over a year.

A More Mature Person

Ortiz's pilot study tracked the progress of just four kids. We can't draw major conclusions from the results. It's doubtful any psychological intervention will ever work universally. But the results do suggest that more study is warranted—which is precisely what Ortiz hopes to do in a forthcoming randomized controlled trial. We hope others will begin researching how wide-ranging the benefits of independence therapy could be.

But we don't have to wait for results before kids can try to be more independent. The Let Grow Experience implementation guide is free at LetGrow.org. So is Ortiz's manual for clinicians.[21] And anyone can implement this simple idea: Start giving kids back what our culture of extreme caution took away.

The two of us sometimes compare this to putting the whole wheat back into bread. As society modernized and could make softer, whiter, lighter bread, it felt like a great advance. But the fiber removed to make bread "better" was actually what made it nutritious. Now, it's time to put it back in. The same is true for childhood independence.

In 2021, a high school sophomore wrote this note to his seventh-grade teacher, who had tasked her students with 20 Let Grow Projects over the year.

> Hi, Mrs. Maurici, I thought I would give you a little bit of insight into the person I am growing up to be right now partially thanks to the program you started with us.
>
> I feel like since the last time we talked about 2 years ago I have become a much more mature person who excepts [sic]

responsibilities. I have been a lot happier in general than I used to be when I think things like depression and anxiety were still hovering over my head. I feel like I have become much much closer to being a mature adult and my parents are super proud of the person I am becoming.

When it comes to sports I still remember that day I was stressing in your room over my tennis tryouts, and now I am the top singles player on boys varsity and made it to divisions last year. I can't wait to hear back from you on how you are doing! Get back to me when you can.

That transformation cost his school about 20 minutes of class time, if that, every couple of weeks. It cost the administration nothing for the materials. It took no training. It cost his parents nothing.

Even when independence therapy is practiced by psychologists on kids with an actual diagnosis of anxiety, the treatment takes less time than talk therapy or cognitive behavioral therapy, which also means it's cheaper—and more immediately gratifying. A therapist can learn the technique for free by reading Ortiz's manual.

Any parents interested in boosting their kids' morale can start giving them a little more independence as soon as today. Just teach your children to cross the street safely and tell them that while they can *talk* to anyone, they can't *walk off* with anyone. Then open the door and say they have to be back home at a certain time, be it in half an hour or by dinner or by dark. It really is that simple, though it's a lot more fun if there's another kid your child can hang out with.

Here's the bottom line: Kids are hardwired for independence. Thwarting it has thwarted the natural development of their curiosity and confidence. You'd doubt yourself, too, if the people who loved you never trusted you to be safe or successful without their assistance. (And you're probably glad that's not how you grew up.)

So let's stop undermining kids by overprotecting them. Giving them back some old-fashioned freedom could be the cheapest, fastest, and easiest way for schools, therapists, and parents to prevent or even turn around the anxiety ruining today's childhood. It's time to step back and let our kids step up.

Notes

1. Camilo Ortiz and Lenore Skenazy, "This Simple Fix Could Help Anxious Kids," *New York Times*, September 4, 2023, https://www.nytimes.com/2023/09/04/opinion/anxiety-depression-teens.html.

2. German Lopez, "Crime on the Decline," *New York Times*, January 11, 2024, https://www.nytimes.com/2024/01/11/briefing/us-crime-rate.html.

3. Claire Cain Miller, "The Relentlessness of Modern Parenting," *New York Times*, December 25, 2018, https://www.nytimes.com/2018/12/25/upshot/the-relentlessness-of-modern-parenting.html.

4. University of Michigan Health, C. S. Mott Children's Hospital, "Mott Poll Report: Promoting Children's Independence: What Parents Say vs Do," October 16, 2023, https://mottpoll.org/sites/default/files/documents/101623_Independence.pdf.

5. University of Michigan Health, C. S. Mott Children's Hospital, "Mott Poll Report."

6. Louise Bates Ames and Frances L. Ilg, *Your Six-Year-Old: Loving and Defiant* (New York: Delacorte Press, 1979).

7. Kelly Wallace, "From '80s Latchkey Kid to Helicopter Parent Today," CNN, March 30, 2016, https://www.cnn.com/2016/03/30/health/the-80s-latchkey-kid-helicopter-parent/index.html.

8. Joe Pinsker, "The Cult of Homework," *The Atlantic*, March 28, 2019, https://www.theatlantic.com/education/archive/2019/03/homework-research-how-much/585889.

9. Emily Boudreau, "The Rapid Rise of Private Tutoring," Harvard Graduate School of Education, May 6, 2021, https://www.gse.harvard.edu/ideas/news/21/05/rapid-rise-private-tutoring; and Sean Gregory, "How Kids' Sports Became a $15 Billion Industry," *Time*, August 24, 2017, https://time.com/magazine/us/4913681/september-4th-2017-vol-190-no-9-u-s.

10. Peter Gray, David F. Lancy, and David F. Bjorklund, "Decline in Independent Activity as a Cause of Decline in Children's Mental Well-Being: Summary of the Evidence," *Journal of Pediatrics* 260, no. 2 (February 2023), https://www.researchgate.net/publication/368794518_Decline_in_Independent_Activity_as_a_Cause_of_Decline_in_Children's_Mental_Wellbeing_Summary_of_the_Evidence.

11. Caitlynn Peetz, "Kids' Declining Mental Health Is the 'Crisis of Our Time,' Surgeon General Says," *Education Week*, April 25, 2023, https://www.edweek.org/leadership/kids-declining-mental-health-is-the-crisis-of-our-time-surgeon-general-says/2023/04.

12. Donna St. George, "One School's Solution to the Mental Health Crisis: Try Everything," *Washington Post*, April 28, 2023, https://www.washingtonpost.com/education/2023/04/28/school-mental-health-crisis-ohio.

13. Lenore Skenazy, "Why I Let My 9-Year-Old Ride the Subway Alone," New York Sun, April 1, 2008, https://www.nysun.com/article/opinion-why-i-let-my-9-year-old-ride-subway-alone; and WDAF Kansas City, "Woman Dubbed 'America's Worst Mom' Promotes Free Range Parenting," Yahoo News, September 26, 2018, https://www.yahoo.com/news/woman-dubbed-americas-worst-mom-182432997.html.

14. Lenore Skenazy, *Free-Range Kids: How Parents and Teachers Can Let Go and Let Grow* (Hoboken, NJ: Jossey-Bass, 2021); and Let Grow, website, https://letgrow.org.

15. Katharine B. Parodi et al., "Time Trends and Disparities in Anxiety Among Adolescents, 2012–2018," *Social Psychiatry and Psychiatric Epidemiology* 57, no. 1 (June 2021): 127–37, https://www.ncbi.nlm.nih.gov/pmc/articles/PMC8183580.

16. Let Grow, "Our Mission," https://letgrow.org/about-us.

17. Allison Kresch Levine, "The Mental Health Impact of Intensive Mothering Ideology on Contemporary Mothers" (PsyD diss., Long Island University, New York, 2023), https://digitalcommons.liu.edu/post_fultext_dis/65.

18. Let Grow, "The Let Grow Experience," https://letgrow.org/program/experience.

19. Camilo Ortiz and Matthew Fastman, "A Novel Independence Intervention to Treat Child Anxiety: A Nonconcurrent Multiple Baseline Evaluation," *Journal of Anxiety Disorders* 105 (July 2024), https://www.sciencedirect.com/science/article/abs/pii/S0887618524000690.

20. James Doorley et al., "Psychological Flexibility: What We Know, What We Do Not Know, and What We Think We Know," *Social and Personality Psychology Compass* 14, no. 3 (October 2020): 1–11, https://www.researchgate.net/publication/344597314_Psychological_flexibility_What_we_know_what_we_do_not_know_and_what_we_think_we_know.

21. Let Grow, "Independence Therapy," https://letgrow.org/program/independence-therapy.

11

Fixing the Mental Health Provider Shortage

ALICE LLOYD RAHN

American children and adolescents are anxious and depressed at record levels, and there aren't nearly enough mental health treatment providers to meet the demand. Although not a new problem, it's been worsening for a while; the only difference now is that we're talking about it.

Experts trace the roots of American children's crisis-level psychological stress to any number of causes. Developmental disruptions caused by isolating pandemic lockdowns certainly bear much of the blame for adolescents' increasing rates of anxiety, depression, and suicide. Other experts add that so-called helicopter parents overinvest in their kids' success and thereby hold them back from building the resilience required for thriving.[1] Smartphones and social media have, it is argued, led directly to a substantial rise in anxiety and depression among young people.[2] Community cohesion, by whatever means of measurement, isn't what it once was[3]—and the average age of puberty's onset, with all its attendant psychic stressors, has been steadily declining, particularly for girls.[4]

Whatever the causes, the trends are undeniable: Depressive episodes and panic attacks are consistently rising among American children and teens. And the mental health workforce is insufficient to meet treatment demands.

The Substance Abuse and Mental Health Services Administration, a branch of the US Department of Health and Human Services, reported in its latest annual national survey that more than 20 percent of 12- to 17-year-olds had a major depressive episode in the past year.[5] That's roughly five million tweens and teens, an increase of more than a million since the previous year's report. As in years past, most of these suffering minors—nearly 60 percent—receive no treatment. For depressed Americans over 18, the numbers are flipped, with more than 60 percent receiving treatment for their symptoms at some point in the past year.

Because the number of minors needing mental health treatment has been steadily increasing year over year, the situation is likely even worse than we know. *JAMA Pediatrics* published a study in 2022 linking increased suicide rates to county levels of mental health professional shortages.[6] All across the country, children and adolescents are suffering without adequate help; waiting lists for children's clinical intake and treatment continue to grow, according to the American Psychological Association, meaning it will often take many months for children to get the treatment they need.[7]

Our children need help, and there aren't enough helpers.

Why Are Young Doctors Fleeing Child Psychiatry?

Many providers planning to spend their careers working with kids often don't stick around in the specialty. This is largely because working with adults is just more lucrative. Clinicians and physicians alike—psychiatrists, psychologists, social workers, counselors, therapists, and anyone trained and licensed to listen, diagnose, and treat mental illness—generally graduate, train, and reach the workforce only to confront the discouraging fact that treating young people typically pays less.

Those loyal to the calling tend to have one thing in common: experience of the power of early intervention. Angela Diaz, the director of Mount Sinai's renowned Adolescent Health Center in New York City, is one such provider.

Diaz first came to the East Harlem hospital clinic she now runs in the 1970s as a depressed and traumatized teenager. The mental health counselor she met there helped her unpack her stressors and symptoms. Diaz had moved from the Dominican Republic to the Bronx at age 12 to join her mother after four lonely years apart, and she was working three after-school jobs while juggling an ambitious, science-heavy curriculum. Impressed by Diaz's talent and diligence, her teachers held justifiably high hopes for her—but the stress and loneliness had become too much to bear. She stopped going to school in her senior year; she knew she needed help.[8]

"If you ask the youth that come here, they say they come because they feel welcome, respected, connected, safe, and not judged," says Diaz of the center's role in its patients' lives.[9]

Attending medical school at Columbia University and completing a residency at Mount Sinai led Diaz back to the Adolescent Health Center in 1989—this time as its director. Under her leadership, it has grown into its current form, providing integrated physical and mental health care and other practical services free of charge. "We have 38,000 patients and see 12,000 regularly, up to the age of 26, and not a penny passes hands," Diaz says.[10]

The Adolescent Health Center was one of the first of its kind offering medical care, mental health counseling, and social services all under the same roof. Patients' screenings and referrals are warm, confidential, and blessedly free from the complexities of interagency bureaucracy.

Diaz notes that the mental health crisis among adolescents is not new, but it is getting worse. The Centers for Disease Control and Prevention data from 2009 to 2019 show rates of suicide, sadness, and hopelessness among youth all sharply increased in the decade preceding the pandemic.[11] The demand for mental health services drastically surpasses the supply—even at a center with resources vast enough not to charge its thousands of patients for individual psychotherapy, health care, prescriptions, or transportation. The center has no limit on walk-in appointments. With so much call for care, it feels the effects of the provider shortage acutely.

"We are getting many, many calls from mental health services here—and you can't find psychiatrists to hire even when you have the money. It's very hard," laments Diaz. "The workforce is inadequate for the need."

The rising need for youth providers in recent years has led to more work for specialists, which in turn has decreased their numbers. During the pandemic, many exhausted providers left their youth center careers behind, lured by the promise of growing demand for private-practice telehealth therapy. "The pandemic dispersed a workforce that was short to begin with," Diaz says.[12]

In 2011, New York's state-level redesign of Medicaid did little to improve access to youth behavioral services in practice. In theory, higher reimbursement rates should have made it easier for providers already treating children to afford to continue offering low-cost mental health care to kids and families.[13] But that hasn't been enough to reverse market realities, entice more providers to the profession, or change the fact that treating kids pays less. "Whatever the reimbursement," Diaz says, "mental health providers find it inadequate compared to the private market—where they'd make $400, $500, [or] $800 for one evaluation."[14]

So while mental health providers already specializing in children's care have left in droves, early-career clinicians increasingly avoid the specialty altogether. "Not enough people are going into child and adolescent psychiatry, or mental health broadly," Diaz says.[15]

There are exceptions. Steven Adelsheim, a child and adolescent psychiatrist and professor of clinical psychiatry at Stanford University, worked in school-based clinics before medical school. He credits his calling to child psychiatry to this early-career experience, and he sees the same long-running recruitment problem in child and adolescent mental health.

"We don't do the same groundwork in recruiting people to consider behavioral health fields that we do [in] other health fields," says Adelsheim.[16] "We had a youth mental health crisis way before the pandemic. The data is worse, and there are more young people with more needs—but the crisis is really because we haven't really addressed the workforce shortage." And persistent stigma doesn't help matters. "Even psychiatry is seen as a lesser medical field than being a surgeon, let alone child psychiatry," he adds.

In an ideal world, training for aspiring youth mental health providers—from social workers and counselors to PhD psychologists and MD child psychiatrists—would not only allow for specialization sooner but also come with a clear and robust career path for the trainee.

Adelsheim suggests creating training programs that are child and adolescent focused upfront, with incentives like loan repayment. "If half of all mental illnesses start by 14 and three quarters by 24, why aren't the bulk of our dollars going to child adolescent services?" he asks, invoking foundational findings regarding the onset of mental illness.[17] "And then we can put some into maintenance for people with serious and persistent illness."[18]

After all, children are, as the saying goes, the future. It's widely understood that early intervention works in mental health—with children's depression and anxiety symptoms clearly diminished by preventive treatments.[19] And, likewise, adolescents with untreated mental illnesses are more likely to struggle as adults.[20] It stands to reason that untreated teens grow up to need more from the social safety net, provided they make it to adulthood.

Cameka Hazel, a counseling and psychology professor at the New York Institute of Technology, finds the increased attention to an insufficient youth mental health workforce in the pandemic's wake a welcome opportunity to shed light on a problem she, too, calls "nothing new."[21]

Before Hazel's graduate studies brought her to Boston, she led the peer-support program at the public school system in her native Jamaica—learning what a difference community investment and peer-to-peer counseling could make in the lives of student counselors and their clients alike. In peer-to-peer counseling, kids are taught by mental health professionals how to help each other—and in the process, they learn skills that help them for the rest of their lives. "Students who came for peer counseling would confide in each other about traumas they would never reveal to an adult," Hazel says, "and peer counselors who completed training were honored as community leaders."

Today, Hazel specializes in K–12 school counseling. Training school counselors to build similar peer-support programs has benefits—such as boosting students' morale and confidence, encouraging community buy-in, and combating loneliness—that far outweigh whatever grant money it would cost, she argues. Student-led and counselor-monitored group sessions proved successful in that students modeled for other students the safety and comfort of telling their trained peers and each other what they wouldn't confide in a parent, teacher, or licensed counselor.

Now, Hazel has become a leading advocate for expanding school-based counseling not just in New York but nationally. In the years leading up to lockdowns, youth hospitalization for mental health more than doubled.[22] COVID-19 clearly worsened but did not cause the youth mental health crisis: Cutting kids off from the sense of community and access to counseling they were offered at school deepened a preexisting problem.

"We must prioritize making behavioral care a part of school life, now more than ever," Hazel explains. Simply put, "it's easier for students to get treatment in schools. They have to go to school."[23]

And yet the average ratio nationwide is one licensed school counselor per 400 students, or about half of what the American School Counselor Association recommends.[24] From under-resourced rural districts to turbulent city governments, political factors get in the way: "Here in New York City, we saw a hiring freeze for mental health counselors in schools under Mayor de Blasio at what happened to be the worst possible time," Hazel recalls.[25]

As a way around the institutional discouragements young professionals face, Hazel advocates teaching basic counseling skills to every school teacher. An adolescent presenting with true mental illness needs a clinically trained provider. But in a world with far too few of those, training for non-providers heightens the likelihood of a referral, helping a suffering kid before it's too late.

Diaz agrees, arguing that while "an adolescent with true mental illness needs a trained provider more than a peer counselor, the perfect is the enemy of the good-enough, and for traumatized kids, mentoring is a powerful protective factor."[26] That mentor figure, Hazel and Diaz concur, can be just about anyone.

And there are, of course, those for whom pure loneliness—in the absence of true trauma or any discernible diagnosable mental illness—lies at the root of all other symptoms. For them, the "cure" is community, not necessarily weekly individual therapy with an expensively credentialed provider.

A Peer-to-Provider Pipeline?

An attractively inexpensive and community-centered investment, peer counseling has fans across the political spectrum. Yet in schools, administrative turnover tends to disrupt mental health providers' work with students. "Principals are turning over every year, and the next one comes in and says, *Why are we doing this? We're about education; we're not about health care. We need this space for a classroom*," Adelsheim said, recalling the frustrations of his work in schools.[27]

Sheila Balk, who directs the celebrated peer-counseling program at Pomona High School in eastern Los Angeles County, says she has recently encountered similar setbacks. Balk took over the peer-counseling program in the mid-1990s when conflict mediation was its primary mission. "Back then, I would break up two fights a day," she recalls. Now, students are largely seeking counseling for anxiety. "We have been getting kids in, male and female, with panic attacks—two or three [students] a class period. . . .

The first year back [from the pandemic], we could not keep up with what was coming in our door."[28]

With the return to in-person schooling, however, lost academic progress received more attention than social and emotional development did, Balk recalls. Students once directed to Balk's peer-counseling center for support were instead encouraged by administrators to seek out academic counselors, who are not always equipped to deal with a child suffering from a mental health problem.

So far, the peer-counseling program at Pomona High School has persevered. Trained peer counselors and their counseling clients have kept up the work. Students schooled in basic counseling skills learn they need to keep their grades up to hold on to their helping roles. Their confidence increases, Balk attests, and they know they're part of a legacy of community support.

One student, Olivia, whose brother was killed in a gang shooting during quarantine, came back to campus after lockdown with symptoms of post-traumatic stress, Balk says.

> She'd come in sobbing and ask for her peer counselor, and she would leave ready to go on with the rest of her day—for that particular peer counselor, just sitting next to Olivia, supportive silence was the strongest tool in the toolbox.

Peer counselors can also help themselves with what they learned once they reach adulthood. "I've had peer counselors who have developed severe substance abuse problems as young adults come back and say they used what they learned to dig themselves out of a hole [and have been] sober now for 20 years," Balk reports. The skills and firsthand experiences they developed to help others wound up saving their own lives.[29]

Peer counseling has obvious limitations for those in a true state of crisis. When clients come to peer counseling in severe distress, counselors know to inform Balk that more help is needed. Yet families often resist seeking professional help outside school, seeing their children's need for mental health counseling as a sign that the family has failed to provide adequate support at home and perceiving proposed intervention as being judgmental. Firsthand knowledge of the limits of school-based mental health intervention led Adelsheim to found Allcove, a growing continuum of youth-led community health centers.

Adelsheim was working in school-based health centers in New Mexico and continually confronting structural barriers to confidentiality and continuity of care—and administrators fighting counselors for classroom real estate—when he started looking for a solution. "I found what we really needed was to have a community-based place for young people outside of schools to also come in and get help," he recalled.[30]

Eventually, the Headspace program, a publicly funded network of youth community health centers in Australia, sparked his inspiration more than a decade ago. By then, Adelsheim was director of the Stanford Center for Youth Mental Health and Wellbeing, and Palo Alto was grappling with its second cluster of youth suicides: Six local teens took their own lives in nine months from 2009 to 2010, and from 2010 to 2014, the county saw an annual average of 20 youth suicides.[31] As a result, "there was heightened interest in what else could we be doing for our young people," Adelsheim recalls.[32] County- and state-level funding came pouring in, and the first integrated Allcove centers opened in June 2021.

Young adults age 12 to 25 come to Allcove centers to be treated by mental health providers—weekly individual and group therapy—and physicians. But the centers also offer career counseling, addiction treatment, peer support, and referrals to other services—including art programs, housing, and intensive psychiatric care.

The key ingredient to every Allcove center, as Adelsheim tells it, is its unique composition of youth advisers. "Each Allcove center has a very active youth advisory group that's very focused on determining the appropriate services for *our* place—what groups we should have, then planning and doing the necessary outreach," explains Adelsheim.[33] Youth advisers age 16–25 serve a two-year term and confer with a consortium of local partners supporting and guiding their internal work and referral networks. Active Allcove centers are cropping up across California.

Youth advisers named Allcove and worked with a design firm to plan the layout of the first center in Santa Clara County. In that and other locations, they were responsible for interviewing prospective staff, presenting the model to potential funders, and spreading the word about their available services. In some locations, youth advisers are paid a stipend. Their involvement in these foundational decisions has a healing effect in terms of empowerment, efficacy, and validity, Adelsheim explains.[34]

On a recent visit to Allcove's Los Angeles location, he ran into a former youth adviser who's since taken a job as a peer-support specialist. One generation deep, the pipeline from peer leader to youth mental health provider suggests a promising trend: "Whether it's lived experience or family experience or otherwise, it seems as though being part of these youth advisory groups for some people is becoming an early gateway into moving into a behavioral health workforce role," Adelsheim says.[35]

Some pursue community college or four-year degree programs with a focus on psychology or mental health, then go on to graduate school to become psychologists or counselors. "Of our first cohorts of youth advisors," Adelsheim reflects, "many are going into mental health and health care fields."[36]

If We Can't Make Enough Therapists, Can We Make Do with Too Few of Them?

The only nationwide health care reform in the past 20 years to make a meaningful dent in the youth mental health provider shortage was a product of the Romney administration.

In Massachusetts, under then-Gov. Mitt Romney, Health and Human Services Secretary Ron Preston led a pilot program in response to a class action lawsuit concerning the growing number of children on Medicaid being prescribed powerful, and sometimes multiple, psychotropic medications. Most of these children, Preston's investigation found, were being treated by pediatricians—not psychiatrists.[37] As a result, the state legislature passed the Massachusetts Child Psychiatry Access Program in 2004.

Since then, the program has offered primary care providers access to on-demand consultations with a child psychiatrist, a licensed therapist, and a care coordinator, regardless of a patient's insurance situation. Its regional hubs cover 95 percent of the state's children. At first, the program was unpopular, with providers suspicious of the increased workload associated with this mysteriously free service.[38] But it proved a success and spread across the country. Today, a national network of child psychiatry access programs catalogs similar provider hubs in 46 states and six tribes and territories.[39]

"Additional training for pediatricians in mental health screening and frontline care is key," says Diaz—pointing to New York state's version, founded in 2010.[40] It includes on-demand, free-of-charge online training in pediatric mental health care for physicians, nurses, and other providers.

Filling gaps in access to youth mental health care will mean finding innovative ways to make do without enough credentialed helpers to meet children's needs, such as by training not only medical providers but also teachers and even parents. It will also mean teaching anxious and depressed young people how to help themselves feel better. There's a common notion in the world of psychotherapy that a treatment has been truly effective only once the patient has internalized supportive habits of mind and coping skills fully enough to become their own therapist.

The provider shortage cuts teens' and children's access to the best evidence-based practices. The gold standard in mental health treatment for depression and anxiety, evidence-based practices are those with the richest backing in clinical research. They're therapies, in other words, that have been proved again and again to make a measurable difference. And among evidence-based treatments, cognitive behavioral therapy (CBT)—a form of "talking cure" that targets distorted thoughts and their ill effects on beliefs and behaviors—leads the pack.[41]

"Teens are not getting first-line CBT," says Bernadette Mazurek Melnyk, a pediatric and psychiatric nurse practitioner who encountered the cruelties of the provider shortage firsthand as a teen. "This is very far from a new problem."[42]

Mazurek Melnyk was 15 when her mother "sneezed, stroked out, and died." Traumatized, she struggled to repress her grief. Before any family doctor had heard the words "child psychiatry access program," a young Mazurek Melnyk was prescribed powerful psychotropic medication by a local physician to treat her symptoms. What would have actually helped, she went on to learn, was guidance in developing coping skills to support her grappling with so much underlying suffering.

Instead, her post-traumatic stress disorder went untreated. "But in time, I discovered I was more resilient than I thought," she says, describing a healing trajectory that built on her own innate capacity to overcome immense tragedy.[43]

Helping others has been a central part of that healing: Mazurek Melnyk's personal experience and professional expertise as a CBT provider inspired her to develop a "highly trainable" and self-administered program called Creating Opportunities for Personal Empowerment (COPE). COPE was first piloted, Mazurek Melnyk says, by nurses at in-patient psychiatric treatment centers, with recorded rates of symptom relief surpassing standard treatments right out the gate. Unlike medication-based treatment, the program taught patients skills to help them deal with the stresses and challenges they would encounter after hospitalization. Its 15 hour-long manualized sessions teach CBT techniques and emphasize nutrition, exercise, and behavioral change, with a documented track record of decreasing depressive and anxious symptoms while enhancing self-esteem, healthy habits, and academic retention.

Rural high schools have adopted an abbreviated version of COPE as part of their health curricula. It's gone on to form the backbone of after-school intervention programs and individual therapy in community centers across the country. Most recently, Mazurek Melnyk says, public schools in Washington, DC, used COPE programs to train teachers developing CBT groups.[44]

It's not just COPE's work in CBT that's evidence based. COPE itself has been the subject of more than a dozen research studies, affirming its effectiveness.[45] Survey feedback tends to focus on self-soothing skills, like breathing techniques or replacing negative thoughts with positive ones, and the thinking-feeling-behaving triangle every COPE program presents in some form (Figure 1): "I remember the triangle that shows you how you think is how you feel and behave," one student reported, "because I could see when that actually happened."[46]

Since its inception, COPE has mostly spread by word of mouth, Mazurek Melnyk explains—and she's used research and feedback to adapt it to different populations' developmental needs, retooling the program for age-appropriate goals, content, and delivery. "My next goal is to create a training program for parents," Mazurek Melnyk says. "We're learning that parents don't have these coping skills themselves." Parents have a unique vantage to support children's habits and skill development when

Figure 1. COPE Thinking-Feeling-Behaving Triangle

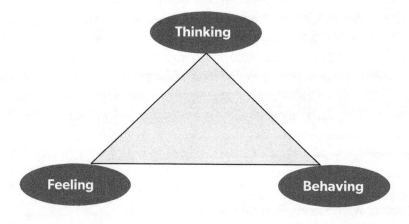

Source: Pamela Lusk and Bernadette Mazurek Melnyk, "COPE for Depressed and Anxious Teens: A Brief Cognitive-Behavioral Skills Building Intervention to Increase Access to Timely, Evidence-Based Treatment," *Journal of Child and Adolescent Psychiatric Nursing* 26, no. 1 (February 2013): 23–31, Figure 1, https://www.ncbi.nlm.nih.gov/pmc/articles/PMC4293698/figure/F1.

it comes to replacing distorted automatic thoughts. Parents' behaviors reinforce and model their children's habits of mind and behaviors. "I'm also working on a new version of COPE for preschoolers," Mazurek Melnyk says.[47]

Already on the market, the self-administered version of the program—available for children and families to download—is relatively affordable at $79. In institutional contexts, grants and reimbursements make the program easily accessible to providers on the front lines, including primary care providers, like the physician who mistreated Mazurek Melnyk, and increasingly high school teachers. A manualized or self-administered program like COPE offers the clearest available answer to the provider shortage: The program, in essence, takes the place of the provider.

Experts like Mazurek Melnyk and Adelsheim are hopeful that the new attention youth mental health has received in recent years will help America's legions of struggling children and adolescents. And yet, as with so many topics of national conversation, the youth mental health provider shortage predates the current burst of attention it's enjoying. And it will, in all likelihood, outlast it too. "We have this brief window to build on the resources that are briefly available and expand access," Adelsheim says, "but I don't know that we're moving quickly enough to address the need."[48]

Notes

1. Julia Schønning Vigdal and Kolbjørn Kallesten Brønnic, "A Systematic Review of 'Helicopter Parenting' and Its Relationship with Anxiety and Depression," *Frontiers in Psychology* 13 (2022): 872–981, https://www.ncbi.nlm.nih.gov/pmc/articles/PMC9176408.

2. Abderrahman M. Khalaf et al., "The Impact of Social Media on the Mental Health of Adolescents and Young Adults: A Systematic Review," *Cureus* 15, no. 8 (2023), https://www.ncbi.nlm.nih.gov/pmc/articles/PMC10476631.

3. US Department of Health and Human Services, "Our Epidemic of Loneliness and Isolation: Key Takeaways from the U.S. Surgeon General's Advisory on the Healing Effects of Social Connection and Community," 2023, https://www.hhs.gov/sites/default/files/sg-social-connection-general.pdf.

4. Azeen Ghorayshi, "Puberty Starts Earlier Than It Used To. No One Knows Why.," *New York Times*, May 19, 2022, https://www.nytimes.com/2022/05/19/science/early-puberty-medical-reason.html.

5. Substance Abuse and Mental Health Services Administration, "Highlights for the 2021 National Survey on Drug Use and Health," https://www.samhsa.gov/data/sites/default/files/2022-12/2021NSDUHFFRHighlights092722.pdf.

6. Jennifer A. Hoffmann et al., "Association of Youth Suicides and County-Level Mental Health Professional Shortage Areas in the US," *JAMA Pediatrics* 177, no. 1 (November 2022): 71–80, https://jamanetwork.com/journals/jamapediatrics/fullarticle/2798887.

7. Heather Stringer, "Providers Predict Longer Wait Times for Mental Health Services. Here's Who It Impacts Most," *American Psychological Association* 54, no. 3 (2023), https://www.apa.org/monitor/2023/04/mental-health-services-wait-times.

8. Karen Brown, "A Survivor's Empathy: HSPH Alumna's Immigrant Journey Inspires Career Transforming Teens' Health," *Harvard Public Health*, Spring 2014, 38–49, https://www.hsph.harvard.edu/magazine/magazine_article/a-survivors-empathy.

9. Angela Diaz (director, Mount Sinai Adolescent Health Center), interview with the author, July 27, 2023.

10. Diaz, interview.

11. Centers for Disease Control and Prevention, *Youth Risk Behavior Survey: Data Summary & Trends Report 2009–2019*, https://www.cdc.gov/healthyyouth/data/yrbs/pdf/YRBSDataSummaryTrendsReport2019-508.pdf.

12. Diaz, interview.
13. Jeanmarie Evelly, "Years After NY Medicaid Overhaul, Kids' Access to Mental Health Care Still in Crisis: Report," City Limits, November 30, 2021, https://citylimits.org/2021/11/30/years-after-ny-medicaid-overhaul-kids-access-to-mental-health-care-still-in-crisis-report.
14. Diaz, interview.
15. Diaz, interview.
16. Steven Adelsheim (director, Stanford Center for Youth Mental Health and Well-being), interview with the author, August 15, 2023.
17. Ronald C. Kessler et al., "Lifetime Prevalence and Age-of-Onset Distributions of DSM-IV Disorders in the National Comorbidity Survey Replication," *Archives of General Psychiatry* 62, no. 6 (June 2005): 593–602, https://jamanetwork.com/journals/jamapsychiatry/fullarticle/208678.
18. Adelsheim, interview.
19. Jai K. Das et al., "Interventions for Adolescent Mental Health: An Overview of Systematic Reviews," *Journal of Adolescent Health* 59, no. 4 (October 2016): S49–S60, https://www.ncbi.nlm.nih.gov/pmc/articles/PMC5026677/pdf/main.pdf.
20. Robert Schlack et al., "The Effects of Mental Health Problems in Childhood and Adolescence in Young Adults: Results of the KiGGS Cohort," *Journal of Health Monitoring* 6, no. 4 (December 2021): 3–19, https://www.ncbi.nlm.nih.gov/pmc/articles/PMC8734087/pdf/johm-6-4-03.pdf.
21. Cameka Hazel (assistant professor of counseling and psychology, New York Institute of Technology), interview with the author, July 24, 2023.
22. Centers for Disease Control and Prevention, *Youth Risk Behavior Survey*.
23. Hazel, interview.
24. American School Counselor Association, "School Counselor Roles & Ratios," https://www.schoolcounselor.org/About-School-Counseling/School-Counselor-Roles-Ratios.
25. Hazel, interview.
26. Diaz, interview.
27. Adelsheim, interview.
28. Sheila Balk (peer counseling teacher, Pomona High School), interview with the author, July 19, 2023.
29. Balk, interview.
30. Adelsheim, interview.
31. Hanna Rosin, "The Silicon Valley Suicides: Why Are So Many Kids with Bright Prospects Killing Themselves in Palo Alto?," *The Atlantic*, December 2015, https://www.theatlantic.com/magazine/archive/2015/12/the-silicon-valley-suicides/413140.
32. Adelsheim, interview.
33. Adelsheim, interview.
34. Adelsheim, interview.
35. Adelsheim, interview.
36. Adelsheim, interview.
37. Wendy Holt, "The Massachusetts Child Psychiatry Access Project: Supporting Mental Health Treatment in Primary Care," Commonwealth Fund, March 2010,

https://www.commonwealthfund.org/publications/case-study/2010/mar/massachusetts-child-psychiatry-access-project-supporting-mental.

38. John H. Straus and Barry Sarvet, "Behavioral Health Care for Children: The Massachusetts Child Psychiatry Access Project," *Health Affairs* 33, no. 12 (December 2014): 2153–61, https://www.healthaffairs.org/doi/10.1377/hlthaff.2014.0896.

39. National Network of Child Psychiatry Access Programs, website, https://www.nncpap.org.

40. Diaz, interview.

41. Stefan G. Hofmann, Alice T. Sawyer, and Angela Fang, "The Empirical Status of the 'New Wave' of Cognitive Behavioral Therapy," *Psychiatric Clinics of North America* 33, no. 3 (September 2010): 701–10, https://www.sciencedirect.com/science/article/abs/pii/S0193953X10000481.

42. Bernadette Mazurek Melnyk (Helene Fuld Health Trust Professor of Evidence-Based Practice, Ohio State University), interview with the author, July 25, 2023.

43. Mazurek Melnyk, interview.

44. Mazurek Melnyk, interview.

45. Creating Opportunities for Personal Empowerment, "Evidence-Based Studies Supporting Positive Effects of the COPE Program," https://www.cope2thrive.com/published-papers.

46. Pamela Lusk and Bernadette Mazurek Melnyk, "COPE for Depressed and Anxious Teens: A Brief Cognitive-Behavioral Skills Building Intervention to Increase Access to Timely, Evidence-Based Treatment," *Journal of Child and Adolescent Psychiatric Nursing* 26, no. 1 (February 2013): 23–31, https://onlinelibrary.wiley.com/doi/10.1111/jcap.12017.

47. Mazurek Melnyk, interview.

48. Adelsheim, interview.

12

Our Generational Challenge: A Gen Z Perspective

KATE FARMER

It's no coincidence that some call us "iGen."
The term, coined by San Diego State University psychologist Jean Twenge, refers to all individuals born between 1995 and 2012.[1] We're more commonly referred to as Gen Z, but Twenge's label hits at something undeniable: This generation has been defined largely by its familiarity with—or, perhaps more accurately, its dependence on—the internet, social media, and smartphones.

This is my generation. I was born in 2001, putting me right at the heart of Gen Z. I created my first social media account at 13, amassed over 100 followers by 14, and walked into my first day of eighth grade with a newly minted smartphone in hand. Looking back on this early exposure to the virtual world, I have a hard time imagining adolescence without the internet, middle and high school without Instagram, or college without total digital interconnectivity. If anything, many researchers and pundits of our generation don't emphasize nearly enough just how much the online world has shaped us.

Yet as of late, this digital imprint has become harder to ignore. According to a 2023 Gallup survey, over half of US teenagers spend at least four hours a day on social media platforms, such as Instagram, TikTok, and YouTube. The national average for teens age 13–19 was 4.8 hours daily, with 17-year-olds spending the most time on social media—averaging a whopping 5.7 hours.[2] In a separate 2022 survey, nearly half of Gen Z teens admitted they were online "almost constantly."[3]

These numbers alone are staggering, but they pale in comparison to the mental health crisis that has come with them. According to Twenge and colleagues, depression among teens rose by 33 percent from 2010 to 2015, and the number of teens reporting at least one suicide-related outcome (meaning suicidal ideation, plans, and attempts) rose by 12 percent.[4] It's therefore no surprise that in 2023, the Office of the Surgeon General pointed to social media as the main driver behind the youth mental health crisis. In the words of Surgeon General Vivek Murthy, social media overuse is "the defining public health issue of our time."[5]

The outlook for my generation—and likely also for Generation Alpha following us—appears bleak. Many of my fellow Gen Zers, sometimes even I, feel powerless to course correct our slanted relationship with phones and social media.[6] And yet, I'm optimistic about my generation's ability to do just that.

Gen Z's Generational Assets

Yes, Gen Z is overdependent on smartphones. Yes, our mental health is worsening. But the internet age has undeniably brought many unique benefits to our lives. Being born and raised in the internet age has left us with an array of skills, resources, and positive character traits that we can use to our advantage. Perhaps we can even leverage these internet-born gifts to save ourselves from the very crisis we've inherited.

Gen Z, in part because of its early internet exposure, is often referred to as a "coddled" generation. To be sure, many in our generation have delayed various adult milestones, like dating and getting a driver's license, potentially due to digital overuse.[7] It would do many of us good to unplug and catch up a little to the world around us. But that's only one part of the story.

To Roberta Katz, a senior research scholar at the Center for Advanced Study in the Behavioral Sciences at Stanford University, the portrayal of Gen Z as a generation of snowflakes frequently falls short. She and her colleagues conducted in-depth interviews with 120 Gen Z students across the US and UK and arranged surveys, hosted focus groups, and compiled a digital repository of millions of spoken and written language entries from individuals age 16 to 25. The resulting image Katz drew was of a generation that values communication and collaboration with people of different backgrounds. She tied this generational open-mindedness largely to Gen Z's technological upbringing:

> Gen Zers . . . developed an early facility with powerful digital tools that allowed them to be self-reliant as well as collaborative. Similarly, because they could learn about people and cultures around the globe from an early age, they developed a greater appreciation for diversity and the importance of finding their own unique identities.[8]

The internet and social media have certainly left many of us addicted, but they've also made many of us creative, entrepreneurial, and tech savvy. Not all of Gen Z has a healthy relationship with technology. And yet, many in Gen Z demonstrate how technology and tech fluency can be wielded in incredible ways and as a force for self-betterment. A recent report by the Innovation Group at J. Walter Thompson Intelligence and Snap, for example, examines dozens of Gen Z content creators who have developed an online following. The report paints a picture of a creative, interconnected, and technologically skilled generation developing business ideas and advancing social causes.[9] But it has a deeper point: We were born with social media at our fingertips, so we're deeply familiar with this technology. If we can use it to reach multitudes, it's certainly possible for us to reorient our tech savviness to improve our overall approach to social media.

Gen Z's values are also a major tool in our tool kit. While Gen Z certainly faces a serious mental health crisis, the data also show that we take mental health more seriously as a result—significantly more so than older generations have.[10] Gen Z is the generation most likely to talk about mental health struggles, seek therapy, and work to reduce stigma around mental health.[11] Gen Z also displays a strong sense of generational unity, and although we vary politically, we remain highly cohesive in our social values.[12] All these factors contribute to our ability to identify and rally behind important issues—and, I hope, come together and fix them.

But how might we go about doing that?

How Gen Z Can Change Our Tech-Obsessed Culture

To help Gen Z, I believe there are two necessary pathways for change. The first is at the personal level, led by members of Gen Z themselves. The second is at a greater, societal level—that all generations, but especially Gen Z, can contribute to.

On the personal level, members of Gen Z can push screenless hobbies and pastimes into cultural normalcy. Consider, for example, the resurgence of a once-presumed dead technology: the flip phone. Over the past five years, Google searches for the term "flip phone" have gone up by more than 140 percent.[13] On TikTok, #FlipPhone has collected over 627 million views. Recent reporting suggests that some Gen Zers today are ditching their iPhones and Androids altogether and switching back to a dumbphone. A student at the University of Illinois Urbana-Champaign told CNN that the flip phone "eliminates all the bad things about college and brings all of the good things about a phone. Which is connecting with people and taking photos and videos."[14]

This old-school fascination extends beyond everyday tech. Gen Z has surprised market watchers with its interest in reviving objects and pastimes from previous decades. This includes a growing affinity for knitting, crocheting, baking, film photography, and charcuterie-board picnics.[15] Gen Z's appetite for screenless experiences does more than reflect consumer trends or a nostalgic bend. It reflects a genuine appetite for social change, moving away from constant digital interconnectivity toward a more hands-on, multifaceted life.

Gen Z should not let these practices lose momentum. I'm not saying that we all must forfeit our digital powers for a dumbphone or take up knitting in place of watching sports or chatting online. Rather, I urge other Gen Zers to be more mindful of the ways screens can be swapped for more human, hands-on alternatives to bring about a healthier and more fulfilling life balance.

I also encourage other Gen Zers to make these changes in their social groups. More than ever, Gen Z is aware of social media's false promises, addictive powers, and potential to damage in-person relationships. Gen Zers hungry for social lives free of constant smartphone exposure can lead their peers toward an increasingly screenless lifestyle by sharing their favorite hobbies and pastimes with friends. This would make for healthy "influencing" and contribute to a greater mission: building social traditions around things that are not screens or phones and enjoying a day-to-day with fewer pressures from the digital world.

Gen Z can also further this goal through reviving group membership at in-person social and cultural organizations. Admittedly, some generational trajectories suggest that forming these customs and revitalizing these institutions will take time and effort. Gen Z is increasingly nonreligious, for example, which makes it less likely to reap the benefits of one of the main institutions of social capital.[16] Moreover, Gen Zers are less likely to volunteer or donate to charity, especially in their own communities.[17] Rather than engaging in these once formative and essential social environments, much of my generation has replaced membership in in-person institutions with time spent online.

That said, these challenges should not scare us away from the potential benefits that community building can bring. Gen Zers have a tremendous opportunity to lead their peers into more robust and frequent social interaction. Whether it's by attending religious services regularly, volunteering for community service groups, or starting new clubs, members of Gen Z can find ways to reduce the time they spend on digital social networks. Or, tapping into Gen Z's creative edge, they can start something completely new of their own. For example, Gen Zers have designed local platforms such as the Girls NYC, Skip the Small Talk, and the Dinner Party Project that connect local strangers for dinner parties, bar mixers, or meals out.[18]

Tech-savvy Gen Zers have an especially important role to play. Social media sites grow smarter, and therefore more addictive, every year. Yet with these advancements has come smart technology designed to help users cut their dependency—and much of it is coming from Gen Z. Young designers are creating anti-addiction phone apps, software, and browser extensions to help their peers fight social media overuse. Content creators are also spreading tips that worked for them, such as putting one's phone in black and white and taking periodic "dopamine detoxes."[19] These efforts are positive examples of Gen Zers harnessing their tech savviness for good.[20]

Many Gen Z–led organizations have already taken this effort nationwide. Organizations like LookUp.live and the Log Off Movement use social media platforms to educate their peers on how to maintain a healthy online-offline balance. They hope to create Gen Z–led movements to educate others on the dangers of internet overuse and promote healthier relationships with social media. Log Off's founder, Emma

Lembke, has even testified before Congress about the dangers of youth social media addiction.[21]

Gen Z can also lead major changes at the societal level that will benefit from, and likely even rely on, cross-generational support. The most obvious one is legislation. Gen Z and older generations would benefit from collaborating on commonsense legislative reform around social media. Age-verification laws for tech are controversial, but many well-supported, bipartisan bills could also help.

The Kids Online Safety Act, for example, would expand protections for minors online while allowing them to disable product features that drive addiction. By creating a "duty of care," it would require social media companies to take reasonable steps to prevent harm in its underage users. This would mean requiring major platforms to disable addictive product settings, limit features that encourage excessive and sustained use, and allow users to opt out of personalized algorithmic recommendations.[22] As of September 2024, the bill has passed the Senate and awaits a vote in the House. In the meantime, at least 15 states have already banned or restricted cellphone use in schools, with more states actively considering similar legislation.[23]

While age-verification laws would require state or federal legislation, other cross-generational efforts at the local level can be tremendously impactful. Growing up, my peers and I were presented with plenty of anti-bullying campaigns at school, which reinforced good habits and norms to address a rising problem. And it reaped benefits. In 2009, 28 percent of middle and high school students reported being bullied; that number dropped to 22 percent in 2019.[24]

Internet and social media overuse should be the next big social education campaign at schools. Teaching healthy habits for social media use and educating students of its potential dangers will help prepare kids for what's in store when they first log on. Obviously, this guidance should also come from parents, but social education curricula have always been around for those who may not receive such lessons at home.

Schools could integrate such lessons through their existing physical fitness and health education curricula. Even better, states and localities could collaborate with research organizations to draft curricula based on the recent science of social media overuse and offer it to teachers for their lesson plans. I call such programming "social media literacy": equipping students with the knowledge and tools they need to cultivate healthier relationships with online media. This includes setting kids straight on social media's addictive powers and teaching them methods to balance their need for digital tools with a healthy lifestyle. Absent greater educational scaffolding, though, teachers can still teach such values individually, initiating group discussions about social media and creating phone-free classrooms.

Gen Z's Road Ahead

My generation's mental health is in a precarious position. Rising rates of depression and self-harm reflect an anxious generation whose problems cannot be ignored any further. Research like Twenge's and the alarm sounded by the surgeon general show that if there was ever a time when these issues could be ignored, it has long passed. The best research shows there's a close relationship between these disorders and smartphones and social media becoming common markers of American adolescence.

And yet, those rightfully worried about modern technology's impact on declining mental health outcomes often overlook my generation's resiliency and potential. Our challenge going forward will be to use our familiarity with the internet and smartphones to our advantage as we seek healthier ways to deal with the technology at our fingertips.

It's an important and difficult challenge, but there's real ground for optimism. Gen Z possesses many of the resources it needs to change our relationship with the online world for the better—and not just for ourselves. Future generations will almost certainly grow up in a world where social media and smartphones are ubiquitous. But if we Gen Zers can step up and use our unique assets to our advantage, we have the chance to pave the way for a happier and healthier future for all of us.

Notes

1. See Jean M. Twenge, *iGen: Why Today's Super-Connected Kids Are Growing Up Less Rebellious, More Tolerant, Less Happy—and Completely Unprepared for Adulthood—and What That Means for the Rest of Us* (New York: Atria Books, 2017).

2. Jonathan Rothwell, "Teens Spend Average of 4.8 Hours on Social Media per Day," Gallup, October 13, 2023, https://news.gallup.com/poll/512576/teens-spend-average-hours-social-media-per-day.aspx.

3. Annie E. Casey Foundation, "What the Statistics Say About Generation Z," November 1, 2023, https://www.aecf.org/blog/generation-z-statistics.

4. Jean M. Twenge et al., "Increases in Depressive Symptoms, Suicide-Related Outcomes, and Suicide Rates Among U.S. Adolescents After 2010 and Links to Increased New Media Screen Time," *Clinical Psychological Science* 6, no. 1 (January 2018): 3–17, https://journals.sagepub.com/doi/10.1177/2167702617723376.

5. Erika Edwards and Hallie Jackson, "Social Media Is Driving Teen Mental Health Crisis, Surgeon General Warns," NBC News, May 23, 2023, https://www.nbcnews.com/health/health-news/social-media-mental-health-anxiety-depression-teens-surgeon-general-rcna85575.

6. Alex Pena, "Gen Z Has Lived Their Entire Lives Online. Some Are Fed Up.," CBS News, May 5, 2022, https://www.cbsnews.com/news/gen-z-internet-social-media; and Hannah Hadley, "Spending Too Much Time on Social Media Is and Has Been Harmful to Gen Z—yet I Am Still Addicted," *The Reflector*, May 1, 2023, https://reflector.uindy.edu/2023/05/01/spending-too-much-time-on-social-media-is-and-has-been-harmful-to-gen-z-yet-i-am-still-addicted.

7. Jean M. Twenge and Heejung Park, "The Decline in Adult Activities Among U.S. Adolescents, 1976–2016," *Child Development* 90, no. 2 (March–April 2019): 638–54, https://srcd.onlinelibrary.wiley.com/doi/epdf/10.1111/cdev.12930.

8. Roberta Katz, "Gen Z Are Not 'Coddled.' They Are Highly Collaborative, Self-Reliant and Pragmatic, According to New Stanford-Affiliated Research," interview by Melissa De Witte, Stanford Report, January 3, 2022, https://news.stanford.edu/stories/2022/01/know-gen-z.

9. J. Walter Thompson Intelligence, Innovation Group, and Snap, *Into Z Future: Understanding Generation Z, the Next Generation of Super Creatives*, https://assets.ctfassets.net/inb32lme5oo9/5DFlqKVGIdmAu7X6btfGQt/44fdca09d7b630ee28f5951d54feed71/Into_Z_Future_Understanding_Gen_Z_The_Next_Generation_of_Super_Creatives_.pdf.

10. Christian Brown, "The Rise of Mental Health Awareness Among Gen-Z: What This Means for Brand Marketing," *Forbes*, March 10, 2023, https://www.forbes.com/sites/forbesbusinesscouncil/2023/03/10/the-rise-of-mental-health-awareness-among-gen-z-what-this-means-for-brand-marketing.

11. Arlin Cuncic, "Why Gen Z Is More Open to Talking About Their Mental Health," Verywell Mind, December 30, 2023, https://www.verywellmind.com/why-gen-z-is-more-open-to-talking-about-their-mental-health-5104730.

12. Amanda Edelman and Andrea Hagelgans, "Gen Z's Voting Habits Are All the Proof Companies Need to Act on Societal Issues," *Fortune*, December 7, 2022, https://fortune.com/2022/12/07/gen-z-voting-habits-proof-societal-issues-abortion-gun-climate-culture-politics-values-edelman-hagelgans; and Samuel J. Abrams, "Gen Z's Pragmatic Politics Could Be a Key to Ending Polarization," *Los Angeles Times*, November 19, 2022, https://www.latimes.com/opinion/story/2022-11-19/gen-z-politics-midterm-elections-voting.

13. Marc Saltzman, "Why Are Flip Phones Coming Back? Gen Z Is Powering a Renaissance for the Forgotten Device," *USA Today*, January 21, 2023, https://www.usatoday.com/story/tech/2023/01/21/flip-phone-samsung-nokia-tracfone/11088551002.

14. Ramisha Maruf, "Gen Z Has a New 'Vintage' Technology to Obsess Over," CNN, January 16, 2023, https://www.cnn.com/2023/01/15/business/flip-phone-gen-z-ctrp/index.html.

15. Jada Jones, "Flip Phones to Digital Cameras, Gen Z's Love of Retro Gadgets Is Smarter Than You Realize," ZDNet, February 12, 2023, https://www.zdnet.com/article/flip-phones-and-digital-cameras-gen-zs-need-for-retro-gadgets-is-much-wiser-than-you-realize; Tate Moyer, "The Return to Retro: Why Gen Z Is Making a Return to Vintage Technology," *Michigan Daily*, February 23, 2023, https://www.michigandaily.com/opinion/the-return-to-retro-why-gen-z-is-making-a-return-to-vintage-technology; and Ellie Sivins, "How TikTok and 'Knit-Fluencers' Are Making Knitting and Crochet 'Trendy and Cool Again,'" *Big Issue*, January 18, 2024, https://www.bigissue.com/life/tiktok-knitting-crochet-gen-z-fashion.

16. Daniel A. Cox, "Generation Z and the Future of Faith in America," Survey Center on American Life, March 24, 2022, https://www.americansurveycenter.org/research/generation-z-future-of-faith.

17. Cone Communications, "Gen Z Sees Social Media Activity as More Effective Than Community Involvement According to New Research by Cone Communications," PR Newswire, September 13, 2017, https://www.prnewswire.com/news-releases/gen-z-sees-social-media-activity-as-more-effective-than-community-involvement-according-to-new-research-by-cone-communications-300518245.html; and Sarah D. Sparks, "Volunteerism Declined Among Young People," *Education Week*, July 17, 2018, https://www.edweek.org/leadership/volunteerism-declined-among-young-people/2018/07.

18. Sam Stone, "The 'Loneliest Generation' Is Transforming the Dinner Party," *Bon Appétit*, June 10, 2024, https://www.bonappetit.com/story/gen-z-dinner-party-boom.

19. Sophie Thompson, "I Tried TikTok's 'Dopamine Detox' to Kick My Social Media Obsession," Indy100, December 24, 2023, https://www.indy100.com/tiktok/dopamine-detox-mental-health-review.

20. Billy Perrigo, "This App Could Fix Your Social Media Addiction," *Time*, December 14, 2022, https://time.com/6240981/social-media-addiction-app; Shalene Gupta, "Meet the Gen Z Founder Who Wants to Save You from a Life of Smartphone Distraction," *Fast Company*, July 13, 2023, https://www.fastcompany.com/90921176/gen-z-founder-interview-tj-driver-brick-app-blocking-device; and Sophia Rascoff, "Battling Gen-Z's Social Media Problem, One App at a Time," *Forbes*, June 9, 2022, https://www.forbes.com/councils/forbesbusinesscouncil/2022/06/09/battling-gen-zs-social-media-problem-one-app-at-a-time.

21. Log Off Movement, "About Us," https://www.logoffmovement.org/about; and Emma Lembke, testimony before the Senate Committee on the Judiciary, February 14, 2023, https://www.c-span.org/video/?c5058357/emma-lembke-logoff-movement-founder.

22. Barbara Ortutay, "What to Know About the Kids Online Safety Act That Just Passed the Senate," Associated Press, July 31, 2024, https://apnews.com/

article/congress-social-media-kosa-kids-online-safety-act-parents-ead646422cf84cef0d0573c3c841eb6d.

23. Arianna Prothero, Lauraine Langreo, and Alyson Klein, "Which States Ban or Restrict Cellphones in Schools?," *Education Week*, September 24, 2024, https://www.edweek.org/technology/which-states-ban-or-restrict-cellphones-in-schools/2024/06; and Nirmita Panchal and Sasha Zitter, "A Look at State Efforts to Ban Cellphones in Schools and Implications for Youth Mental Health," KFF, accessed October 8, 2024, https://www.kff.org/mental-health/issue-brief/a-look-at-state-efforts-to-ban-cellphones-in-schools-and-implications-for-youth-mental-health.

24. US Department of Education, Institute of Education Sciences, National Center for Education Statistics, "Bullying," https://nces.ed.gov/fastfacts/display.asp?id=719.

12

Conclusion

SALLY SATEL AND NAOMI SCHAEFER RILEY

In the spring of 2024, amid the drafting and revisions process for *Mind the Children*, two major books were published, both with a strong bearing on the debate over youth mental health.

Journalist Abigail Shrier published *Bad Therapy: Why the Kids Aren't Growing Up*, a book premised on the idea that the therapeutic culture has heavily contributed to, perhaps even created, the youth mental health crisis. Relentless focus on children's feelings by parents, schools, and poorly qualified therapists has made things worse, Shrier contends.[1]

Next came Jonathan Haidt's *The Anxious Generation: How the Great Rewiring of Childhood Is Causing an Epidemic of Mental Illness*. A deep examination of the relationship between smartphones and teen mental health led Haidt to conclude that 10–15 percent of the variation in teens' well-being can be traced to the 2010 introduction of Instagram and the front-facing (selfie-enabling) phone camera.[2] He urges tech companies and Congress to make it harder for kids to access these platforms, particularly before age 16.

Both books were bestsellers, a barometer of avid public concern surrounding the well-being of American teens.

Though Shrier and Haidt acknowledge the complex nature of the causal picture, each, nonetheless, strongly emphasizes a specific aspect of it. In contrast, *Mind the Children* explores a suite of determinants and their collective impact on youth mental health. We cover a range of influences on American childhood—from eroded trust in institutions, such as marriage and parenthood, to the waning power and uniformity of cultural scripts that serve as guides for maturity, such as the benefits of organized religion, especially for kids.

In their place, other scripts have emerged. One presumes that young people are fragile, a state brought on, in part, by alarmism. The idea of the endangered child has given rise to a cult and culture of overprotection and restrictive parenting. Schools and the media, for example, are prominent conduits of disillusionment, reminding young people that they were born into a world that is overheating and overpopulated and that America is racist to its core, founded on documents that were untrue when written, and a country whose democratic principles are threadbare.

Another burgeoning script is that millions of youth are inhabiting a wrong-gendered body and that parents, schools, and professionals need to quickly affirm their perception and seek body modification. Add to this the availability of potent marijuana, which can precipitate psychosis. Meanwhile, the opportunity cost of so much time spent alone on screens—the declines in sleeping, reading, experiencing nature, and socializing face-to-face and in real time—complicates the transition to adulthood.

These myriad influences, we contend, have compromised the psychological immune systems of young people and, having predated the rise of social media, created fertile ground in which the phone-based childhood, as Haidt calls it, could take root. Once it became established, a heavy diet of social media further exacerbated the unhealthy trends that led to its proliferation in the first place.

Yet even as these harmful patterns have taken hold, there are a number of remedies within reach that can help loosen their grip on today's teens and keep those patterns from threatening the next generation. These remedies involve renewing some traditional scripts, creating novel ones, and equipping children with the strategies they need to move confidently in the world.

First, we must allow children to build confidence in their own abilities. Lenore Skenazy and Camilo Ortiz suggest allowing children to do more on their own, through tasks such as running errands for the family or navigating public spaces alone. These simple acts can reduce anxiety and build a child's resilience, self-sufficiency, and willingness to embrace the challenges of life.

Robert Pondiscio speaks to the power of "primal beliefs" in shaping a child's mental health, showing how teachers and parents must begin with the premise that the world is a generally safe and positive place to be. Without this belief, children can lose their confidence when the world inevitably fails to live up to this expectation. Teachers and parents can help by quelling the apocalyptic rhetoric and couching their lessons and conversations with kids in a language of resilience and possibility.

Next, children need basic norms to thrive. Whether it is the loss of faith in humanity's most fundamental institutions—marriage and the family, as Kay Hymowitz notes—or the diminishing rates of religious participation among youth and families, children in modern society increasingly lack opportunities to understand the world and their own identities in the context of a cohesive community. While religion cannot, as Michelle Shain notes, "be prescribed like a pill," the elements of religious practice that encourage mental well-being—such as creating supportive and loving communities, providing avenues for helping others, and helping youth find meaning and purpose in their lives—are valuable assets.

While the threshold for medicalizing normal angst is too low in our culture, millions of children who are suffering would nonetheless benefit from sophisticated professionals. They could address, for example, the task of distinguishing between the effects of marijuana use and underlying psychiatric disturbance, as Ken C. Winters and Holly B. Waldron prescribe, or carefully untangle complaints of gender dysphoria from distress rooted primarily in anxiety, depression, or other conditions, as Leor Sapir recommends. Because these clinical pictures are often difficult to analyze, providers must be knowledgeable and discerning.

Lawrence H. Diller suggests a number of interventions to increase the effectiveness of mental health treatment, including allowing school psychologists and counselors to include parents in treating children at school and limiting harmful insurance company practices, such as requiring wasteful neuropsychological evaluations to fund certain treatments. Paul E. Weigle details the profound effect of limiting screen use on teen mental health. Zach Goldberg shows how a barrage of hyperbolic news—often spread on social media—is especially harmful to some young people.

Finally, the growing deficit of mental health professionals may be offset by training teens to help other teens, as Alice Lloyd Rahn documents. The goal is to leverage kids' resilience and boost their coping skills. Redirecting children whose problems are not clinically significant allows trained mental health professionals to focus their efforts on the children who need them most.

Fortunately, the ground is starting to shift. The number of educated parents who are deeply concerned has reached a critical mass. For better or worse, depending on one's view of state power, federal legislation is beginning to address access to cell phones for those under age 16.[3] In addition, a sizable cohort of teachers have had enough of poor behaviors and constant distractions. Indeed, many young people themselves have realized the harms these devices are doing and have become part of the movement to limit their use.

These attitudes and actions will almost surely serve as a corrective influence on Generation Alpha, born between 2010 and 2024. But for children who matured in the past decade, change may come too late. Even if parents have managed to protect their children from the worst ravages of screens, kids are still surrounded by peers whose gentle parents have stifled any achievement of independence. The 23-year-old Kate Farmer gives us hope for some members of Gen Z, expressing optimism about her generation's ability to change its relationship with the online world. We will learn soon enough if her outlook is vindicated.

Notes

1. Abigail Shrier, *Bad Therapy: Why the Kids Aren't Growing Up* (New York: Sentinel, 2024).

2. Jonathan Haidt, *The Anxious Generation: How the Great Rewiring of Childhood Is Causing an Epidemic of Mental Illness* (New York: Penguin, 2024).

3. Kids Online Safety Act, S. 1409, 118th Cong., 1st. sess. (2023).

About the Authors

Lawrence H. Diller has practiced behavioral-developmental pediatrics in Walnut Creek, California, for 44 years. He is an associate clinical professor in pediatrics at the University of California, San Francisco. He is the author of four books (most recently *Remembering Ritalin: A Doctor and Generation Rx Reflect on Life and Psychiatric Drugs*) and numerous articles for the professional and lay press. His series in HuffPost, The United States of Adderall, was the basis of a Netflix documentary, *Take Your Pills*, in which he appears.

Kate Farmer is a senior undergraduate student at Washington University in St. Louis and a freelance writer and commentator for Young Voices, a PR agency for budding writers under 35. Her writing centers broadly on topics in mental health, Gen Z, and homelessness, and she has appeared in various national publications including *RealClearPolitics*, the *American Spectator*, and the *Washington Examiner*. She is a former intern for AEI President Robert Doar. Following graduation, she will attend Harvard Law School after a gap period.

Zach Goldberg is a research fellow at the Manhattan Institute (MI) who completed a PhD in political science from Georgia State University. His dissertation focused on the "Great Awokening," closely examining the role that the media and collective moral emotions have played in recent shifts in racial liberalism among white Americans. At MI, his work deals with a range of issues, including identity politics, criminal justice, and the sources of American political polarization. Some of Goldberg's previous writing on identity politics in America can be found at Tablet and on his Substack.

Kay Hymowitz is the William E. Simon Fellow at the Manhattan Institute and contributing editor at *City Journal*. She has been researching and writing about changes in the experience of children, adolescents, and families for all of her career and has published widely on those subjects. She is the author of five books, including *Manning Up: How the Rise of Women Has Turned Men into Boys* and *Marriage and Caste in America: Separate and Unequal Families in a Post-Marital Age.*

Camilo Ortiz is an associate professor in the clinical psychology doctoral program at Long Island University Post. He is also a fellow with the Flourishing in Action project at the Archbridge Institute's Human Flourishing Lab. His scholarship focuses on parenting, disruptive behavior problems in children, child anxiety, elimination disorders, and cognitive behavior therapy for child and adult psychiatric disorders. Ortiz is the developer of independence therapy for the treatment of child anxiety. He is a licensed psychologist in New York state and maintains a private psychology practice where he sees adults and children. He received a PhD in clinical psychology from the University of Massachusetts Amherst.

Robert Pondiscio is a senior fellow at the American Enterprise Institute, where he focuses on K–12 education, curricula, teaching, school choice, and charter schooling.

Alice Lloyd Rahn is a therapist and writer. She has worked at the Addiction Institute of Mount Sinai and the *Weekly Standard*. Her writing has appeared in the *New York Times*, the *Washington Post*, and the *Boston Globe*.

Naomi Schaefer Riley is a senior fellow at the American Enterprise Institute, where she focuses on child welfare and foster care issues. Specifically, her work analyzes the role of faith-based, civic, and community organizations in changing the foster care and adoption services landscape.

Leor Sapir is a fellow at the Manhattan Institute for Policy Research, where his work focuses on research and policy related to youth gender transition. Dr. Sapir is a regular contributor to *City Journal*, and his writings have appeared in *The Hill*, *National Review*, and the *Wall Street Journal*'s opinion column. His academic work has been published in the *Archives of Sexual Behavior*. Dr. Sapir received his PhD in political science from Boston

College and completed a postdoctoral fellowship at the Program on Constitutional Government at Harvard University.

Sally Satel is a senior fellow at the American Enterprise Institute; the medical director of a local methadone clinic in Washington, DC; and a lecturer at Yale University School of Medicine. She earned a BS from Cornell University, an MS from the University of Chicago, and an MD from Brown University. After completing her residency in psychiatry at Yale University School of Medicine, she was an assistant professor of psychiatry from 1988 to 1993. From 1993 to 1994, she was a Robert Wood Johnson Foundation Health Policy Fellow with the Senate Labor and Human Resources Committee.

Michelle Shain is director of research at the Jewish Nonprofit Planning and Research Institute and a visiting research scientist at Brandeis University. She conducts applied social research and program evaluation for Jewish nonprofit organizations. Before committing herself to nonprofit work, Dr. Shain conducted academic research at Brandeis University's Cohen Center for Modern Jewish Studies and published extensively on religion, gender, and family formation. She holds a PhD in social policy from Brandeis University, an MA in contemporary Jewry from the Hebrew University of Jerusalem, and a BA in anthropology and Judaic studies from Brandeis University.

Lenore Skenazy is the president of Let Grow, a nonprofit promoting childhood independence. She is also the author of *Free-Range Kids: How Parents and Teachers Can Let Go and Let Grow*, now in its second edition. Before this, she was a *New York Daily News* reporter and columnist. She received a BA from Yale University in American studies.

Holly B. Waldron is a senior scientist at Oregon Research Institute and the director of the Center for Family and Adolescent Research, with adolescent drug-abuse treatment programs in Albuquerque, New Mexico. She has nearly 30 years of experience in clinical work and research with adolescents and their families involving randomized clinical trials evaluating individual and group treatment approaches, including motivational enhancement, cognitive behavioral therapies, and technology-based strategies for adolescent substance abuse and related mental health problems. She is widely published and a frequent speaker and trainer.

Paul E. Weigle is a child and adolescent psychiatrist and associate medical director at Natchaug Hospital of Hartford HealthCare, and he cares for children and teens suffering mental health conditions at the Joshua Center in Mansfield, Connecticut. For over 20 years, he has taught and written extensively on the effects of screen media habits on the mental health of youth. Weigle is a distinguished fellow of the American Academy of Child and Adolescent Psychiatry, having served for 20 years on its Media Committee, including eight years as committee chair. He has also served on the National Scientific Advisory Board of the Institute of Digital Media and Child Development for over a decade.

Ken C. Winters is a senior scientist at Oregon Research Institute in Falcon Heights, Minnesota, and a consultant to the Native Center for Behavioral Health at the University of Iowa. He previously was a professor in the Department of Psychiatry at the University of Minnesota, where he founded and directed the Center for Adolescent Substance Abuse Research for 25 years. He also is the cofounder of Smart Approaches to Marijuana Minnesota, a statewide community public health awareness initiative. His primary research interest is the prevention and treatment of youth substance use and coexisting mental health disorders. He is a widely published author, a frequent trainer and speaker, and a member of several community and professional boards.

Index

AARP Brain Health and Mental
    Well-Being Survey, 61, 62–63,
    64
ABA. *See* Applied behavior analysis
ACEs. *See* Adverse childhood
    experiences
Addiction, 101, 108–10, 123–24,
    179–83
Adelsheim, Steven, 164, 168–69,
    172–73
ADHD. *See* Attention deficit hyper-
    activity disorder
Adolescents
    Adolescent Health Center, 163
    Allcove centers for, 168–69
    in brain imaging, 108–9
    communication with, 178–79
    with depression, 126–27
    dopamine detoxes by, 181
    on drugs, 142n6
    Gen Z as, 82
    health of, 116–18
    mental health of, 25–26, 164, 183
    motivation in, 100–1
    neurology of, 99–100, 121
    play for, 120
    politics of, 88
    with pornography, 122–24
    in postmarital culture, 39–40
    psychology of, 28, 40–41, 187–90
    psychosis in, 103–4
    with religious optimism, 131–34,
        132–33
    screen time and, 116–18, 127
    self-agency for, 69–70
    on social media, 51, 177
    sociopolitical awareness among,
        65
    Stanford Center for Youth
        Mental Health and Wellbeing,
        168
    substance abuse by, 2
    in suburbs, 147–48
    suicide by, 161, 168
    Surgeon General on, 178
    THC for, 100–1
    transgender phenomenon in,
        80–81
    in US, 39–40
    video game use among, 118–21
    vulnerability of, 100–3, 109–11
    wokeness for, 75n50
    youth vulnerability in, 100–3
Adulthood, 164
Adverse childhood experiences
    (ACEs), 17
Aegrescit medendo, 1
Aesthetic perspectives, 10–11
Age-verification laws, 182, 190
Agreeableness, 53, 56, 59–60
Alarmism, 187–88
Allcove centers, 168–69

American Academy of Pediatrics, 82, 89
American Educational Research Association, 14–15
American Families of Faith Project, 132–33
American Trends Panel (Pew Research Center), 55, 56–57, 58
Animal studies, 103
Anti-hierarchy ideology, 58
Anxiety
    in AARP Brain Health and Mental Well-Being Survey, 61, 62–63, 64
    children with, 40
    clinical, 151
    depression and, 6, 23, 71n11, 161–62
    disorders, 135
    eagerness compared to, 10
    without freedom, 149
    independence therapy for, 157
    Prozac for, 32
    psychology of, 149–52
    screening for, 31
    self-harm and, 2
    social, 126–27
    from social media, 55
    stress and, 140
    students with, 17–18, 166–67
The Anxious Generation (Haidt), 33, 187
Applied behavior analysis (ABA), 32
Aristotle, 23
ASD. *See* Autism spectrum disorder
Asher, Jay, 13

Attention deficit hyperactivity disorder (ADHD), 26–29, 32, 78, 126
Attitudinal wokeness. *See* Wokeness
Augustine (saint), 139
Australia, 168
Autism spectrum disorder (ASD), 26–27, 77–78, 83–84
Avoidance, 25–26, 151–52

The Bachelor (TV show), 44
The Bachelorette (TV show), 44
Bad Therapy (Shrier), 187
Balk, Sheila, 166–67
Bara, Anissa, 109
Barry, Herbert, 42
Behavior disorders, 126–27
Big Cannabis, 102
Big Five personality traits, 52–55, 73n35
Big Tobacco, 102
Black Lives Matter, 64
Boredom, 3
Brain imaging, 108–9
Brazil, 106
Brooks, Arthur C., 20

C. S. Mott Children's Hospital, 147–48
Call of Duty (video game), 119, 125
Cannabis
    cannabis use disorder, 100, 104, 107–8, 110
    psychosis and, 99–100, 103–9, 188
    in US, 100–2, 109–11

withdrawal symptoms, 109–10
youth vulnerability with, 102–3
Careers, 40–41
Caregivers, 3, 25
Cass, Hilary, 81, 85, 89–90
Catholic Church, 48n9
CBT. *See* Cognitive behavioral therapy
Cell phones. *See* Smartphones
Centers for Disease Control and Prevention, 16–17, 23, 86, 142n6, 163
Chakrabarti, Meghna, 90
Children. *See specific topics*
Choices, with identity, 3–4
Christianity, 131–34, 132–33, 135, 137–40
See also Religion
Civic education, 14
Clifton, Jeremy, 10–12, 17, 19–20
Climate change, 5, 17–18
Clinical anxiety, 151
Clinicians. *See* Psychology/psychiatry
The Coddling of the American Mind (Haidt and Lukianoff), 15–16
Cognitive behavioral therapy (CBT), 151–52, 170–72, 172
Collins, Suzanne, 13–14
Commager, Henry Steele, 12
Communication, 3, 178–79
Communism, 47
Community, 4, 24–25, 189
Compulsion loops, 118–21
Concerta, 32
Confessions (St. Augustine), 139

Confidentiality, 29
Conscientiousness, 53–54, 56, 58–60, 69
Conservatives
liberals and, 60, 61, 65, 66, 69–70, 88
in US, 100–1
See also Politics
COPE. *See* Creating Opportunities for Personal Empowerment
COVID
for families, 116
mental health in, 18, 23–24
politics during, 111
schools during, 2
screen time during, 115
Creating Opportunities for Personal Empowerment (COPE), 171–72, 172
Critical race theory, 15

Danger, 10, 20
de Blasio, Bill, 166
Denmark, 81, 107–8, 110
Department of Education, New York, 87
Department of Health and Human Services, 81
DePaulo, Bella, 47
Depression
adolescents with, 126–27
anxiety and, 6, 23, 71n11, 161–62
from drugs, 137–38
loneliness and, 57, 57–58
Prozac for, 32
risk of, 39

screening for, 31
suicide and, 2, 11, 62
support for, 122
Di Forti, Marta, 106
Diagnostic and Statistical Manual of Mental Disorders (DSM), 16, 27, 79
Diaz, Angela, 162–64, 166, 170
Dinner Party Project, 181
Disney World, 152
Divorce, 41
  See also Postmarital culture
Doernbecher Children's Hospital, 80
Dollahite, David C., 132–33, 135, 138, 140
Doomscrolling, 58
Dopamine detoxes, 181
Drugs, 2, 137–38, 142n6, 161
  See also Cannabis
DSM. *See Diagnostic and Statistical Manual of Mental Disorders*
Dystopian entertainment, 13–14

Economics
  of health insurance, 5
  in Hollywood, 13–14
  of insurance companies, 36n15
  of mental health, 163–66
  of neuropsychiatric evaluations, 29
  of private schools, 30–31
  socioeconomics, 66
  winner-takes-all, 149
Education
  academic achievement, 125

American Educational Research Association, 14–15
civic, 14
educators, 41
health, 182–83
higher, 140, 169
homework and, 148–49
IDEA, 30, 33
IEPs, 29–30, 33–34
K–12, 9–11, 15–16, 18–20, 87, 152, 165
mainstream, 14
in modernity, 1
NCTE, 14
New York State Department of Education, 87
with parents, 190
Parents Defending Education, 88
philosophy of, 12
in private schools, 30–31
psychoeducational evaluations, 29
special education services, 30
therapeutic, 15–19
in US, 15–16, 178
  See also Schools
Emotional development, 1
Emotional responsiveness, 58
Errands, 152–53
Euphoria (TV show), 45–46
Europe, 48n9, 106–7, 110
Excessive supervision, 147–48, 150–51
Extended family, 43–44
Extroverts, 54–55, 56

INDEX 199

Facebook, 121–22
Families
    COVID for, 116
    extended family, 43–44
    identity in, 90
    marriage for, 42–43
    mental health in, 34–35
    parents and, 31
    in postmarital culture, 44–46
    as sacred, 135
    in US, 4, 39–40
Fastman, Matt, 154
Fear, 20, 25–26, 118
Feminism, 86–87
50 Shades of Grey (film), 45–46
Finland, 81, 83
FOMO, 118
Fortnite (video game), 119
Free-Range Kids movement, 149–50
Freud, Sigmund, 131
From Paralysis to Fatigue (Shorter), 85
Furedi, Frank, 24–25
Future of Dating 2023 report, 46

Gallup surveys, 177
Gang violence, 167
Gap, Darién, 46
Gen Z
    as adolescents, 82
    as adults, 79
    men, 45–46
    Millennials and, 44–45
    psychology of, 177–83, 190
    puberty for, 84–85
    reputation of, 43–44
Gender
    binary, 26
    dysphoria, 78–81, 83–85, 90
    Gender Identity Development Service, 79–80, 83
    gender-affirming care, 77–82, 89–90
    ideology, 18
    for insurance companies, 82
    interventions, 89
    minority stress and, 83–85
    of parents, 31–32
    pediatric gender clinics, 80
    personality traits and, 59–61, 61–63, 64
    in schools, 87–90
    sex and, 3
    sexting and, 124
    on TikTok, 46
    tomboys, 86–87
    transgender phenomenon, 79–83, 89–90
    in US, 47, 77–78, 83, 85–87, 91
    Xenogenders, 77
Generation Alpha, 178, 190
Genital surgery, 80–81
Gentile, Emilio, 140
Girls NYC, 181
Go Ask Alice (Sparks), 13
Grand Theft Auto (video game), 125
Gray, Peter, 150
Great Recession, 132
Greek philosophy, 23
Gurri, Martin, 42–43

Haidt, Jonathan, 15–17, 33, 84, 187–88
Happiness
  of children, 2–3
  memory and, 31–34
  mental health and, 27–29
  in philosophy, 23–24
  psychology of, 29–31
  tyranny of, 24–27, 32–35
Harris Poll, 44
The Hate U Give (Thomas), 13
Hazel, Cameka, 165–66
Headspace program, 168
Health care, 169–70
  See also specific topics
Health education, 182–83
Health insurance, 5
  See also Insurance companies
Helicopter parents, 5–6
Henderson, Rob, 43
Higher education, 140, 169
Hinton, S. E., 13
Hollywood, 13–14
Homework, 148–49
Homosexual men, 48n9
Hopelessness, 163
Human anthropology, 41–43
Human biology, 42
The Hunger Games series (Collins), 13–14
Hyperbolic news
  ideology from, 59–61, 61–63, 64
  mental health with, 64, 65, 66, 67–68, 69–70
  psychology of, 55, 56–57, 57–58
  in US, 51–55, 70

IDEA. *See* Individuals with Disabilities Education Act
Identity
  choices with, 3–4
  in families, 90
  Gender Identity Development Service, 79–80, 83
  psychology of, 91
  self-identity, 25
  in transgender phenomenon, 89–90
  See also Gender
Ideology
  anti-hierarchy, 58
  in feminism, 86–87
  from hyperbolic news, 59–61, 61–63, 64
  politics and, 47, 59
  sex and, 60, 61, 65
  of wokeness, 64, 65, 66, 67–68, 69–70
IEPs. *See* Individualized Educational Programs
Independence
  in Let Grow Experience, 152–53
  maturity with, 156–57
  mental health with, 149–52, 187–90
  with over-parenting, 148–49
  psychology of, 6
  safety and, 147–48
  therapy, 153–57
Individualized Educational Programs (IEPs), 29–30, 33–34
Individuals with Disabilities Education Act (IDEA), 30, 33

Infants, 44–45
Innovation Group, 179
In-person socialization, 181, 188
Instagram, 39, 187
Insurance companies
　children for, 26–27
　economics of, 36n15
　gender for, 82
　mental health professionals and, 32–33
　policies of, 34
Intellect, 53, 56, 59
Internet access, 1, 122–24
　See also specific topics
Interventions
　with parents, 154
　school-based mental health, 167–68
　in schools, 33–34
Intimacy, 46
Introverts, 54–55
Islam, 133, 139–40

James, William, 131–32
Johnson, John, 59
Judaism, 133–34, 135, 140
Julian, Kate, 46
Justice sensitivity, 52–53, 59–60, 71n11

K–12 education, 9–11, 15–16, 18–20, 87, 152, 165
Kaiser Family Foundation, 59–60
Kaiser Permanente, 16–17
Kajonius, Petri, 59
Katz, Roberta, 178

Kaufmann, Eric, 87–88
Kids. *See specific topics*
Kids Online Safety Act, 182

The Last Normal Child (Diller), 27–28
Learning
　about climate change, 5
　disabilities, 5
　psychology of, 1
　SEL, 11–12, 16, 18–19
　by students, 4–5
Lembke, Emma, 181–82
Lemov, Doug, 1
Let Grow Experience, 149–50, 152–53, 156–57
Liberals, 60, 61, 65, 66, 69–70, 88
　See also Politics
Liminal space, 42–43
Littman, Lisa, 84
Log Off Movement, 181–82
Loneliness, 57, 57–58, 136, 137
Lukianoff, Greg, 15–17

Mainstream education, 14
Marconi, Arianna, 105–6
Marks, Loren D., 132–33, 135, 138, 140
Marriage
　for families, 42–43
　for Gen Z, 43–44
　parents and, 40–41
　in US, 41–43
　See also Postmarital culture
Mary Bridge Children's Hospital, 80

Massachusetts Child Psychiatry
    Access Program, 169–70
Maturity, 156–57, 187
McGuffy reader, 12–13
Medicaid, 163–64
Medical practitioners, 34
Medication
    for ADHD, 32
    limitations of, 31
    psychiatric drugs, 28
    rates, 26–27
Meindl, Peter, 11–12
Melnyk, Bernadette Mazurek,
    170–73, 172
Memory, 31–34
Mental health
    ADHD and, 126
    of adolescents, 25–26, 164, 183
    behavior disorders from, 126–27
    in COVID, 18, 23–24
    data on, 179
    disorders, 134
    economics of, 163–66
    in families, 34–35
    with gender-affirming care,
        78–82
    happiness and, 27–29
    in higher education, 169
    with hyperbolic news, 64, 65, 66,
        67–68, 69–70
    with independence, 149–52,
        187–90
    after independence therapy,
        153–57
    industry, 28–29
    mental illness, 135
    of parents, 4
    peer-to-provider pipeline for,
        166–69
    personality traits and, 52–55
    politics and, 75n50
    primal world beliefs and, 19,
        188–89
    professionals, 5–6, 32–33
    providers, 161–62, 169–73, 172,
        189
    psychology and, 31–34
    public health and, 17
    reading and, 12–15
    reform with, 169–70
    school-based mental health
        interventions, 167–68
    in schools, 9, 29–31
    screen time and, 2–3, 177–78
    sleep for, 117–18
    social media and, 5, 55, 56–57,
        57–58, 74n37
    sources of, 27
    Stanford Center for Youth Mental
        Health and Wellbeing, 168
    Substance Abuse and Mental
        Health Services Administration, 161
    Surgeon General on, 183
    with THC, 100
    treatment, 31–32
    in US, 2, 141
    in YA literature, 12–15
    youth health, 116–18
Millennials
    in higher education, 140
    reputation of, 44–45

surveys with, 131–37, 132–33, 136–37, 141
Minecraft (video game), 120
Minority stress, 78, 83–85
Money, for children, 153
Moore, Theresa H. M., 105–6
Moral outrage, 51–52
Motivation
    in adolescents, 100–1
    psychology of, 27–28
    with video games, 118–19
MultiCare health system, 77–78
multiple-baseline designed experiments, 154
Murthy, Vivek, 84, 178

National Academy of Sciences, 102
National Council of Teachers of English (NCTE), 14
National Health Service (England), 81, 85
National Institute on Drug Abuse, 102
National Study of Youth, 132, 132–33
NCTE. *See* National Council of Teachers of English
Neo-Marxism, 14
Netherlands, 91
Neurology
    of adolescents, 99–100, 121
    brain imaging, 108–9
    neuropsychiatric evaluations, 29
Neuroticism, 52, 56, 59–60
New Zealand, 102
Nonreligious organizations, 138

Obesity, 117
The Odyssey (Homer), 127
1-2-3 Magic (parenting manual), 33
Online habits, 115–18, 126
    See also Screen time
Online social skills, 119
Openness, 53, 56, 59–60
The Outsiders (Hinton), 13
Over-parenting, 148–49

Pac Man (video game), 118
Parents
    caregivers and, 3, 25
    education with, 190
    excessive supervision by, 147–48, 150–51
    families and, 31
    gender of, 31–32
    helicopter, 5–6
    of infants, 44–45
    interventions with, 154
    marriage and, 40–41
    mental health of, 4
    over-parenting, 148–49
    parenting, 26, 33
    Parents Defending Education, 88
    pessimism in, 20
    in postmarital culture, 41–43
    schools and, 157, 187–88
    screen time monitoring by, 124–27
    students and, 30
    in surveys, 147–48
    teachers and, 19, 32–33, 152, 188–89

204 MIND THE CHILDREN

transgender phenomenon for, 79
trust in, 9
unhappy, 24
in US, 6
video game monitoring by, 121, 126
PARF. *See* Population attributable risk fraction
Parodi, Katharine, 150
Pedagogy, 12, 16
Pediatric gender clinics, 80
Pediatricians, 170
Peer-to-provider pipeline, 166–69
The Perks of Being a Wallflower (Chbosky), 13
Personality traits
    gender and, 59–61, 61–63, 64
    mental health and, 52–55
    social media and, 73n35
Pessimism, 20
Pew Research Center, 55, 56–57, 58, 73n35, 101, 137–38
Philosophy
    of Clifton, 19–20
    of education, 12
    of emotional resilience, 15–16, 19
    Greek, 23
    happiness in, 23–24
Pietzke, Tamara, 77–78
Play, 120
Policymakers, 32–34, 111
Politics
    of adolescents, 88
    of age-verification laws, 190
    climate change in, 17–18
    during COVID, 111

ideology and, 47, 59
mental health and, 75n50
neo-Marxism, 14
racial, 11, 15
religiosity in, 66, 68, 69–70
sacralization of, 140
social media in, 181–82
sociopolitical awareness, 65
in US, 60, 61
of wokeness, 64, 65, 66, 67–68, 69–70
Polycules, 47
Polygamy, 41–42
Population attributable risk fraction (PARF), 108
Pornography, 122–24
Postmarital culture
    adolescents in, 39–40
    families in, 44–46
    Gen Z in, 43–44
    parents in, 41–43
    in US, 46–47
Post-traumatic stress disorder, 25
Poverty, 11, 24
Primal world beliefs
    mental health and, 19, 188–89
    research on, 10–12
    in schools, 18–20
Private schools, 30–31
Prozac, 32
Psychology/psychiatry
    after ACEs, 17
    of addiction, 101, 108–10, 123–24
    of adolescents, 28, 40–41, 187–90
    from aesthetic perspectives, 10–11

of anxiety, 149–52
after avoidance, 151–52
of boredom, 3
of compulsion loops, 120–21
conscientiousness, 53–54
of danger, 10
in DSM, 16
of Gen Z, 177–83, 190
gender dysphoria, 78–81, 83–85, 90
of happiness, 29–31
human anthropology and, 41–43
human biology and, 42
of hyperbolic news, 55, 56–57, 57–58
of identity, 91
of independence, 6
intimacy, 46
of Islam, 133
of justice sensitivity, 52–53, 71n11
of learning, 1
Massachusetts Child Psychiatry Access Program, 169–70
mental health and, 31–34
of motivation, 27–28
neuroticism, 52
psychiatric drugs, 28
psychoeducational evaluations, 29
psychological flexibility, 155–56
psychologists, 5
psychosis, 99–100, 103–9, 188
psychotherapy, 36n15
of religion, 138–41, 141
of religious belief, 135–38, 136–37
of religious optimism, 131

of resilience, 150, 189
from SEL, 11–12
sex in, 89–90
with social media, 59–61, 61–63, 64, 74n38, 121–22
of social skills, 117, 127
of tomboys, 86–87
of unmarried couples, 47
for young doctors, 162–66
Puberty, 80, 84–85, 102
Public health, 17

Racial politics, 11, 15
Racial wokeness. *See* Wokeness
Rafferty, Jason, 82
Reading, 12–15
Real-world problems, 9
Religion
  of Catholic Church, 48n9
  community and, 4, 24–25, 189
  psychology of, 138–41, 141
  religiosity, 66, 68, 69–70
  religious belief, 135–38, 136–37
  religious optimism, 131–34, 132–33
Resilience, 15–16, 19, 150, 189
Rhetoric (Aristotle), 23
Romantic relationships, 123–24
Romney, Mitt, 169

Sadness, 163
Safe world beliefs, 11–12
Safety, 147–48
Salerno, Steve, 15
Schools
  counseling in, 165–67

during COVID, 2
gender in, 87–90
homework in, 148–49
in IDEA, 30
interventions in, 33–34
Let Grow Experience in, 156–57
meetings at, 29–30
mental health in, 9, 29–31
NCTE, 14
parents and, 157, 187–88
policymakers in, 32–34
primal world beliefs in, 18–20
private, 30–31
psychoeducational evaluations in, 29
school shootings, 17–18
school-based mental health interventions, 167–68
SEL in, 18–19
self-identity in, 25
smartphones in, 1
social justice in, 14
social media literacy in, 182–83
therapeutic education in, 19
trauma-informed practices in, 16–17
in United Kingdom, 178
in US, 4–5
See also Education
Screen time
adolescents and, 116–18, 127
during COVID, 115
mental health and, 2–3, 177–78
monitoring, 124–27
sexually explicit content and, 122–24

SEL. *See* Social and emotional learning
Selective exposure, 58
Selective serotonin reuptake inhibitors (SSRIs), 32
Self-agency, 69–70
Self-esteem, 155–56
Self-harm, 2, 72n11
Self-identity, 25
Sex, biological
at birth, 85–88
gender and, 3
ideology and, 60, 61, 65
in psychology, 89–90
stereotypes, 86–87
in US, 64, 65, 66, 67–68, 69
Sex recession, 45–46
Sexting, 124
Sexual abuse, 77
Sexual assault, 123
Sexual minorities, 42
Sexual trauma, 78
sexually explicit content, 122–24
Shorter, Edward, 85
Shrier, Abigail, 187
Single at Heart (DePaulo), 47
"Singles in America" survey, 44
Sleep, 117–18
Small Talk, 181
Smartphones
dependence on, 178
rebellion against, 180
in schools, 1
social media and, 161, 187–90
Social and emotional learning (SEL), 11–12, 16, 18–19

Social anxiety, 126–27
Social justice, 14–15
Social media
　addiction to, 179
　adolescents on, 51, 177
　anxiety from, 55
　children on, 39–40
　Lemov on, 1
　literacy, 182–83
　mental health and, 5, 55, 56–57, 57–58, 74n37
　moral outrage on, 51–52
　personality traits and, 73n35
　in politics, 181–82
　psychology with, 59–61, 61–63, 64, 74n38, 121–22
　smartphones and, 161, 187–90
　suicide and, 177–78
　video games and, 3, 116–18, 124–25
　See also specific social media
Social networks, 137
Social Psychiatry and Psychiatric Epidemiology (Parodi), 150
Social skills
　for communication, 3
　online, 119
　psychology of, 117, 127
　romantic relationships and, 123–24
　socialization, 181, 188
Socioeconomics, 66
Sociopolitical awareness, 65
Sonic the Hedgehog (video game), 120
Sparks, Beatrice, 13

Special education services, 30
SSRIs. *See* Selective serotonin reuptake inhibitors
Stanford Center for Youth Mental Health and Wellbeing, 168
Stoller, Robert, 85–86
Stranger Things (TV show), 147
Stress
　anxiety and, 140
　of children, 16–17
　minority, 83–85
　in US, 161–62
Students
　with anxiety, 17–18, 166–67
　counseling for, 165–66
　learning by, 4–5
　parents and, 30
　teachers and, 18
　world view of, 12
Substance Abuse and Mental Health Services Administration, 161
Suburbs, adolescents in, 147–48
Suicide
　by adolescents, 161, 168
　Centers for Disease Control and Prevention on, 163
　depression and, 2, 11, 62
　mental health professionals shortage and, 162
　plans, 23
　rates, 83–84
　social media and, 177–78
Surgeon General, 178, 183
Sweden, 81
Switzerland, 102

Teachers
    NCTE, 14
    parents and, 19, 32–33, 152, 188–89
    pedagogy of, 12
    students and, 18
    in United Kingdom, 86
    in US, 87
Technology addiction, 179–83
THC. *See* Cannabis
Therapeutic education, 15–19
Therapists. *See* Psychology/psychiatry
Therapy Culture (Furedi), 24–25
Thirteen Reasons Why (Asher), 13
Thomas, Angie, 13
TikTok, 39, 45, 46, 177, 180
Tinder, 46
Title IX, 90
Tomboys, 86–87
Transgender phenomenon, 79–83, 89–90
See also Gender
Trauma, 11, 16–17, 25
Trump, Donald, 18
Trust, 9, 46
Twenge, Jean, 45, 177, 183
Twitter. *See* X
Tyranny, of happiness, 24–27, 32–35

Unhappy parents, 24
United Kingdom, 81, 83, 85–86, 178
United States (US)
    adolescents in, 39–40
        American Academy of Pediatrics, 82, 89

American Trends Panel, 55, 56–57, 58
cannabis in, 100–2, 109–11
careers in, 40–41
Centers for Disease Control and Prevention, 16–17
Christianity in, 131–34, 132–33
conservatives in, 100–1
culture, 24–25, 101–2
Department of Health and Human Services, 81
DSM in, 16
dystopian entertainment in, 13–14
education in, 15–16, 178
Europe and, 110
families in, 4, 39–40
Gallup surveys in, 177
gender in, 47, 77–78, 83, 85–87, 91
Great Recession, 132
health care reform in, 169–70
hyperbolic news in, 51–55, 70
IDEA in, 30, 33
K–12 education in, 18–20
Kids Online Safety Act, 182
marriage in, 41–43
Medicaid, 163–64
medication rates in, 26–27
mental health in, 2, 141
mental health providers in, 169–73, 172
parents in, 6
pediatric gender clinics in, 80
personality datasets, 59
policymakers in, 111
politics in, 60, 61
polls in, 44

postmarital culture in, 46–47
racial politics in, 11
schools in, 4–5
sex in, 64, 65, 66, 67–68, 69
"Singles in America" survey, 44
society, 15
stress in, 161–62
Substance Abuse and Mental Health Services Administration, 161
suicide rates in, 83–84
Surgeon General, 178, 183
teachers in, 87
technology addiction in, 179–83
Title IX in, 90
transgender phenomenon in, 82–83
unmarried cohabitation in, 43
volunteerism in, 138
Unmarried cohabitation, 43
Unmarried couples, 47
Unmarried women, 48n9
Urban environments, 106–7
US. *See* United States

Video games
online habits with, 115, 126
social media and, 3, 116–18, 124–25
video game compulsion loop, 118–21

Violence
gang, 167
poverty and, 24
sexual assault, 123
Volunteerism, 138, 181

Weddings, 42
Wilks, Isaac, 39
Wilson, E. O., 47
Winner-takes-all economics, 149
Withdrawal symptoms, 109–10
Wokeness, 64, 65, 66, 67–68, 69–70, 75n50
Wood, Peter, 14
World Professional Association for Transgender Health (WPATH), 81, 85
Wright, Colin, 86

X, 64
Xenogenders, 77

YA literature. *See* Young Adult literature
Yancey, George, 69
Young Adult (YA) literature, 12–15
Young doctors, 162–66
Youth. *See* Adolescents
YouTube, 125, 177

Zoomers. *See* Gen Z

The American Enterprise Institute for Public Policy Research

AEI is a nonpartisan, nonprofit research and educational organization. The work of our scholars and staff advances ideas rooted in our commitment to expanding individual liberty, increasing opportunity, and strengthening freedom.

The Institute engages in research; publishes books, papers, studies, and short-form commentary; and conducts seminars and conferences. AEI's research activities are carried out under four major departments: Domestic Policy Studies, Economic Policy Studies, Foreign and Defense Policy Studies, and Social, Cultural, and Constitutional Studies. The resident scholars and fellows listed in these pages are part of a network that also includes nonresident scholars at top universities.

The views expressed in AEI publications are those of the authors; AEI does not take institutional positions on any issues.

BOARD OF TRUSTEES

DANIEL A. D'ANIELLO, *Chairman*
Cofounder and Chairman Emeritus
The Carlyle Group

CLIFFORD S. ASNESS
Managing and Founding Principal
AQR Capital Management LLC

PETER H. COORS
Chairman of the Board
Molson Coors Brewing Company

HARLAN CROW
Chairman
Crow Holdings

RAVENEL B. CURRY III
Chief Investment Officer
Eagle Capital Management LLC

KIMBERLY O. DENNIS
President and CEO
Searle Freedom Trust

DICK DEVOS
President
The Windquest Group

ROBERT DOAR
President
American Enterprise Institute

BEHDAD EGHBALI
Managing Partner and Cofounder
Clearlake Capital Group LP

MARTIN C. ELTRICH III
Partner
AEA Investors LP

TULLY M. FRIEDMAN
Managing Director, Retired
FFL Partners LLC

CHRISTOPHER B. GALVIN
Chairman
Harrison Street Capital LLC

HARVEY GOLUB
Chairman and CEO, Retired
American Express Company
Chairman, Miller Buckfire

FRANK J. HANNA
CEO
Hanna Capital LLC

JOHN K. HURLEY
Founder and Managing Partner
Cavalry Asset Management

DEEPA JAVERI
Chief Financial Officer
XRHealth

JOANNA F. JONSSON
Vice Chair, Capital Group
President, Capital Research
  Management Company

MARC S. LIPSCHULTZ
Co-CEO
Blue Owl Capital

JOHN A. LUKE JR.
Chairman
WestRock Company

DREW MCKNIGHT
Co-CEO and Managing Partner
Fortress Investment Group

BOB MURLEY
Senior Adviser
UBS

PAT NEAL
Chairman of the Executive Committee
Neal Communities

ROSS PEROT JR.
Chairman
Hillwood Development Company

GEOFFREY S. REHNERT
Co-CEO
Audax Group

MATTHEW K. ROSE
Retired CEO/Chairman
BNSF Railway

EDWARD B. RUST JR.
Chairman Emeritus
State Farm Insurance Companies

WILSON H. TAYLOR
Chairman Emeritus
Cigna Corporation

WILLIAM H. WALTON
Managing Member
Rockpoint Group LLC

WILL WEATHERFORD
Managing Partner
Weatherford Capital

EMERITUS TRUSTEES

THE HONORABLE
RICHARD B. CHENEY

JOHN FARACI

ROBERT F. GREENHILL

BRUCE KOVNER

KEVIN B. ROLLINS

D. GIDEON SEARLE

OFFICERS

ROBERT DOAR
President

JASON BERTSCH
Executive Vice President

JOHN CUSEY
Senior Vice President for
External Relations

KAZUKI KO
Vice President;
Chief Financial Officer

KATHERYNE WALKER
Vice President of Operations;
Chief Human Resources Officer

MATTHEW CONTINETTI
Senior Fellow; Director, Domestic
Policy Studies; Patrick and Charlene
Neal Chair in American Prosperity

YUVAL LEVIN
Senior Fellow; Director, Social,
Cultural, and Constitutional Studies;
Beth and Ravenel Curry Chair in Public
Policy; Editor in Chief, National Affairs

KORI SCHAKE
Senior Fellow; Director, Foreign and
Defense Policy Studies

MICHAEL R. STRAIN
Senior Fellow; Director, Economic
Policy Studies; Arthur F. Burns Scholar
in Political Economy

RESEARCH STAFF

SAMUEL J. ABRAMS
Nonresident Senior Fellow

BETH AKERS
Senior Fellow

J. JOEL ALICEA
Nonresident Fellow

JOSEPH ANTOS
Senior Fellow Emeritus

LEON ARON
Senior Fellow

KIRSTEN AXELSEN
Nonresident Fellow

JOHN BAILEY
Nonresident Senior Fellow

KYLE BALZER
Jeane Kirkpatrick Fellow

CLAUDE BARFIELD
Senior Fellow

MICHAEL BARONE
Senior Fellow Emeritus

MICHAEL BECKLEY
Nonresident Senior Fellow

ERIC J. BELASCO
Nonresident Senior Fellow

ANDREW G. BIGGS
Senior Fellow

MASON M. BISHOP
Nonresident Fellow

DAN BLUMENTHAL
Senior Fellow

KARLYN BOWMAN
Distinguished Senior Fellow Emeritus

HAL BRANDS
Senior Fellow

ALEX BRILL
Senior Fellow

ARTHUR C. BROOKS
President Emeritus

RICHARD BURKHAUSER
Nonresident Senior Fellow

CLAY CALVERT
Nonresident Senior Fellow

JAMES C. CAPRETTA
Senior Fellow; Milton Friedman Chair

TIMOTHY P. CARNEY
Senior Fellow

AMITABH CHANDRA
Nonresident Senior Fellow

LYNNE V. CHENEY
Distinguished Senior Fellow

YVONNE CHIU
Jeane Kirkpatrick Fellow

JAMES W. COLEMAN
Nonresident Senior Fellow

PRESTON COOPER
Senior Fellow

ZACK COOPER
Senior Fellow

KEVIN CORINTH
Senior Fellow; Deputy Director, Center on Opportunity and Social Mobility

JAY COST
Gerald R. Ford Nonresident Senior Fellow

DANIEL A. COX
Senior Fellow; Director, Survey Center on American Life

SADANAND DHUME
Senior Fellow

GISELLE DONNELLY
Senior Fellow

ROSS DOUTHAT
Nonresident Fellow

LAURA DOVE
Nonresident Fellow

COLIN DUECK
Nonresident Senior Fellow

MACKENZIE EAGLEN
Senior Fellow

NICHOLAS EBERSTADT
Henry Wendt Chair in Political Economy

JEFFREY EISENACH
Nonresident Senior Fellow

CHRISTINE EMBA
Senior Fellow

ANDREW FERGUSON
Nonresident Fellow

JESÚS FERNÁNDEZ-VILLAVERDE
John H. Makin Visiting Scholar

JOHN G. FERRARI
Nonresident Senior Fellow

JOHN C. FORTIER
Senior Fellow

AARON FRIEDBERG
Nonresident Senior Fellow

JOSEPH B. FULLER
Nonresident Senior Fellow

SCOTT GANZ
Research Fellow

R. RICHARD GEDDES
Nonresident Senior Fellow

ROBERT P. GEORGE
Nonresident Senior Fellow

EDWARD L. GLAESER
Nonresident Senior Fellow

JOSEPH W. GLAUBER
Nonresident Senior Fellow

JONAH GOLDBERG
Senior Fellow; Asness Chair in Applied Liberty

JACK LANDMAN GOLDSMITH
Nonresident Senior Fellow

BARRY K. GOODWIN
Nonresident Senior Fellow

SCOTT GOTTLIEB, MD
Senior Fellow

PHIL GRAMM
Nonresident Senior Fellow

WILLIAM C. GREENWALT
Senior Fellow

ALLEN GUELZO
Nonresident Senior Fellow

PHILIP HAMBURGER
Nonresident Senior Fellow

JIM HARPER
Nonresident Senior Fellow

TODD HARRISON
Senior Fellow

WILLIAM HAUN
Nonresident Fellow

FREDERICK M. HESS
Senior Fellow; Director, Education Policy Studies

CAROLE HOOVEN
Nonresident Senior Fellow

BRONWYN HOWELL
Nonresident Senior Fellow

R. GLENN HUBBARD
Nonresident Senior Fellow

HOWARD HUSOCK
Senior Fellow

DAVID HYMAN
Nonresident Senior Fellow

BENEDIC N. IPPOLITO
Senior Fellow

MARK JAMISON
Nonresident Senior Fellow

FREDERICK W. KAGAN
Senior Fellow; Director, Critical Threats Project

STEVEN B. KAMIN
Senior Fellow

LEON R. KASS, MD
Senior Fellow Emeritus

JOSHUA T. KATZ
Senior Fellow

L. LYNNE KIESLING
Nonresident Senior Fellow

KLON KITCHEN
Nonresident Senior Fellow

KEVIN R. KOSAR
Senior Fellow

ROBERT KULICK
Visiting Fellow

PAUL H. KUPIEC
Senior Fellow

DESMOND LACHMAN
Senior Fellow

PAUL LETTOW
Senior Fellow

DANIEL LYONS
Nonresident Senior Fellow

NAT MALKUS
Senior Fellow; Deputy Director, Education Policy Studies

JOHN D. MAURER
Nonresident Fellow

ELAINE MCCUSKER
Senior Fellow

BRUCE D. MEYER
Nonresident Senior Fellow

BRIAN J. MILLER
Nonresident Fellow

CHRIS MILLER
Nonresident Senior Fellow

THOMAS P. MILLER
Senior Fellow

M. ANTHONY MILLS
Senior Fellow; Director, Center for Technology, Science, and Energy

FERDINANDO MONTE
Nonresident Senior Fellow

CHARLES MURRAY
F. A. Hayek Chair Emeritus in Cultural Studies

STEPHEN D. OLINER
Senior Fellow Emeritus

BRENT ORRELL
Senior Fellow

TOBIAS PETER
Senior Fellow; Codirector, AEI Housing Center

JAMES PETHOKOUKIS
Senior Fellow; Editor, AEIdeas Blog; DeWitt Wallace Chair

ROGER PIELKE JR.
Senior Fellow

EDWARD J. PINTO
Senior Fellow; Codirector, AEI Housing Center

DANIELLE PLETKA
Distinguished Senior Fellow

KENNETH M. POLLACK
Senior Fellow

KYLE POMERLEAU
Senior Fellow

ROBERT PONDISCIO
Senior Fellow

RAMESH PONNURU
Nonresident Senior Fellow

ROB PORTMAN
Distinguished Visiting Fellow in the Practice of Public Policy

ANGELA RACHIDI
Senior Fellow; Rowe Scholar

NAOMI SCHAEFER RILEY
Senior Fellow

WILL RINEHART
Senior Fellow

DALIBOR ROHAC
Senior Fellow

CHRISTINE ROSEN
Senior Fellow

JEFFREY A. ROSEN
Nonresident Fellow

MICHAEL ROSEN
Nonresident Senior Fellow

IAN ROWE
Senior Fellow

MICHAEL RUBIN
Senior Fellow

PAUL RYAN
Distinguished Visiting Fellow in the Practice of Public Policy

SALLY SATEL, MD
Senior Fellow

ERIC SAYERS
Nonresident Fellow

CHRISTOPHER J. SCALIA
Senior Fellow

BRETT D. SCHAEFER
Senior Fellow

DIANA SCHAUB
Nonresident Senior Fellow

ANNA SCHERBINA
Nonresident Senior Fellow

GARY J. SCHMITT
Senior Fellow

MARK SCHNEIDER
Nonresident Senior Fellow

DEREK SCISSORS
Senior Fellow

NEENA SHENAI
Nonresident Fellow

DAN SLATER
Nonresident Fellow

SITA NATARAJ SLAVOV
Nonresident Senior Fellow

THOMAS SMITH
Nonresident Fellow

VINCENT H. SMITH
Nonresident Senior Fellow

CHRISTINA HOFF SOMMERS
Senior Fellow Emeritus

DANIEL STID
Nonresident Senior Fellow

CHRIS STIREWALT
Senior Fellow

BENJAMIN STOREY
Senior Fellow

JENNA SILBER STOREY
Senior Fellow

RUY TEIXEIRA
Nonresident Senior Fellow

SHANE TEWS
Nonresident Senior Fellow

MARC A. THIESSEN
Senior Fellow

JOSEPH S. TRACY
Nonresident Senior Fellow

SEAN TRENDE
Nonresident Fellow

TUNKU VARADARAJAN
Nonresident Fellow

STAN VEUGER
Senior Fellow

ALAN D. VIARD
Senior Fellow Emeritus

DUSTIN WALKER
Nonresident Fellow

PHILIP WALLACH
Senior Fellow

PETER J. WALLISON
Senior Fellow Emeritus

MARK J. WARSHAWSKY
Senior Fellow

MATT WEIDINGER
Senior Fellow; Rowe Scholar

ADAM J. WHITE
Senior Fellow; Laurence H. Silberman Chair in Constitutional Governance

BRAD WILCOX
Nonresident Senior Fellow

THOMAS CHATTERTON WILLIAMS
Nonresident Fellow

SCOTT WINSHIP
Senior Fellow; Director, Center on Opportunity and Social Mobility

AUDRYE WONG
Jeane Kirkpatrick Fellow

JOHN YOO
Nonresident Senior Fellow

BENJAMIN ZYCHER
Senior Fellow

www.ingramcontent.com/pod-product-compliance
Lightning Source LLC
Jackson TN
JSHW022303100525
84207JS00001B/1/J